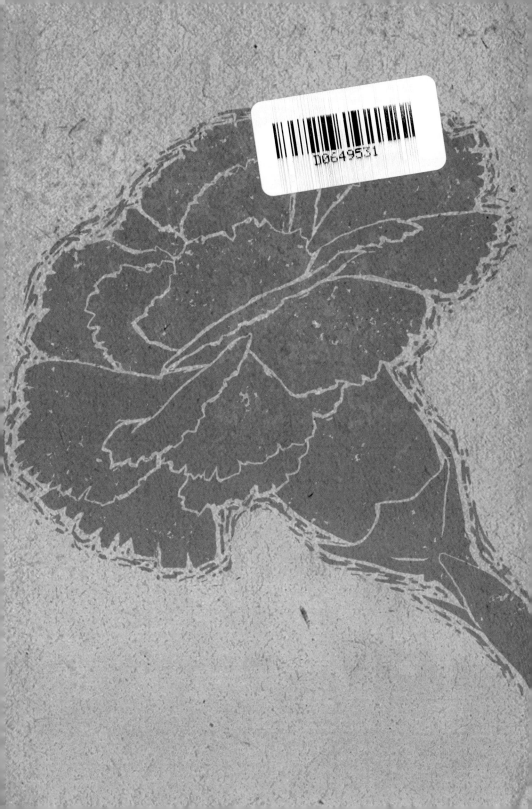

THE RED VIRGIN

AND THE VISION OF UTOPIA

MARY M TALBOT   BRYAN TALBOT

DARK HORSE BOOKS

Utopia (/juːˈtoʊpiə/)

A place of ideal perfection especially in laws, government and social conditions.

'A map of the world that does not include Utopia is not even worth glancing at.'

Oscar Wilde

'Ever tried. Ever failed. No matter. Try again. Fail again. Fail better.'

Samuel Beckett

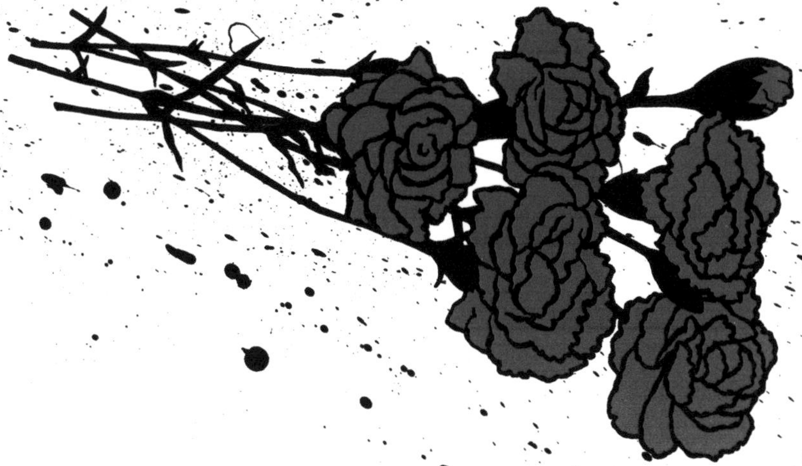

Dedicated to the memory of
Iain (M) Banks,
friend and sorely missed creator
of socialist utopias.

With thanks to
Eric Bufkens, Alex Butterworth, Kate Charlesworth,
Dan Franklin, Stephen Holland, Jose Muñoz,
Madeline Talbot

Thanks to the staff of the HMS
Trincomalee in Hartlepool, Levallois-Perret
cemetery and the following museums in Paris
and Nouméa: Carnavalet Museum, Museum of
Montmartre, Museum of Saint-Denis, Museum
of New Caledonia, Maritime Museum
and City Museum of Nouméa.

Supported using public funding by
ARTS COUNCIL
ENGLAND
LOTTERY FUNDED

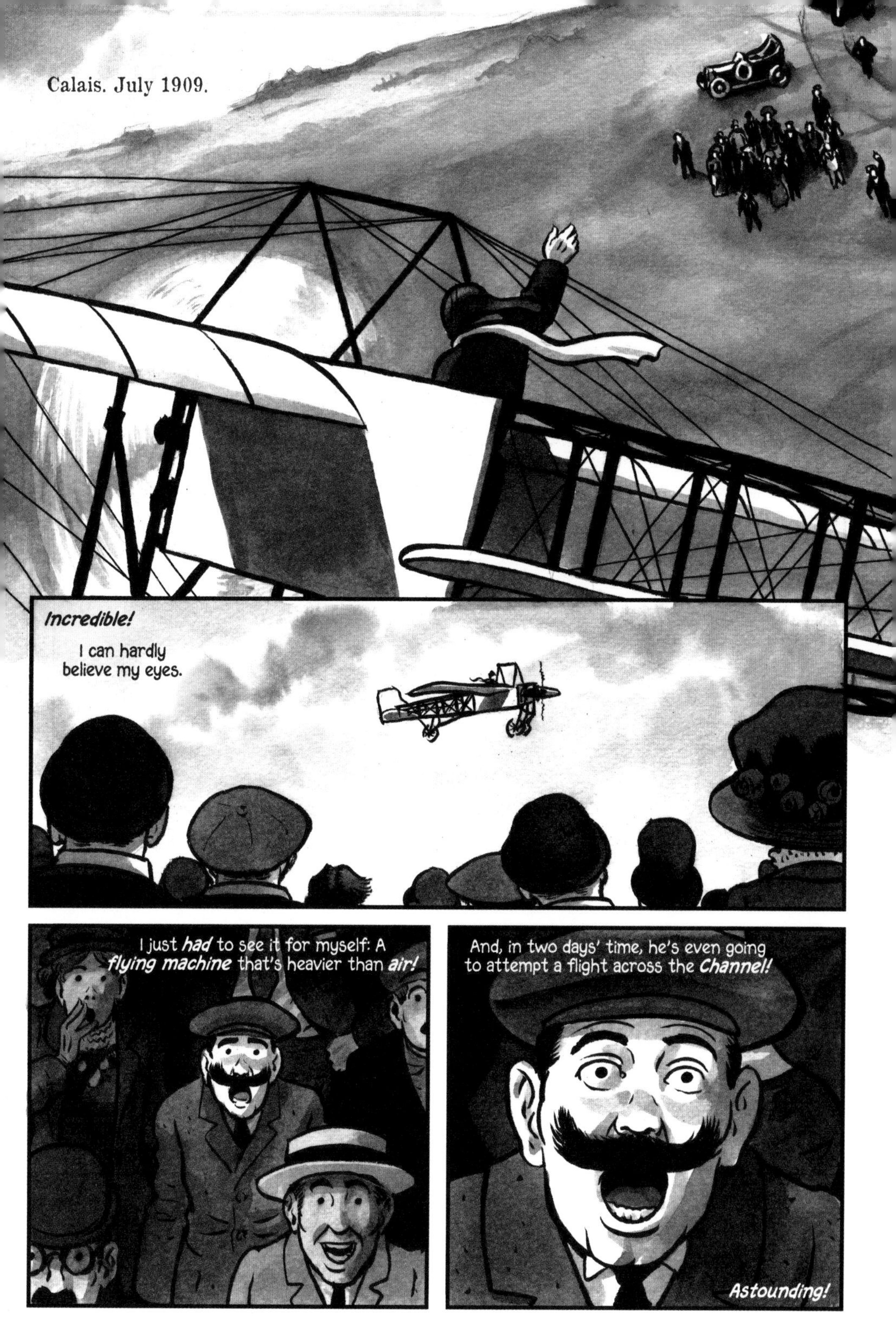

Calais. July 1909.
Incredible!
I can hardly believe my eyes.
I just had to see it for myself: A flying machine that's heavier than air!
And, in two days' time, he's even going to attempt a flight across the Channel!
Astounding!

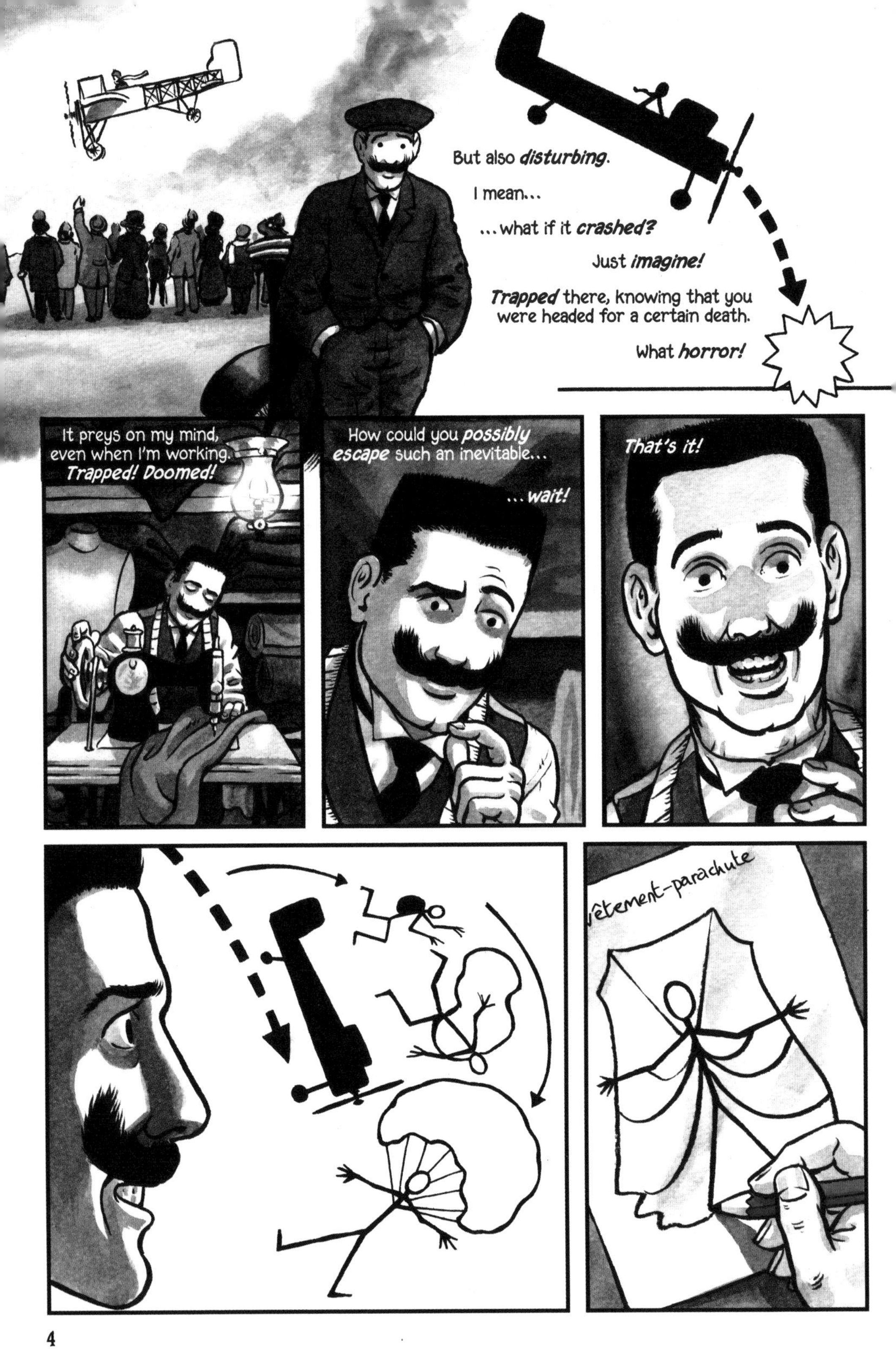

But also *disturbing*.
I mean...
...what if it *crashed?*
Just *imagine!*
Trapped there, knowing that you were headed for a certain death.
What *horror!*
It preys on my mind, even when I'm working. *Trapped! Doomed!*
How could you *possibly escape* such an inevitable...
...*wait!*
That's it!
vêtement-parachute

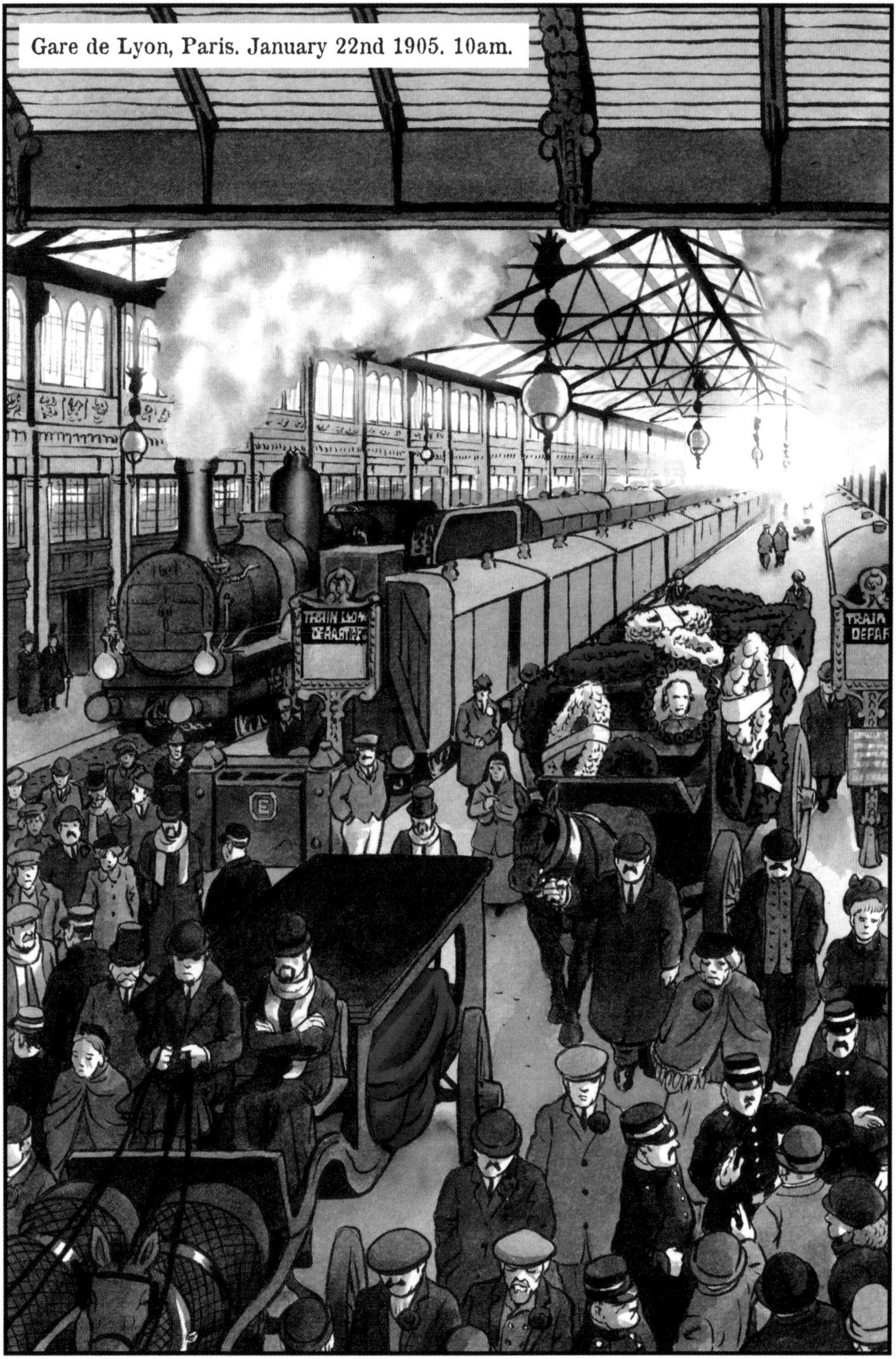
Gare de Lyon, Paris. January 22nd 1905. 10am.

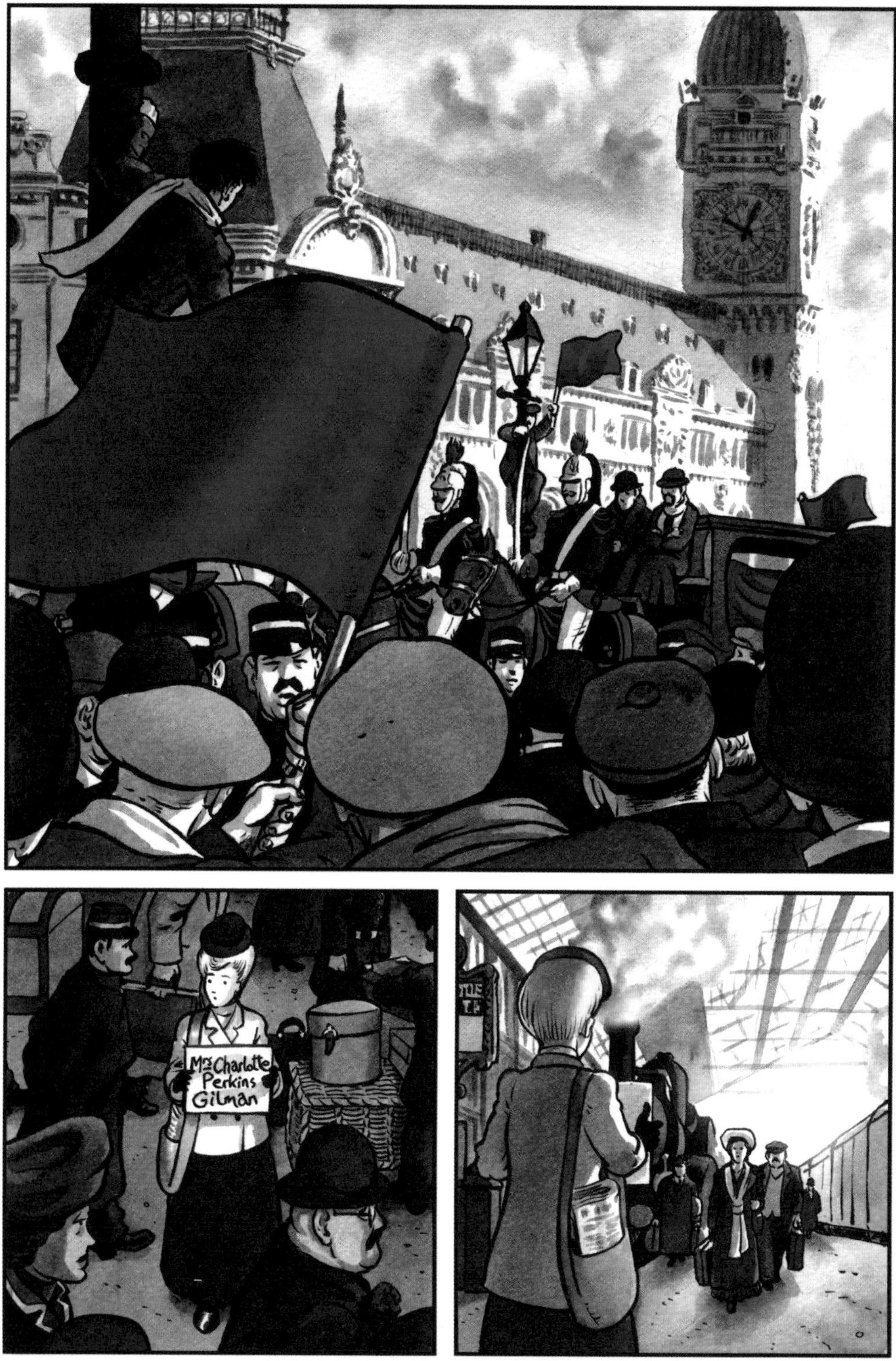
Mrs Charlotte Perkins Gilman

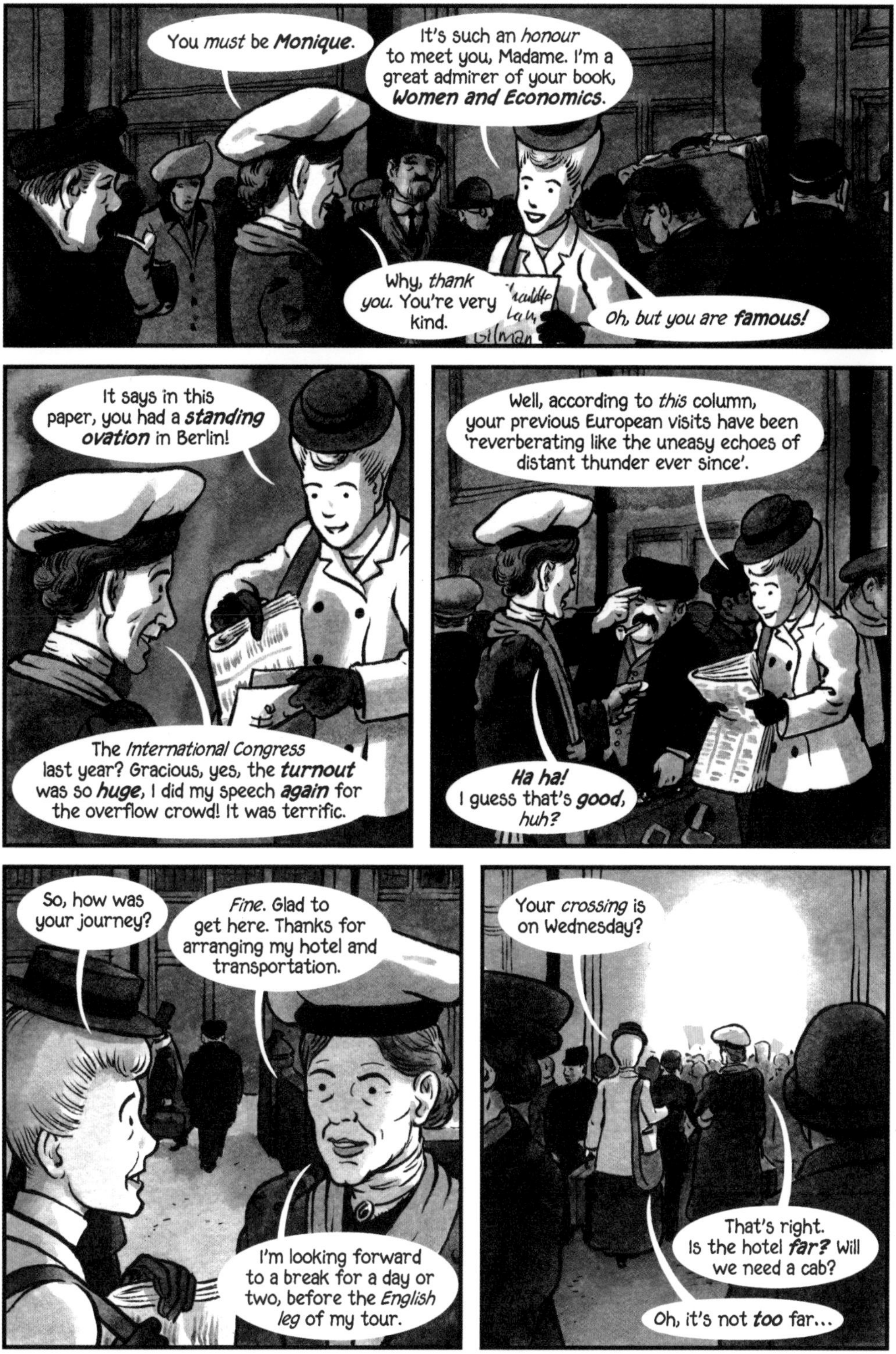
You *must* be **Monique**.
It's such an *honour* to meet you, Madame. I'm a great admirer of your book, ***Women and Economics***.
Why, *thank you*. You're very kind.
Oh, but you are ***famous!***
It says in this paper, you had a ***standing ovation*** in Berlin!
The *International Congress* last year? Gracious, yes, the ***turnout*** was so ***huge***, I did my speech ***again*** for the overflow crowd! It was terrific.
Well, according to *this* column, your previous European visits have been 'reverberating like the uneasy echoes of distant thunder ever since'.
Ha ha! I guess that's ***good***, *huh?*
So, how was your journey?
Fine. Glad to get here. Thanks for arranging my hotel and transportation.
I'm looking forward to a break for a day or two, before the *English leg* of my tour.
Your *crossing* is on Wednesday?
That's right. Is the hotel ***far?*** Will we need a cab?
Oh, it's not ***too*** far...

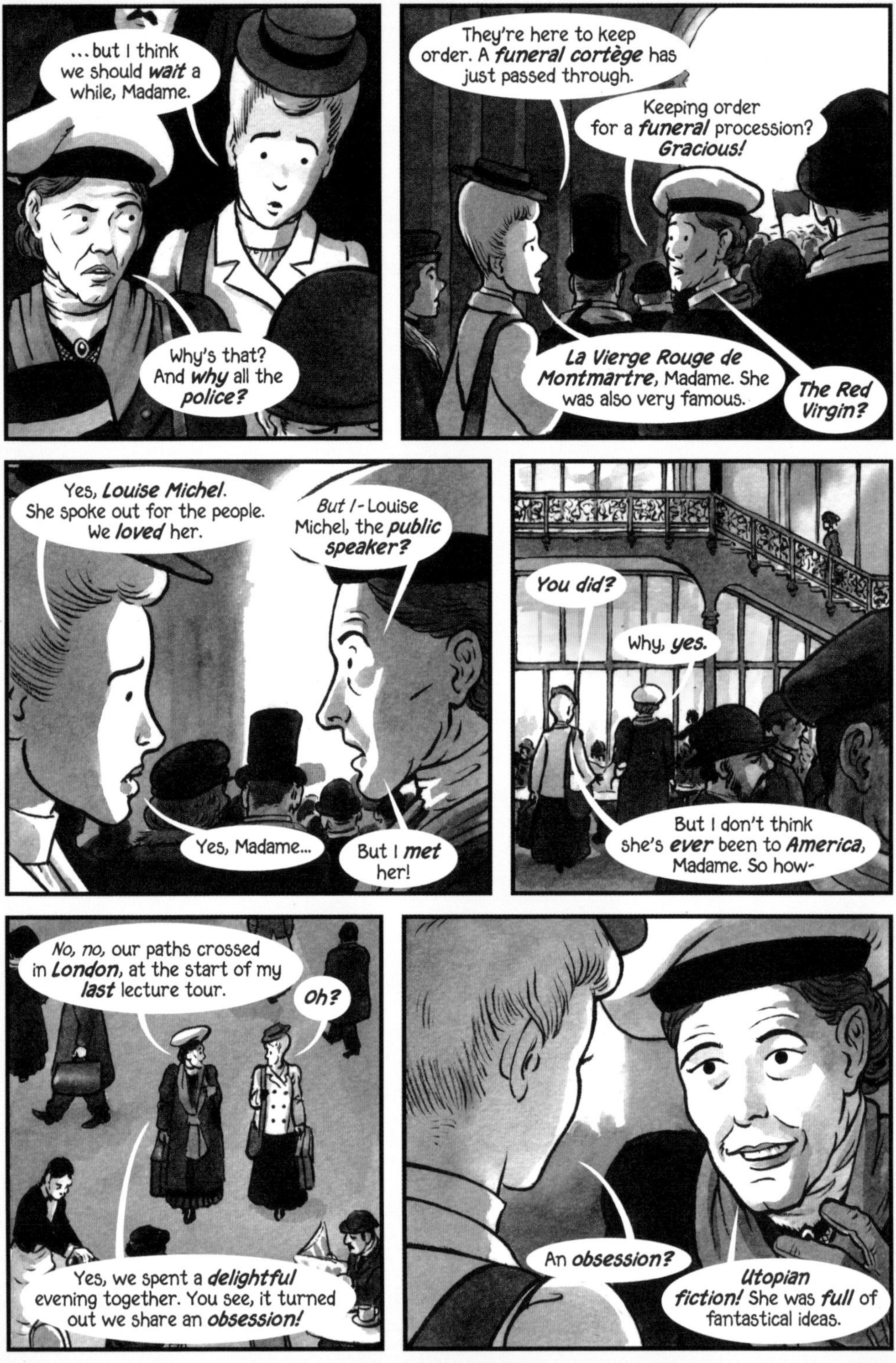
...but I think we should *wait* a while, Madame.
Why's that? And *why* all the *police?*
They're here to keep order. A *funeral cortège* has just passed through.
Keeping order for a *funeral* procession? *Gracious!*
La Vierge Rouge de Montmartre, Madame. She was also very famous.
The Red Virgin?
Yes, *Louise Michel*. She spoke out for the people. We *loved* her.
But I - Louise Michel, the *public speaker?*
Yes, Madame...
But I *met* her!
You did?
Why, *yes.*
But I don't think she's *ever* been to *America*, Madame. So how-
No, no, our paths crossed in *London*, at the start of my *last* lecture tour.
Oh?
Yes, we spent a *delightful* evening together. You see, it turned out we share an *obsession!*
An *obsession?*
Utopian fiction! She was *full* of fantastical ideas.

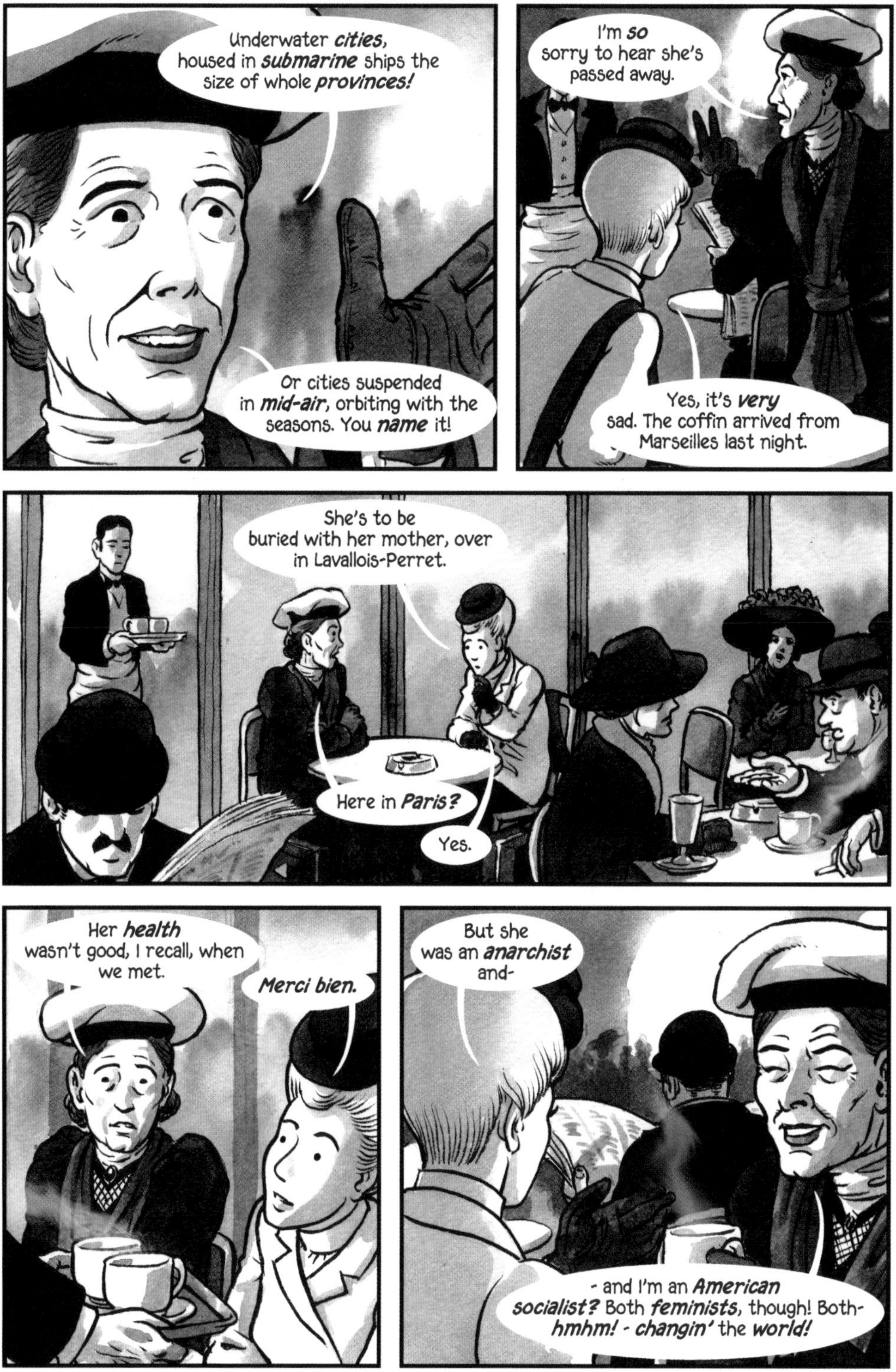
Underwater cities, housed in submarine ships the size of whole provinces!
Or cities suspended in mid-air, orbiting with the seasons. You name it!
I'm so sorry to hear she's passed away.
Yes, it's very sad. The coffin arrived from Marseilles last night.
She's to be buried with her mother, over in Lavallois-Perret.
Here in Paris?
Yes.
Her health wasn't good, I recall, when we met.
Merci bien.
But she was an anarchist and-
- and I'm an American socialist? Both feminists, though! Both- hmhm! - changin' the world!

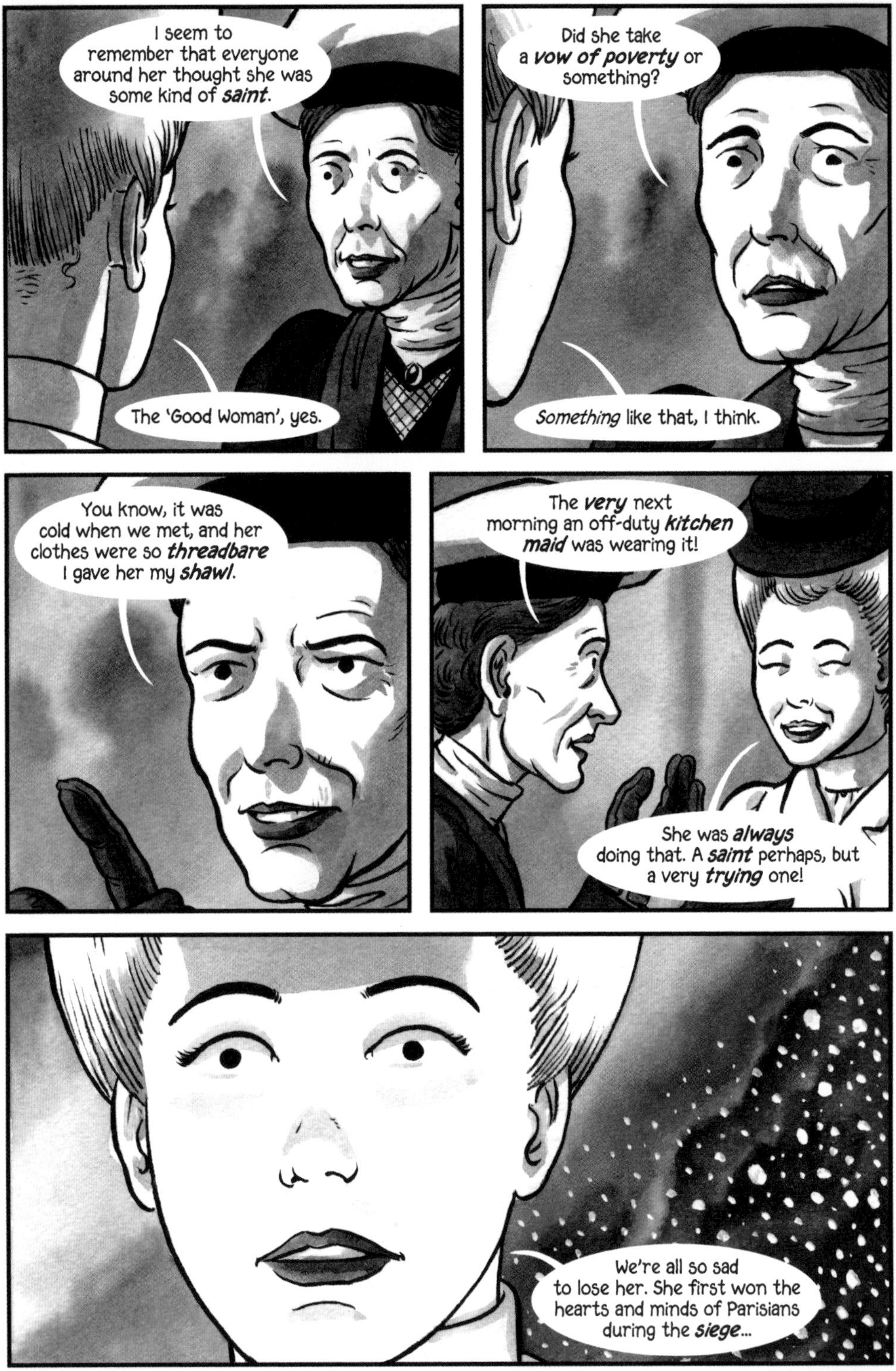
I seem to remember that everyone around her thought she was some kind of *saint*.
The 'Good Woman', yes.
Did she take a ***vow of poverty*** or something?
Something like that, I think.
You know, it was cold when we met, and her clothes were so ***threadbare*** I gave her my ***shawl***.
The ***very*** next morning an off-duty ***kitchen maid*** was wearing it!
She was ***always*** doing that. A ***saint*** perhaps, but a very ***trying*** one!
We're all so sad to lose her. She first won the hearts and minds of Parisians during the ***siege***...

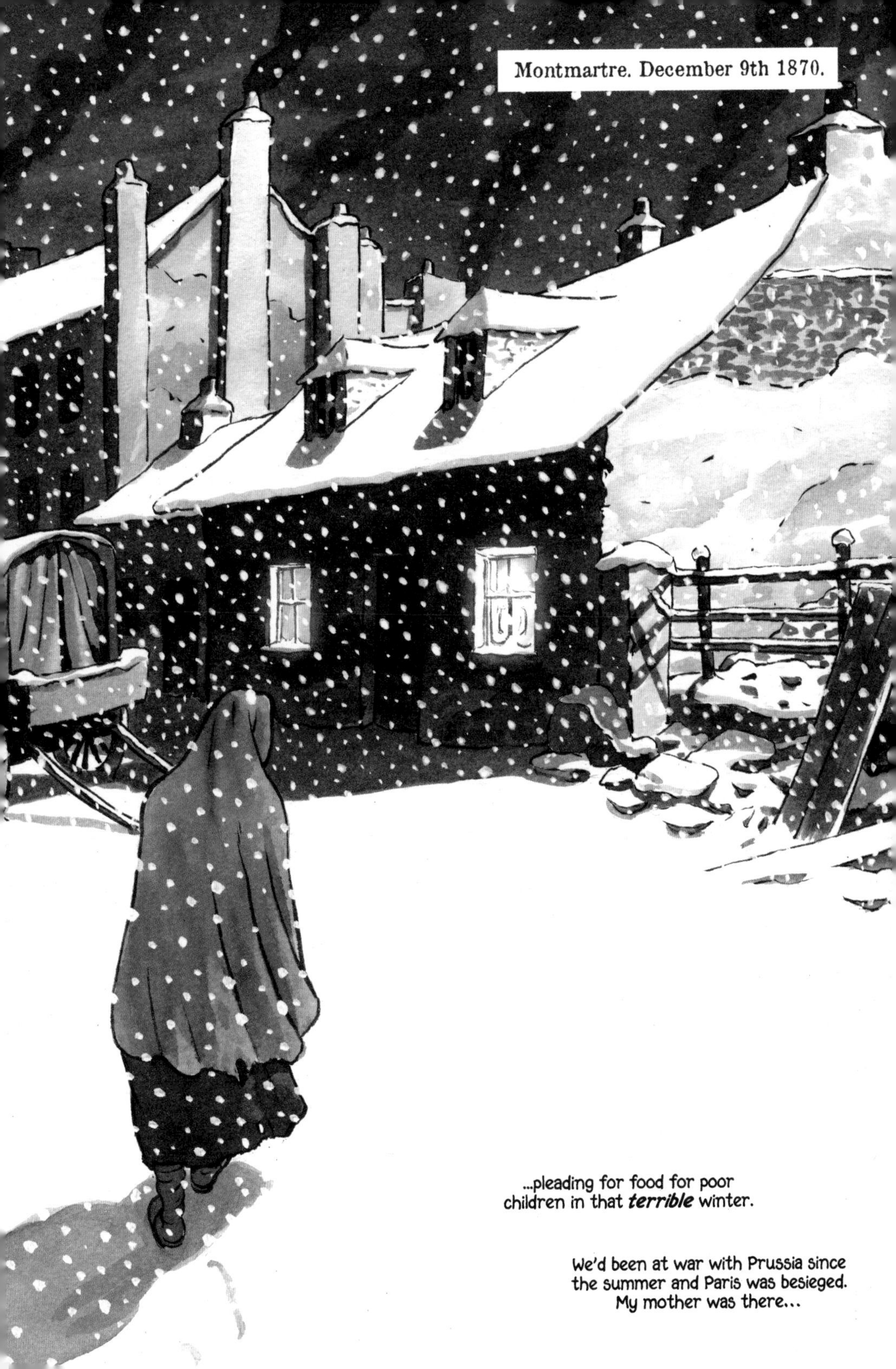
Montmartre. December 9th 1870.
...pleading for food for poor children in that *terrible* winter.
We'd been at war with Prussia since the summer and Paris was besieged. My mother was there...

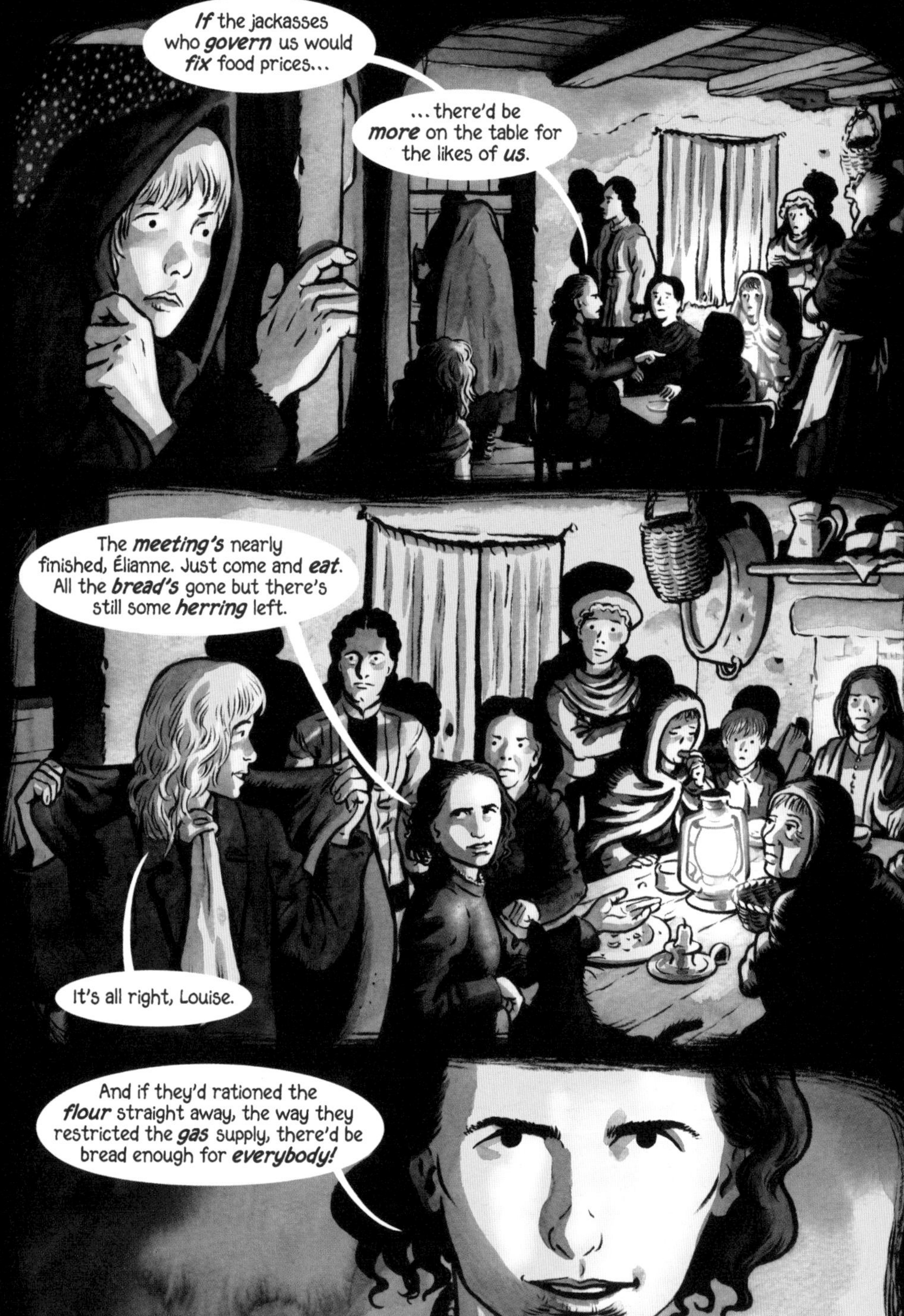

If the jackasses who *govern* us would *fix* food prices...
...there'd be *more* on the table for the likes of *us*.
The *meeting's* nearly finished, Élianne. Just come and *eat*. All the *bread's* gone but there's still some *herring* left.
It's all right, Louise.
And if they'd rationed the *flour* straight away, the way they restricted the *gas* supply, there'd be bread enough for *everybody!*

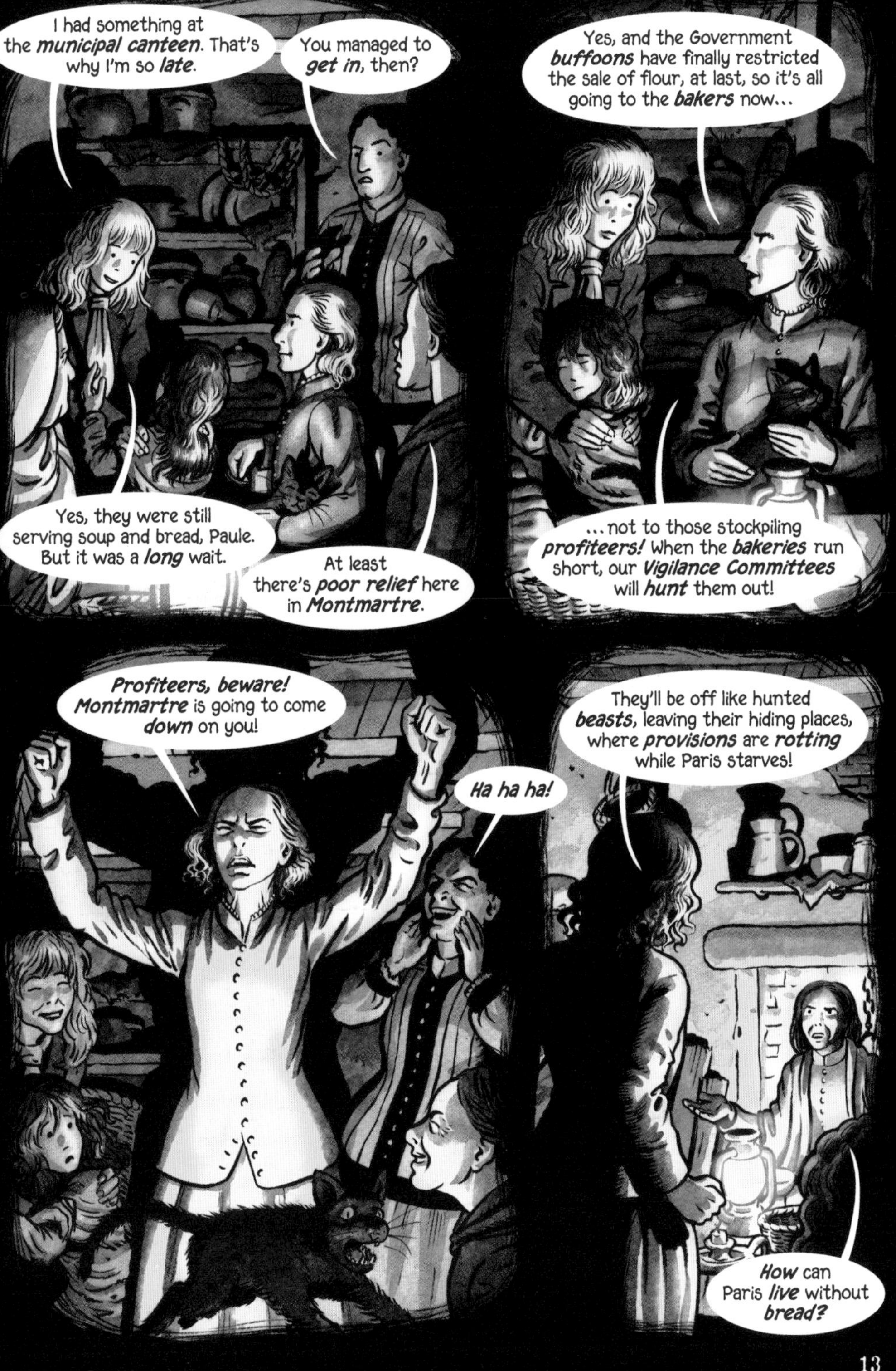

I had something at the municipal canteen. That's why I'm so late.
You managed to get in, then?
Yes, they were still serving soup and bread, Paule. But it was a long wait.
At least there's poor relief here in Montmartre.
Yes, and the Government buffoons have finally restricted the sale of flour, at last, so it's all going to the bakers now...
...not to those stockpiling profiteers! When the bakeries run short, our Vigilance Committees will hunt them out!
Profiteers, beware! Montmartre is going to come down on you!
Ha ha ha!
They'll be off like hunted beasts, leaving their hiding places, where provisions are rotting while Paris starves!
How can Paris live without bread?

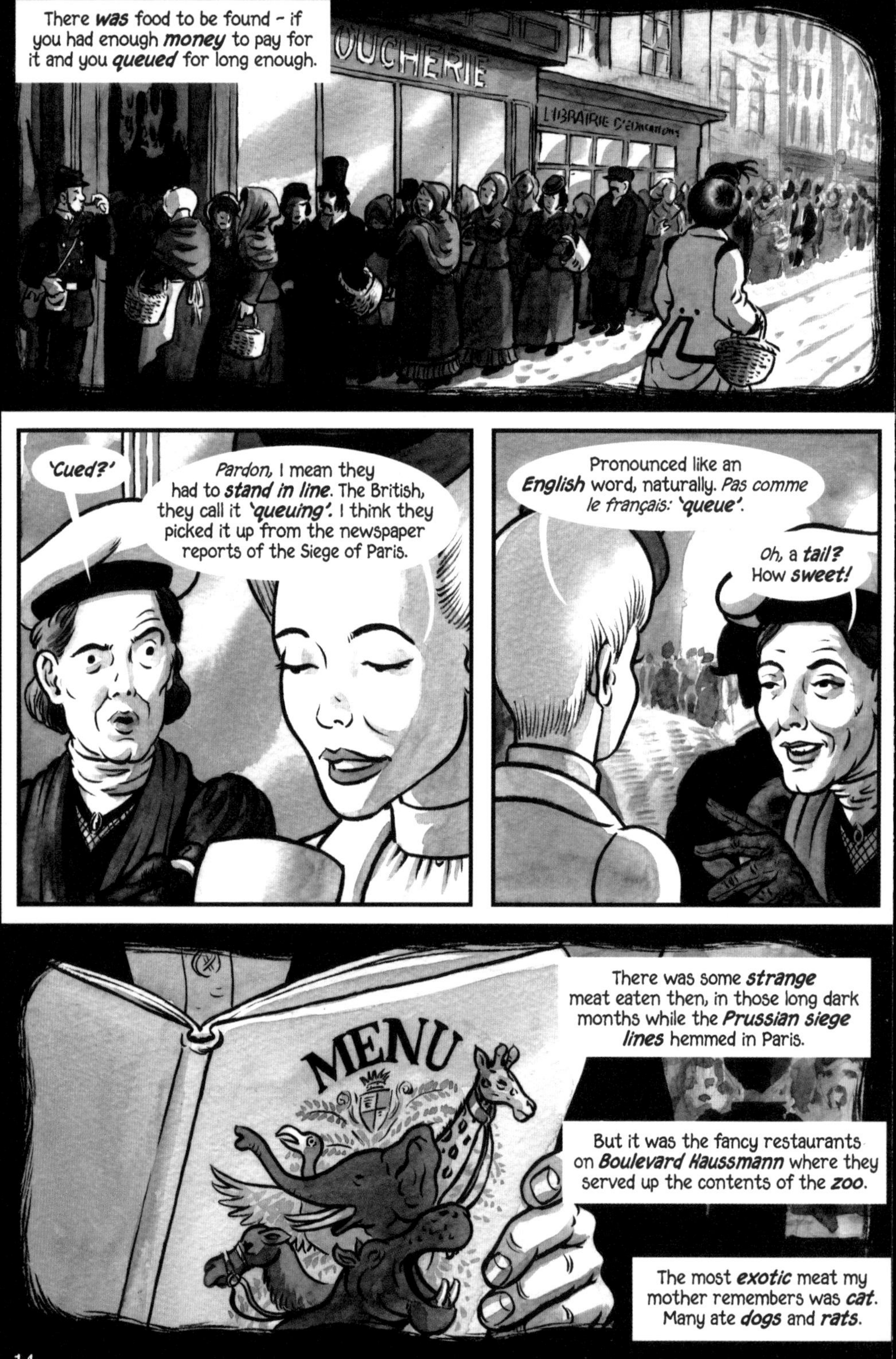
There *was* food to be found – if you had enough *money* to pay for it and you *queued* for long enough.
OUCHERIE
LIBRAIRIE D'EDUCATIONS
'Cued?'
Pardon, I mean they had to *stand in line*. The British, they call it *'queuing'*. I think they picked it up from the newspaper reports of the Siege of Paris.
Pronounced like an *English* word, naturally. *Pas comme le français: 'queue'*.
Oh, a tail? How sweet!
There was some *strange* meat eaten then, in those long dark months while the *Prussian siege lines* hemmed in Paris.
MENU
But it was the fancy restaurants on *Boulevard Haussmann* where they served up the contents of the *zoo*.
The most *exotic* meat my mother remembers was *cat*. Many ate *dogs* and *rats*.

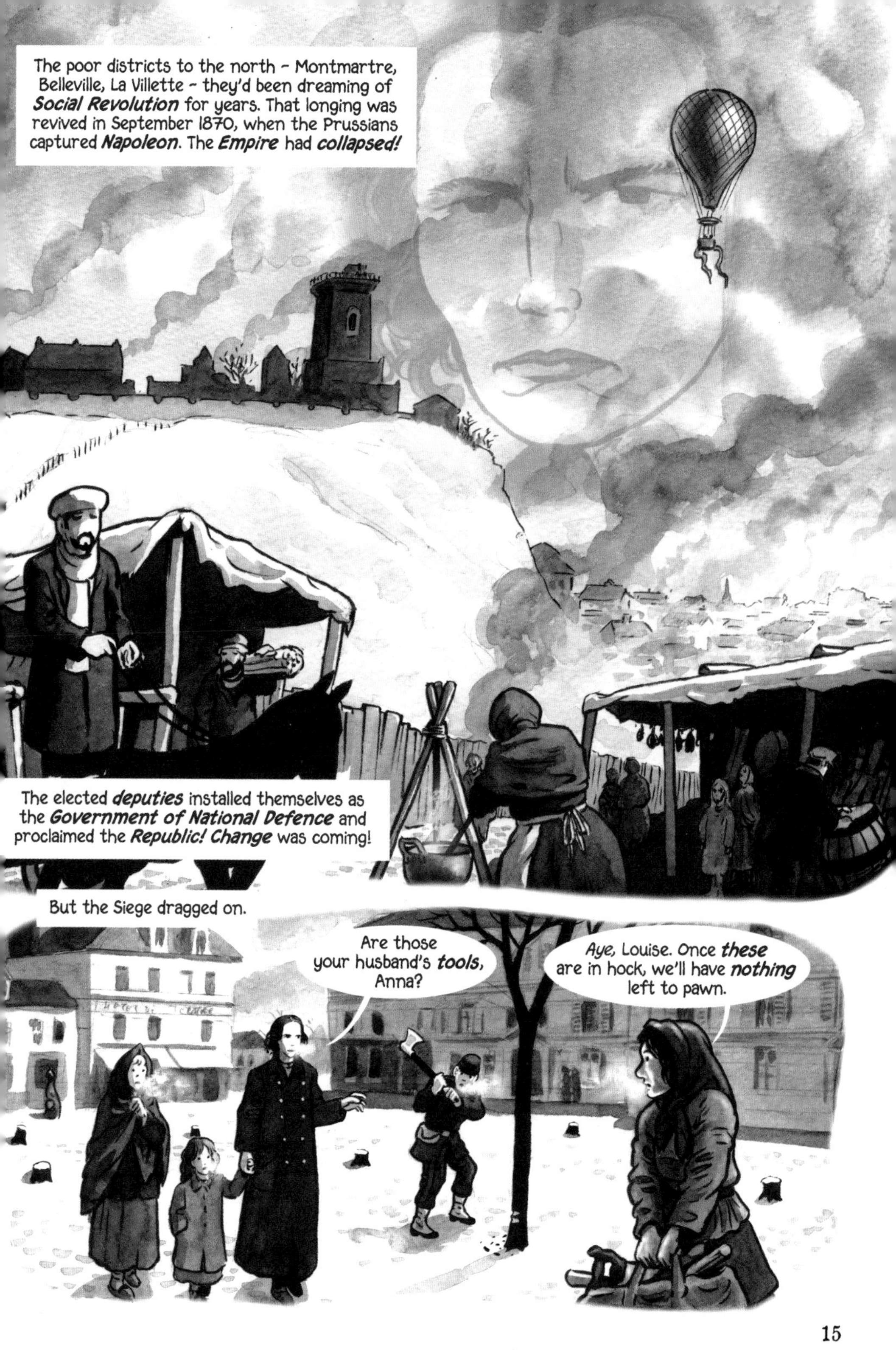
The poor districts to the north - Montmartre, Belleville, La Villette - they'd been dreaming of ***Social Revolution*** for years. That longing was revived in September 1870, when the Prussians captured ***Napoleon***. The ***Empire*** had ***collapsed!***
The elected ***deputies*** installed themselves as the ***Government of National Defence*** and proclaimed the ***Republic! Change*** was coming!
But the Siege dragged on.
Are those your husband's ***tools***, Anna?
Aye, Louise. Once ***these*** are in hock, we'll have ***nothing*** left to pawn.

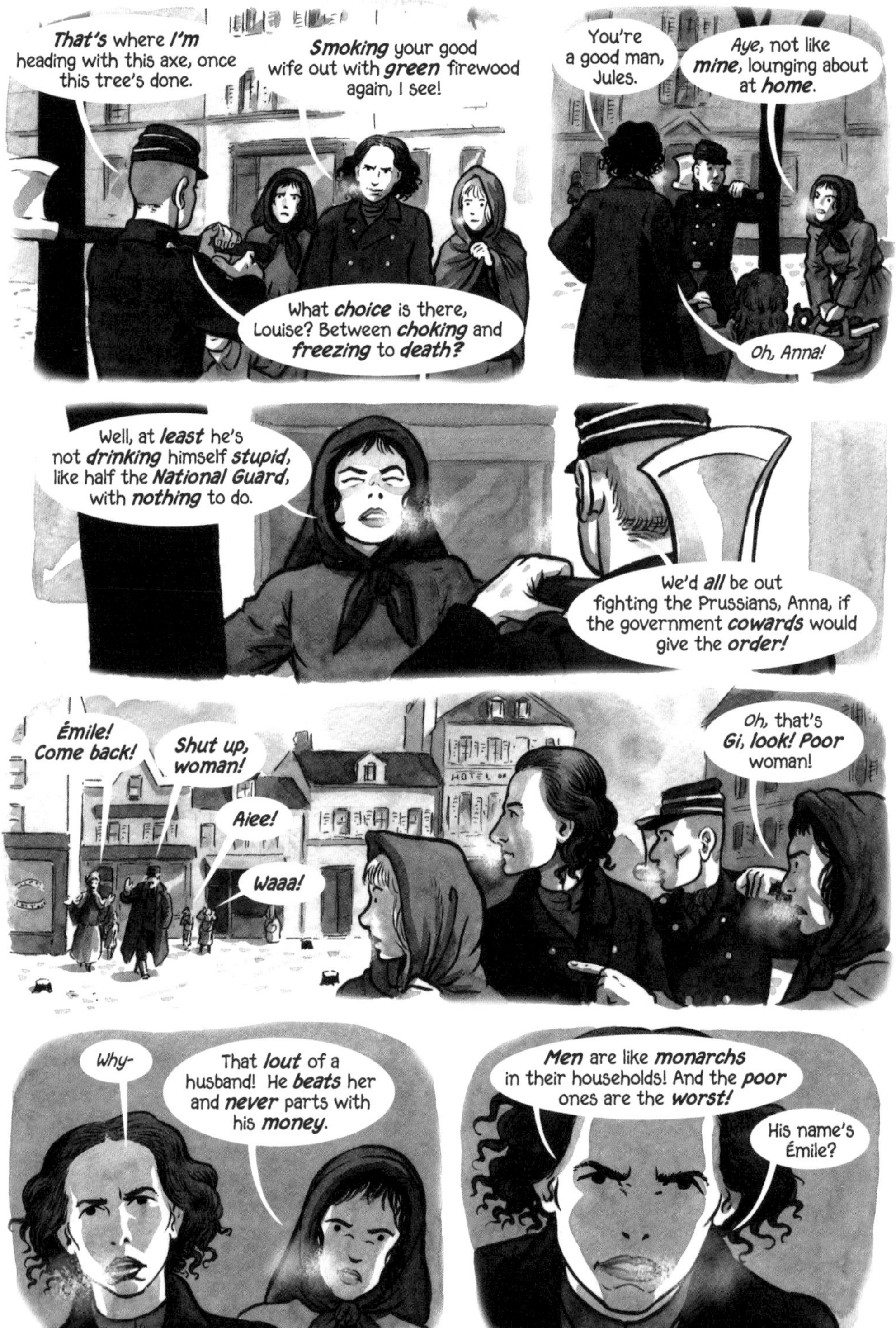
That's where I'm heading with this axe, once this tree's done.
Smoking your good wife out with green firewood again, I see!
What choice is there, Louise? Between choking and freezing to death?
You're a good man, Jules.
Aye, not like mine, lounging about at home.
Oh, Anna!
Well, at least he's not drinking himself stupid, like half the National Guard, with nothing to do.
We'd all be out fighting the Prussians, Anna, if the government cowards would give the order!
Émile! Come back!
Shut up, woman!
Aiee!
Waaa!
HOTEL DE
Oh, that's Gi, look! Poor woman!
Why-
That lout of a husband! He beats her and never parts with his money.
Men are like monarchs in their households! And the poor ones are the worst!
His name's Émile?

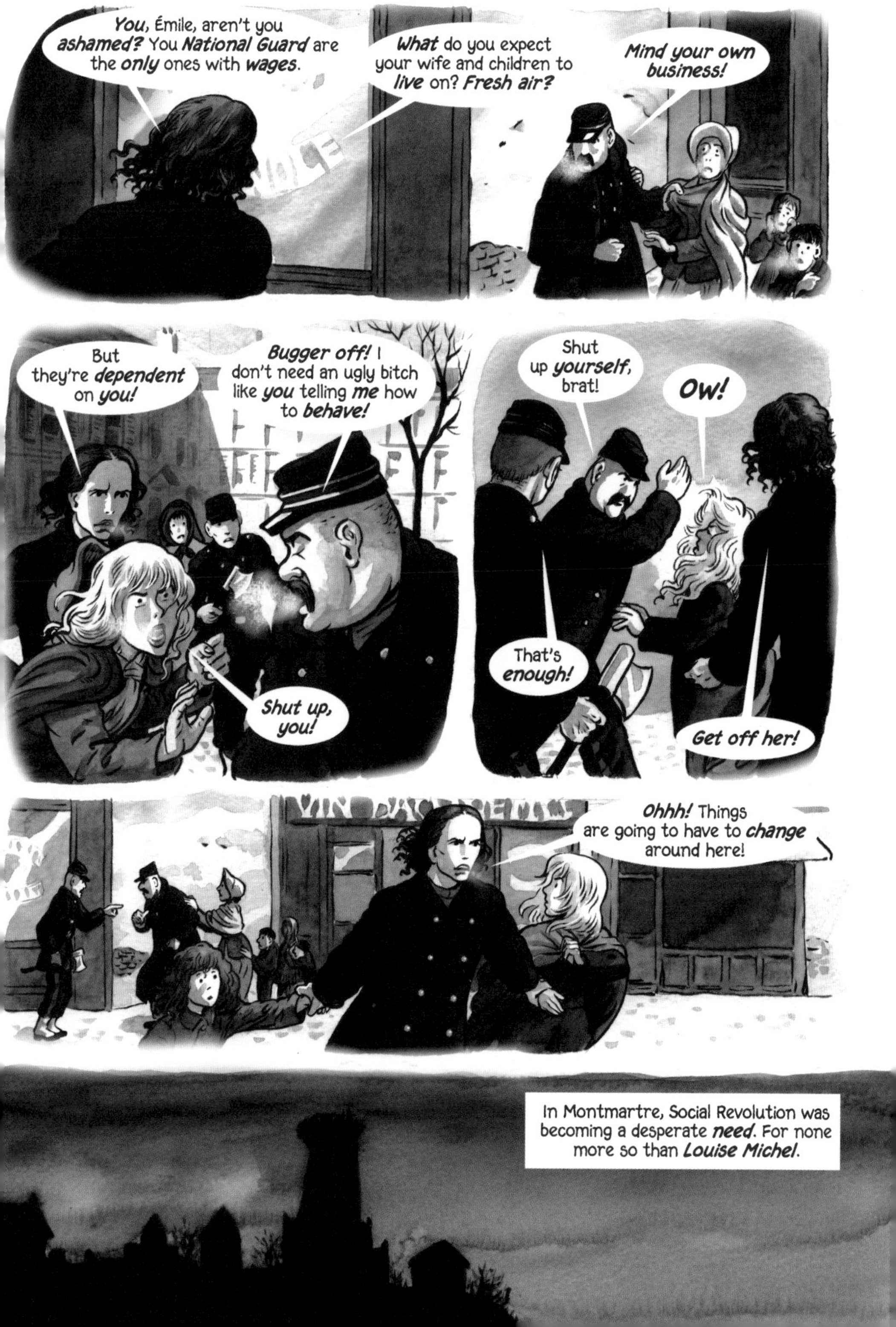
You, Émile, aren't you ashamed? You National Guard are the only ones with wages.
What do you expect your wife and children to live on? Fresh air?
Mind your own business!
But they're dependent on you!
Bugger off! I don't need an ugly bitch like you telling me how to behave!
Shut up, you!
Shut up yourself, brat!
OW!
That's enough!
Get off her!
Ohhh! Things are going to have to change around here!
In Montmartre, Social Revolution was becoming a desperate need. For none more so than Louise Michel.

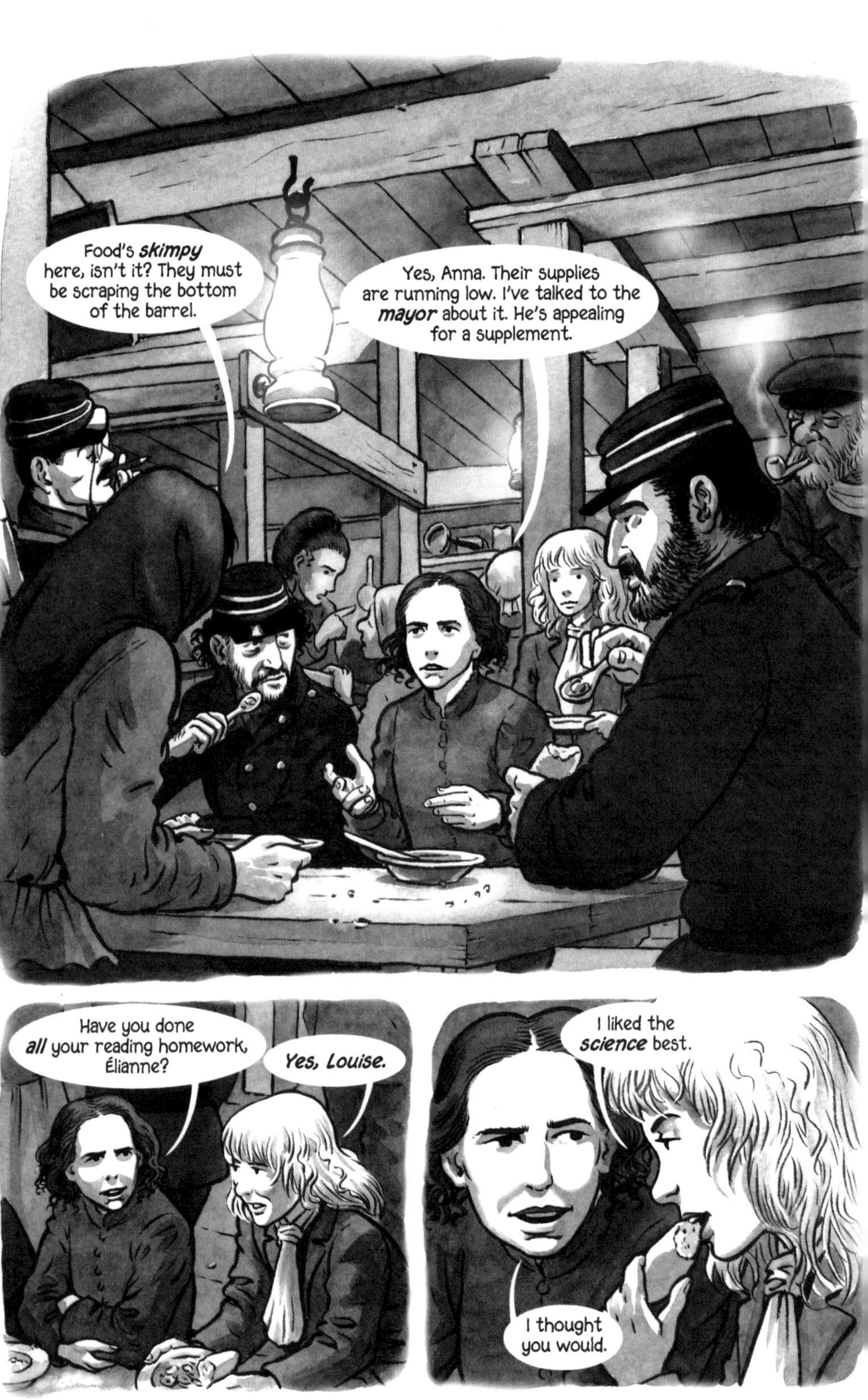
Food's *skimpy* here, isn't it? They must be scraping the bottom of the barrel.
Yes, Anna. Their supplies are running low. I've talked to the *mayor* about it. He's appealing for a supplement.
Have you done *all* your reading homework, Élianne?
Yes, Louise.
I liked the *science* best.
I thought you would.

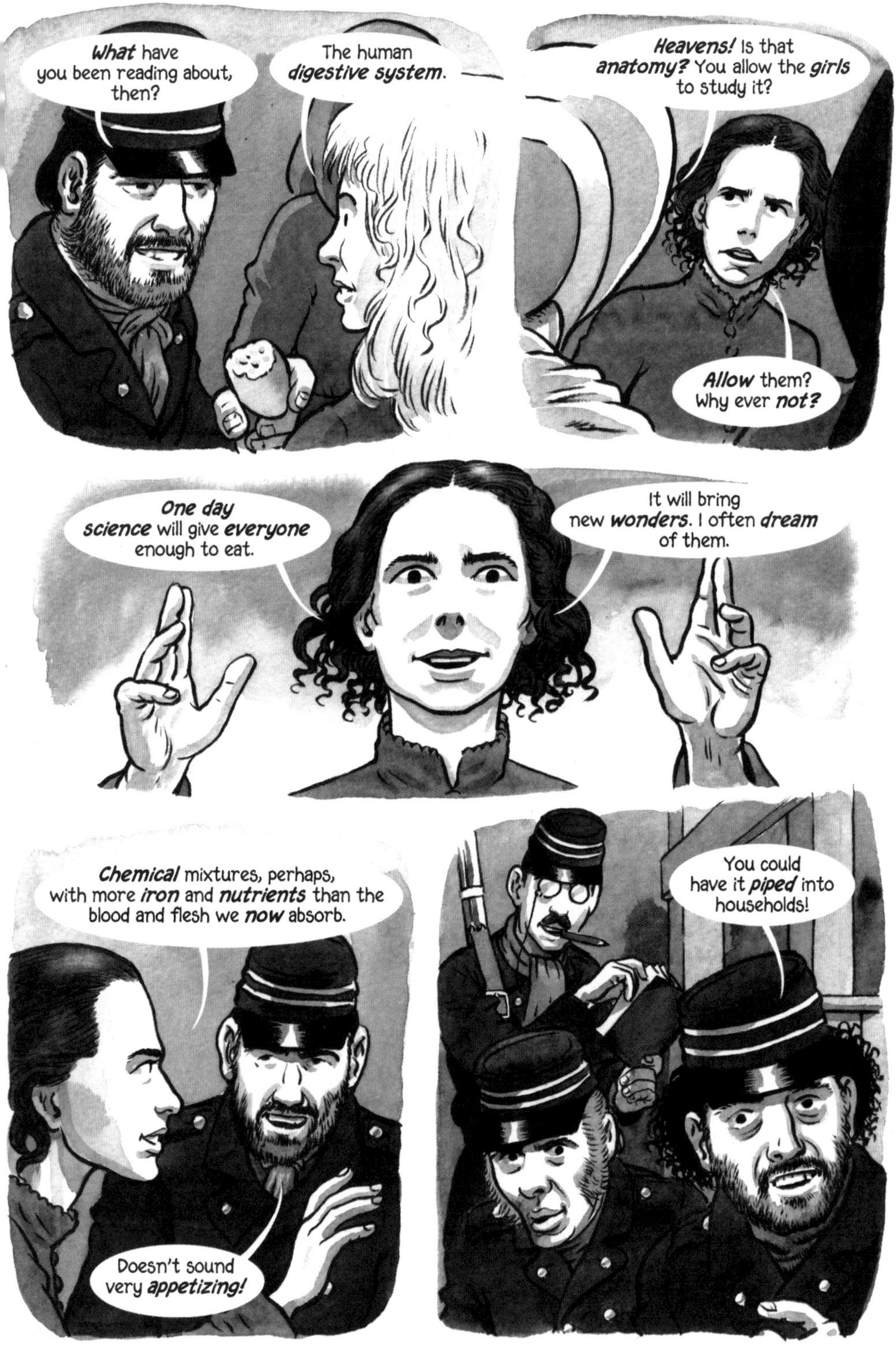
What have you been reading about, then?
The human *digestive system*.
Heavens! Is that *anatomy?* You allow the *girls* to study it?
Allow them? Why ever *not?*
One day science will give *everyone* enough to eat.
It will bring new *wonders*. I often *dream* of them.
Chemical mixtures, perhaps, with more *iron* and *nutrients* than the blood and flesh we *now* absorb.
Doesn't sound very *appetizing!*
You could have it *piped* into households!

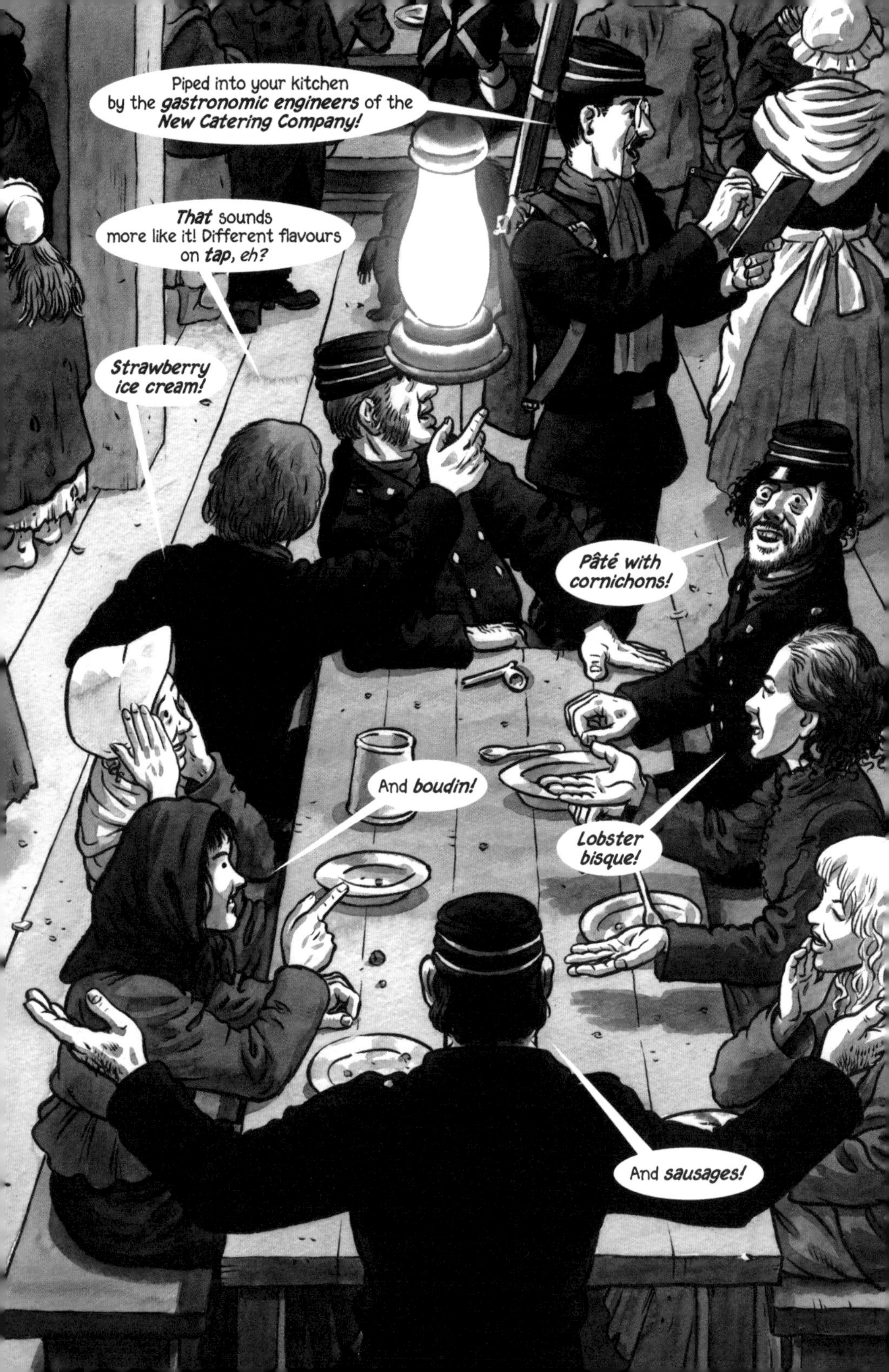

Piped into your kitchen by the *gastronomic engineers* of the *New Catering Company!*
That sounds more like it! Different flavours on *tap, eh?*
Strawberry ice cream!
Pâté with cornichons!
And *boudin!*
Lobster bisque!
And *sausages!*

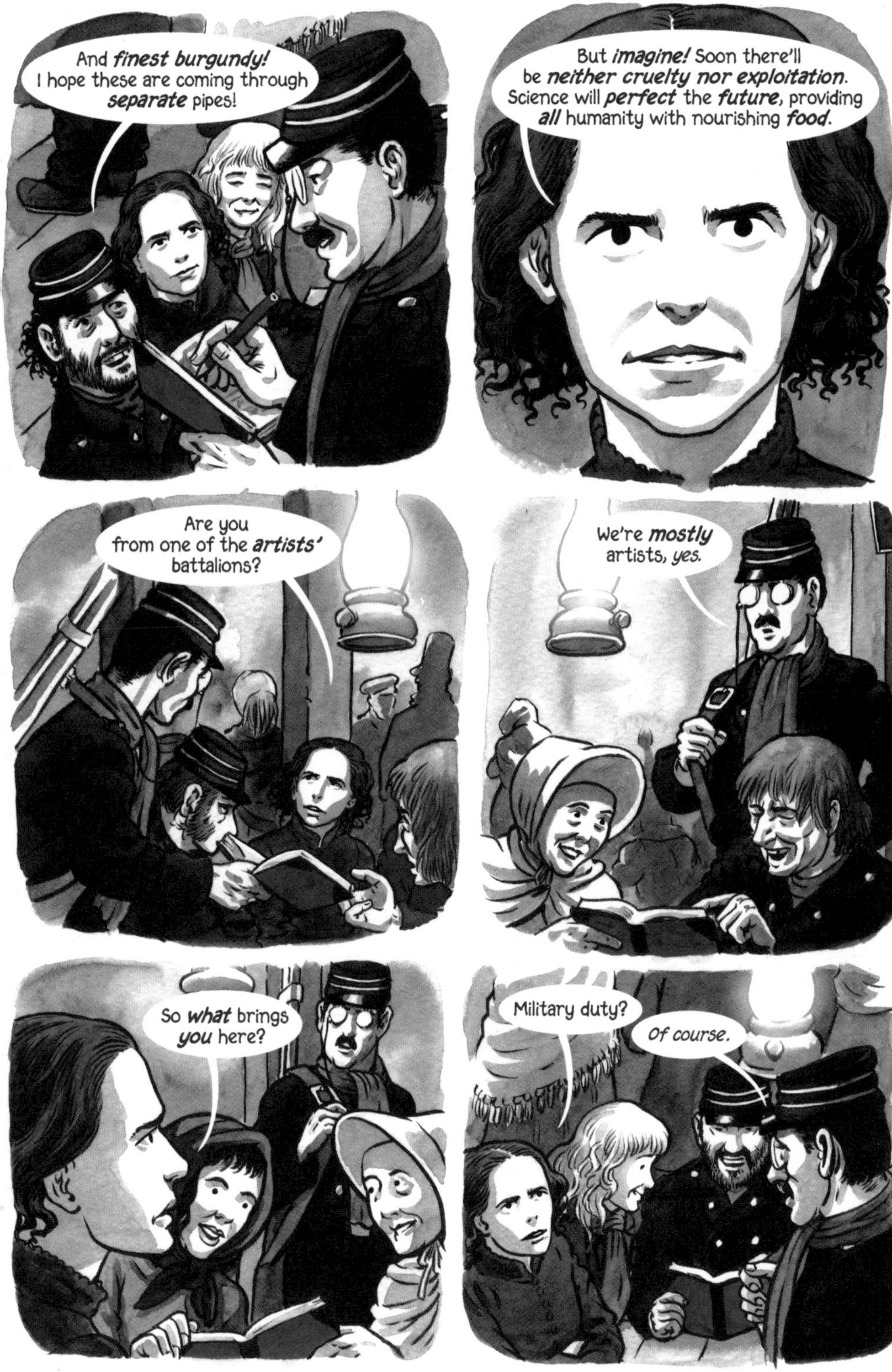
And *finest burgundy!* I hope these are coming through *separate* pipes!
But *imagine!* Soon there'll be ***neither cruelty nor exploitation***. Science will ***perfect*** the ***future***, providing ***all*** humanity with nourishing ***food***.
Are you from one of the ***artists'*** battalions?
We're ***mostly*** artists, *yes*.
So ***what*** brings ***you*** here?
Military duty?
Of course.

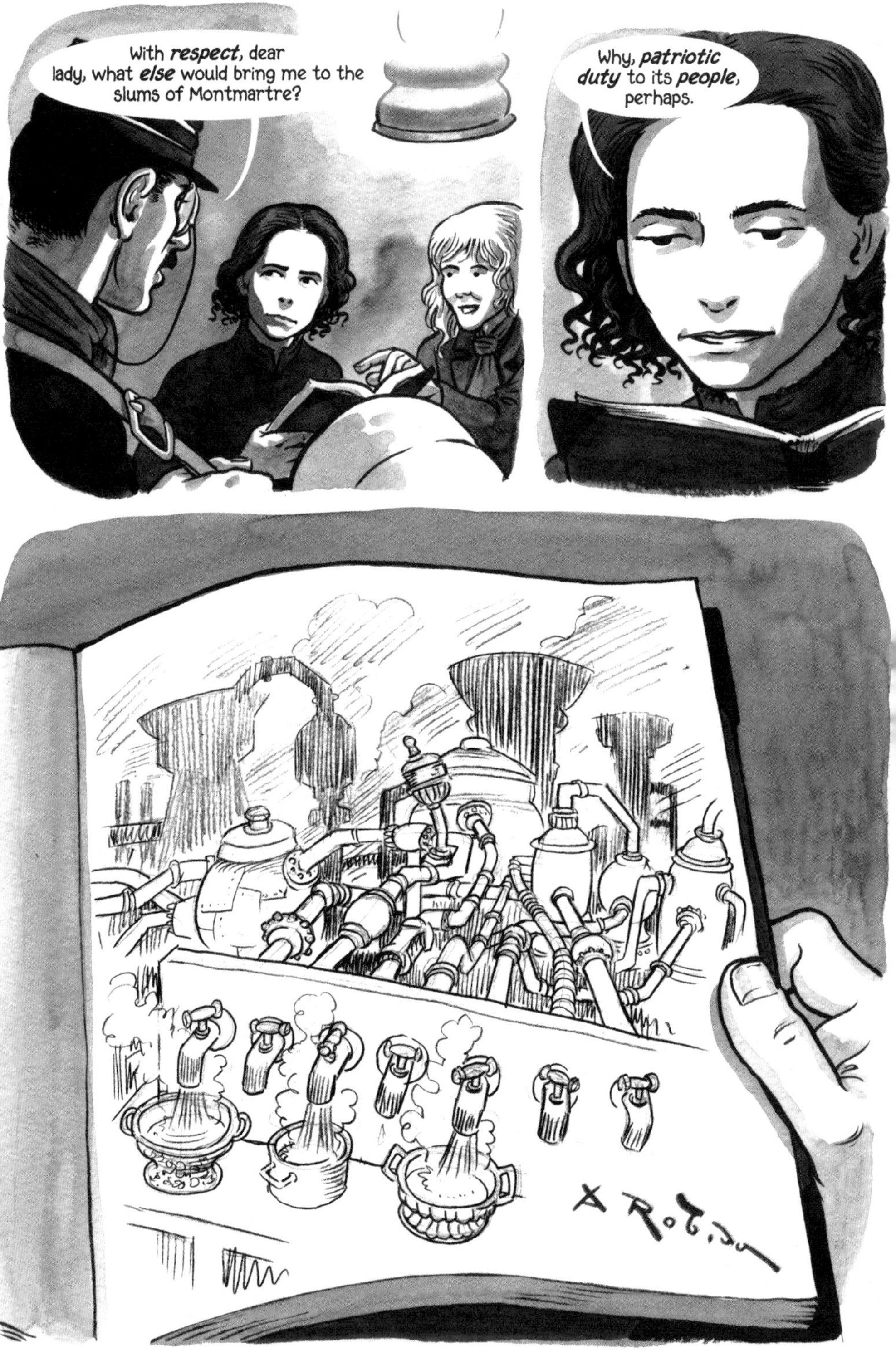
With *respect*, dear lady, what *else* would bring me to the slums of Montmartre?
Why, *patriotic duty* to its *people*, perhaps.
A Robida

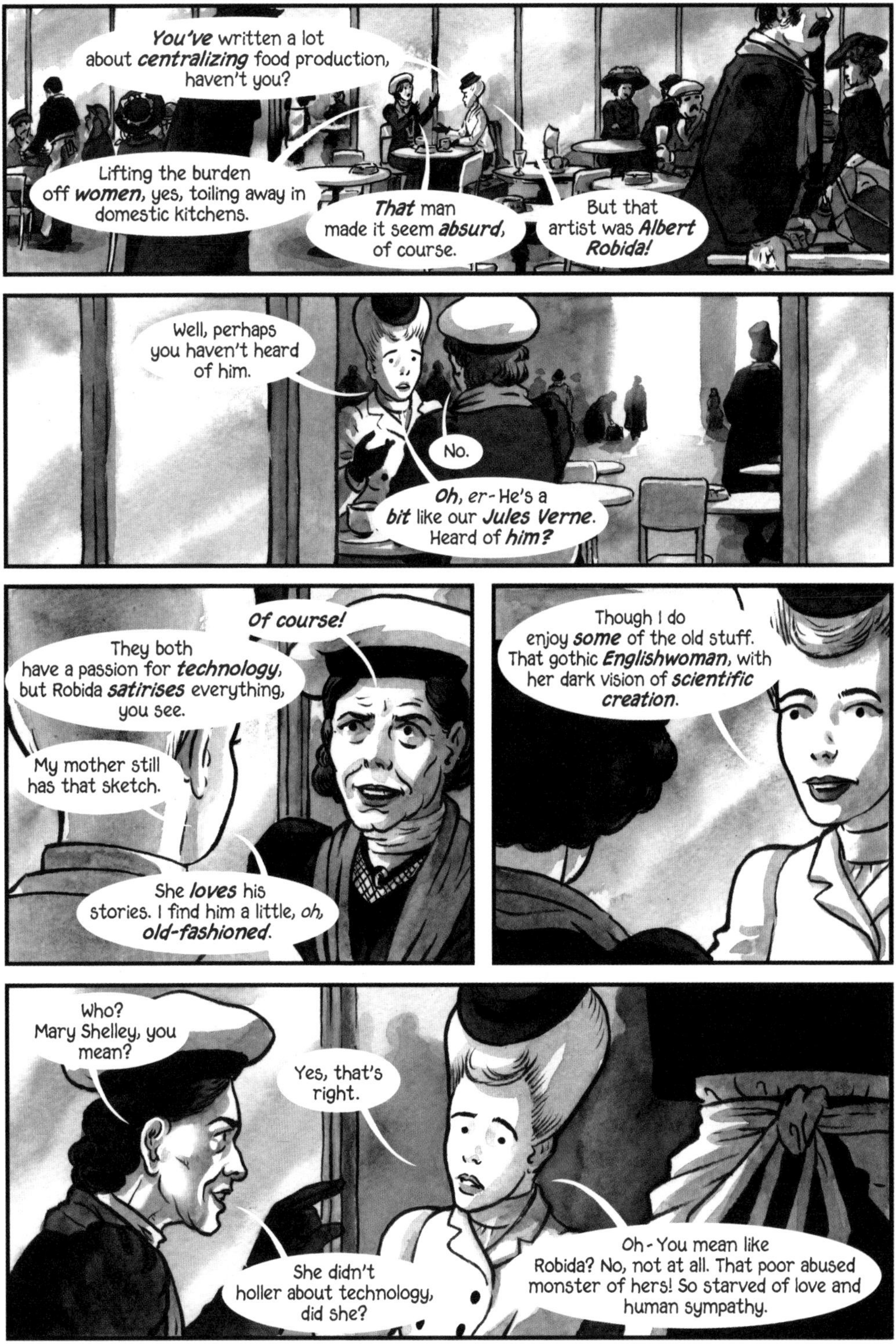
You've written a lot about centralizing food production, haven't you?
Lifting the burden off women, yes, toiling away in domestic kitchens.
That man made it seem absurd, of course.
But that artist was Albert Robida!
Well, perhaps you haven't heard of him.
No.
Oh, er- He's a bit like our Jules Verne. Heard of him?
Of course!
They both have a passion for technology, but Robida satirises everything, you see.
My mother still has that sketch.
She loves his stories. I find him a little, oh, old-fashioned.
Though I do enjoy some of the old stuff. That gothic Englishwoman, with her dark vision of scientific creation.
Who? Mary Shelley, you mean?
Yes, that's right.
She didn't holler about technology, did she?
Oh- You mean like Robida? No, not at all. That poor abused monster of hers! So starved of love and human sympathy.

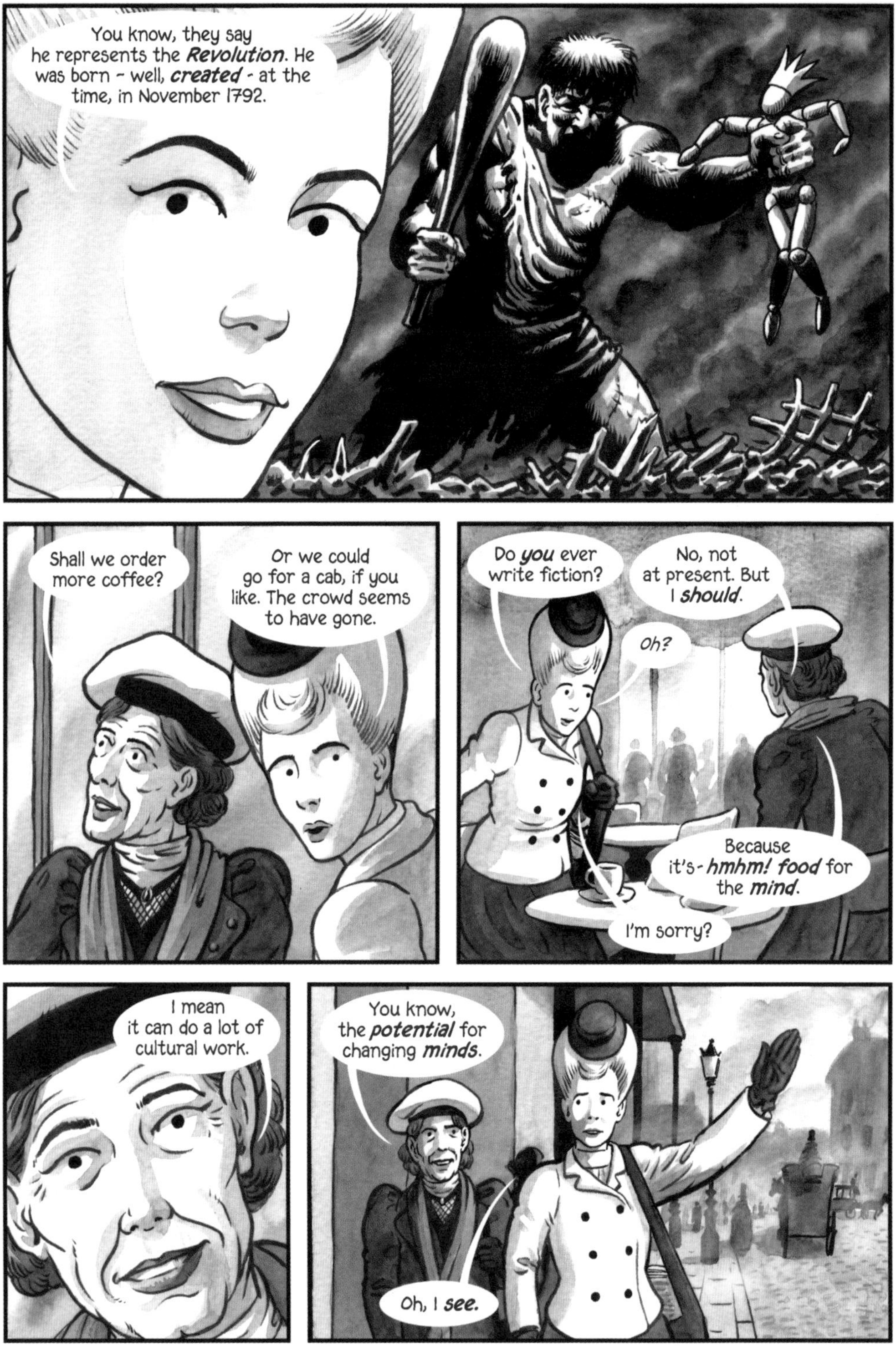
You know, they say he represents the ***Revolution***. He was born - well, ***created*** - at the time, in November 1792.
Shall we order more coffee?
Or we could go for a cab, if you like. The crowd seems to have gone.
Do ***you*** ever write fiction?
No, not at present. But I ***should***.
Oh?
Because it's- ***hmhm! food*** for the ***mind***.
I'm sorry?
I mean it can do a lot of cultural work.
You know, the ***potential*** for changing ***minds***.
Oh, I ***see.***

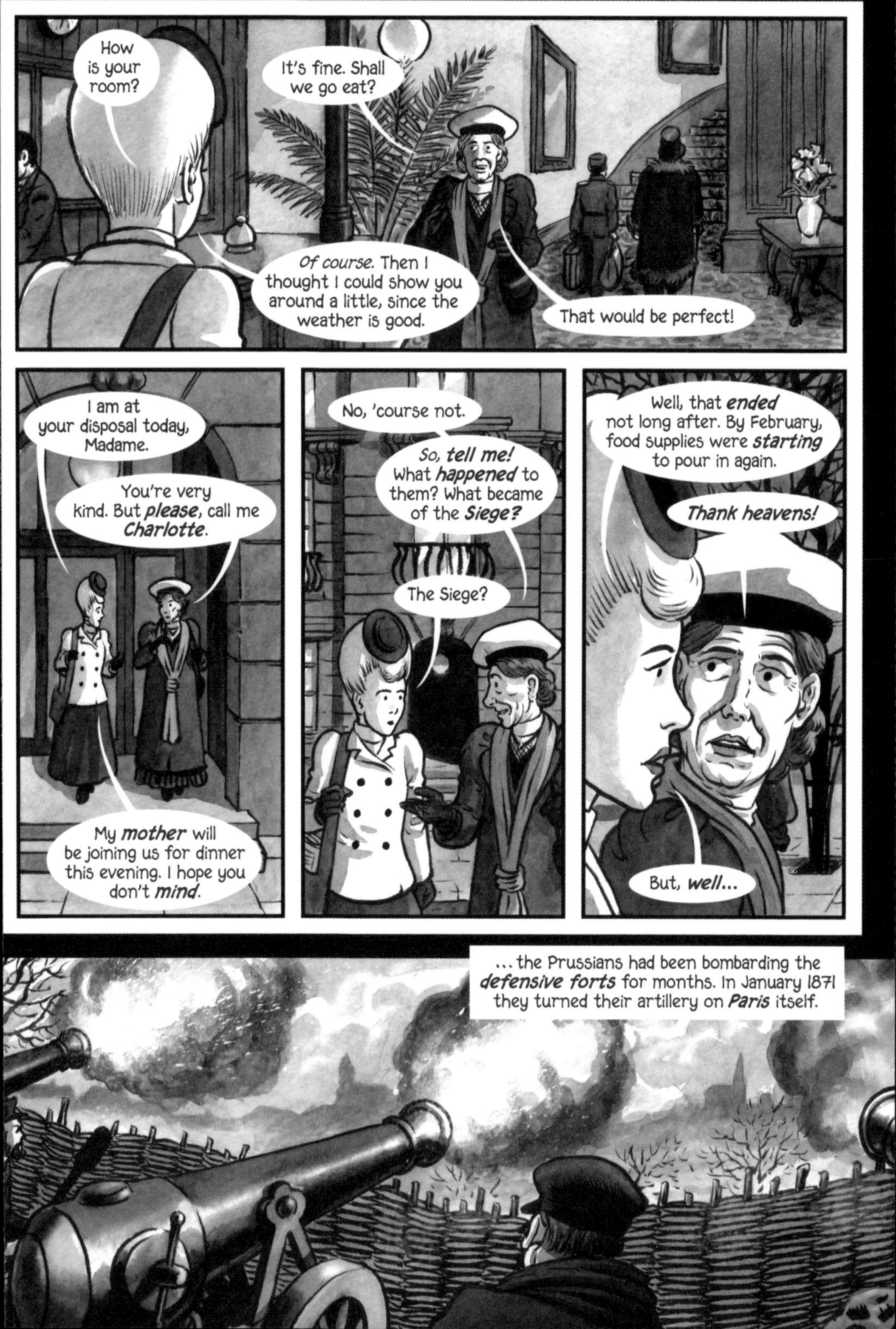
How is your room?
It's fine. Shall we go eat?
Of course. Then I thought I could show you around a little, since the weather is good.
That would be perfect!
I am at your disposal today, Madame.
You're very kind. But please, call me Charlotte.
My mother will be joining us for dinner this evening. I hope you don't mind.
No, 'course not.
So, tell me! What happened to them? What became of the Siege?
The Siege?
Well, that ended not long after. By February, food supplies were starting to pour in again.
Thank heavens!
But, well...
...the Prussians had been bombarding the defensive forts for months. In January 1871 they turned their artillery on Paris itself.

January 6th 1871.

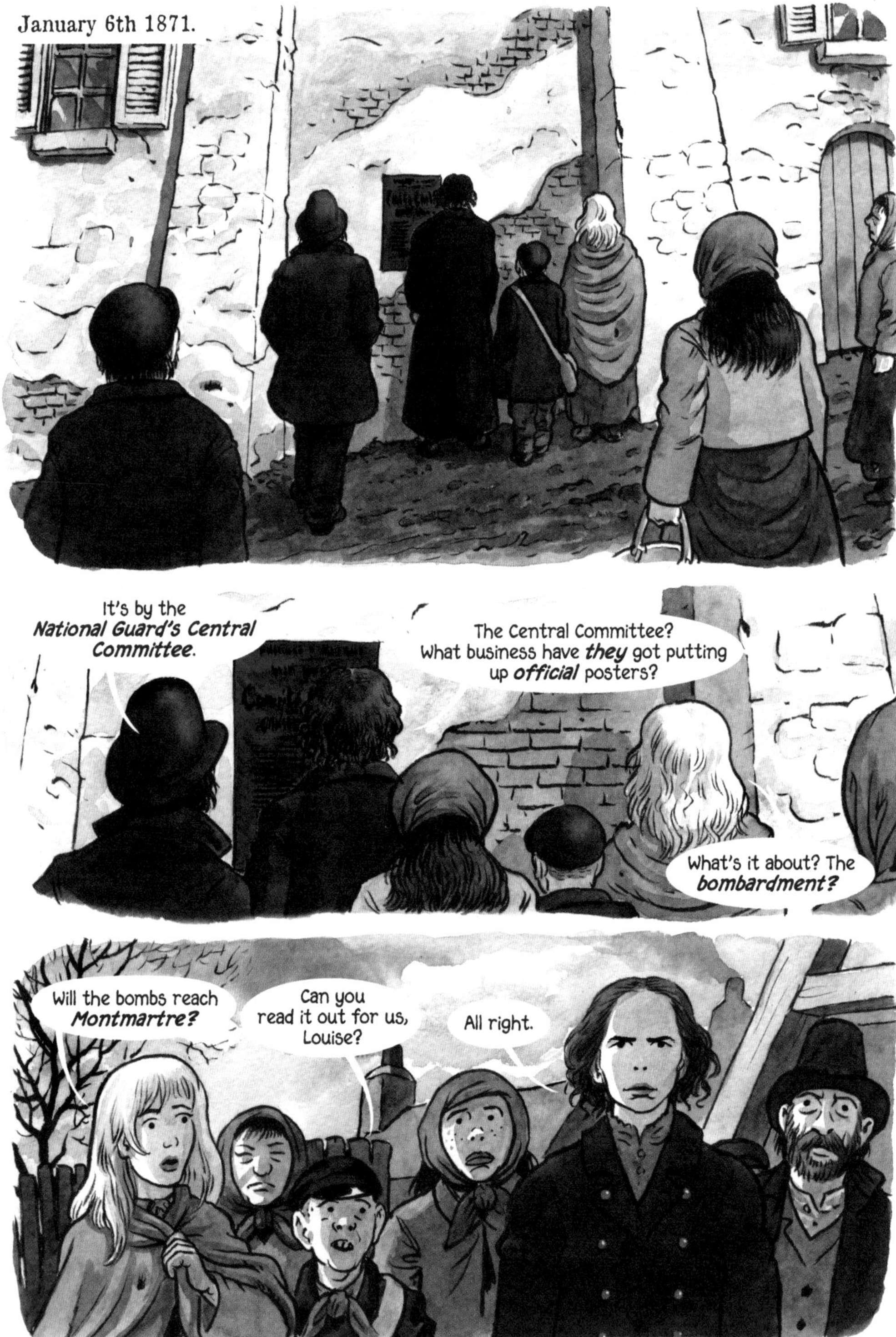
It's by the *National Guard's Central Committee*.
The Central Committee? What business have *they* got putting up *official* posters?
What's it about? The *bombardment?*
Will the bombs reach *Montmartre?*
Can you read it out for us, Louise?
All right.

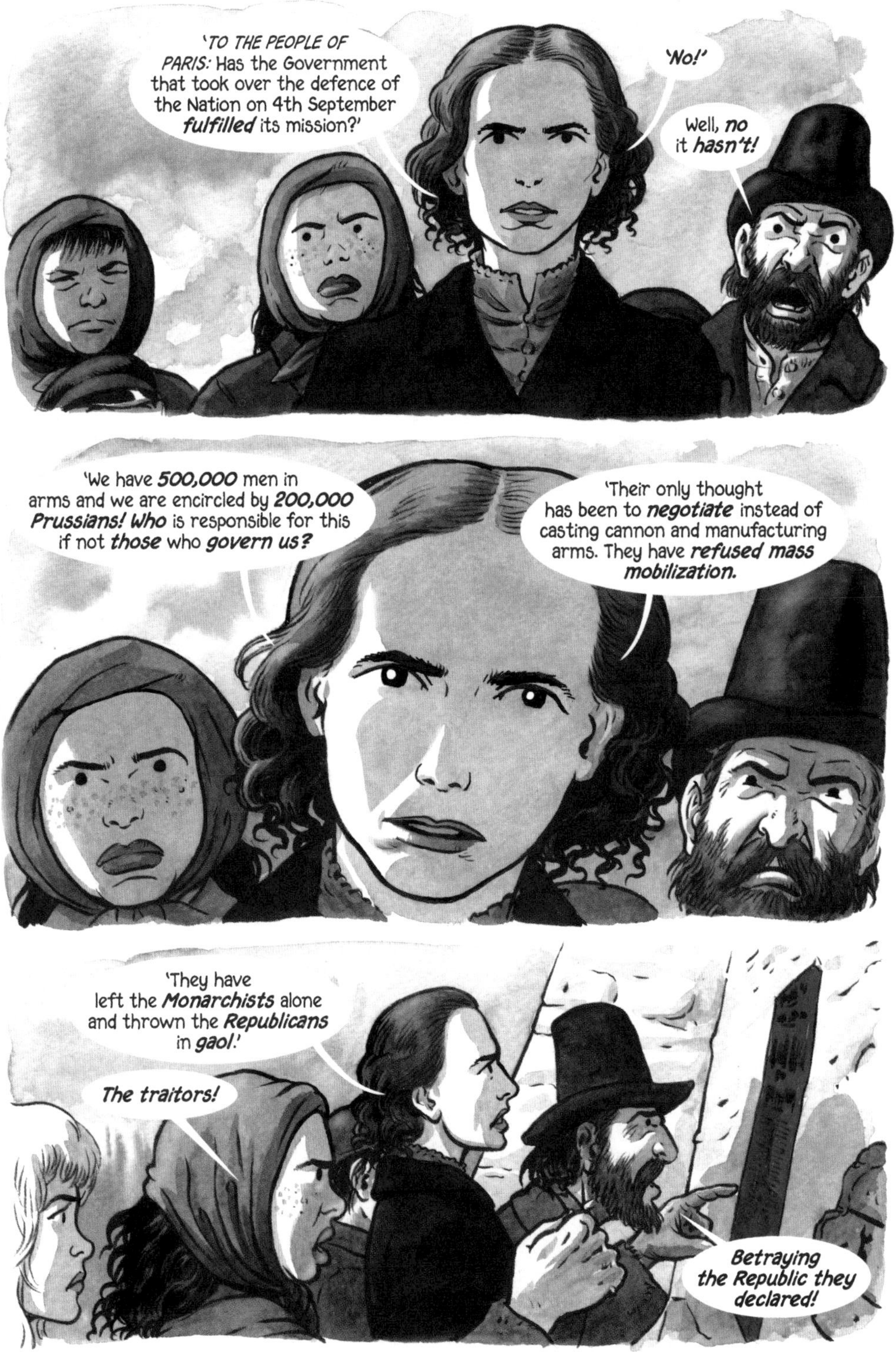
'TO THE PEOPLE OF PARIS: Has the Government that took over the defence of the Nation on 4th September fulfilled its mission?'
'No!'
Well, no it hasn't!
'We have 500,000 men in arms and we are encircled by 200,000 Prussians! Who is responsible for this if not those who govern us?
'Their only thought has been to negotiate instead of casting cannon and manufacturing arms. They have refused mass mobilization.
'They have left the Monarchists alone and thrown the Republicans in gaol.'
The traitors!
Betraying the Republic they declared!

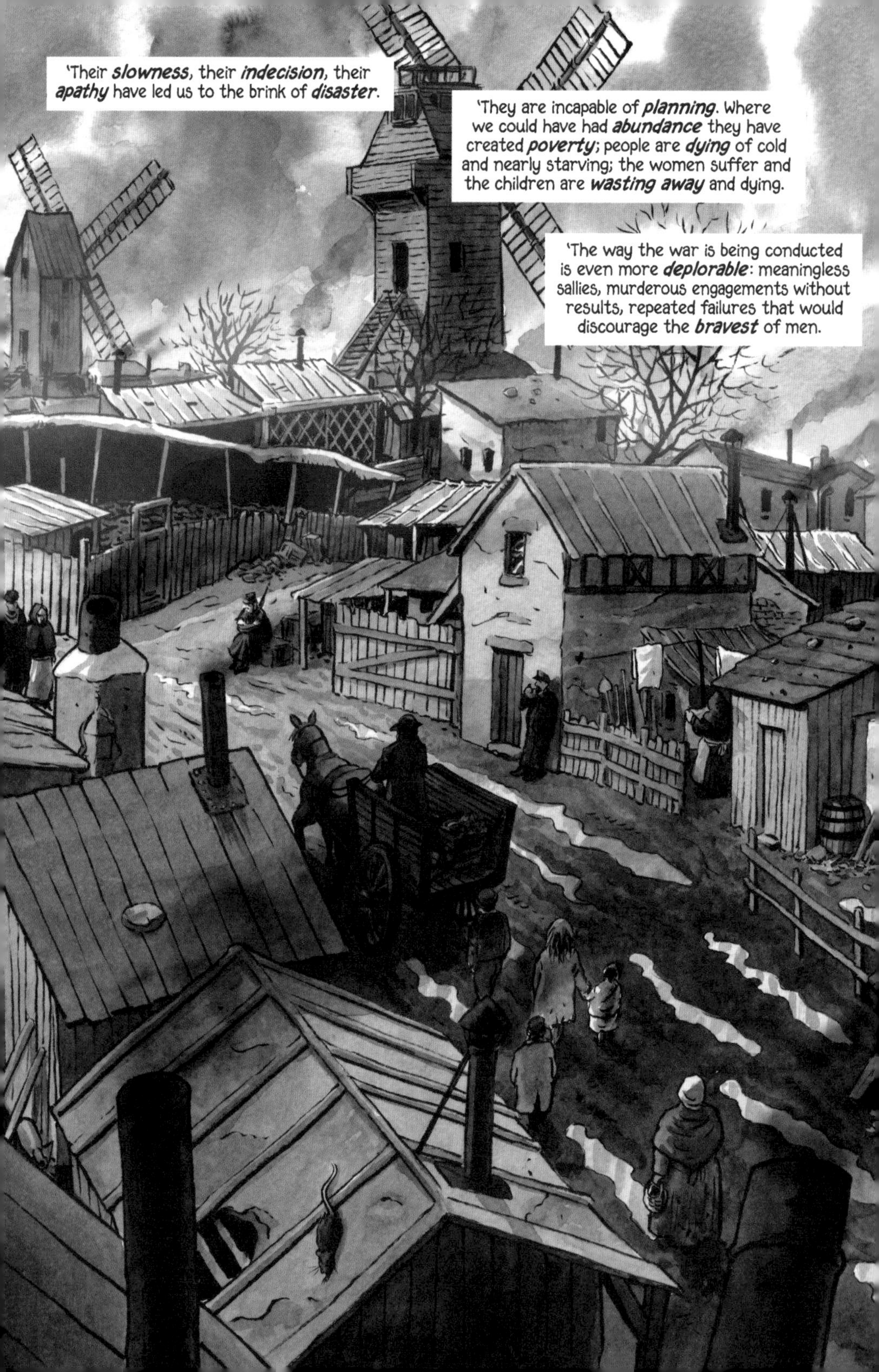
'Their slowness, their indecision, their apathy have led us to the brink of disaster.
'They are incapable of planning. Where we could have had abundance they have created poverty; people are dying of cold and nearly starving; the women suffer and the children are wasting away and dying.
'The way the war is being conducted is even more deplorable: meaningless sallies, murderous engagements without results, repeated failures that would discourage the bravest of men.

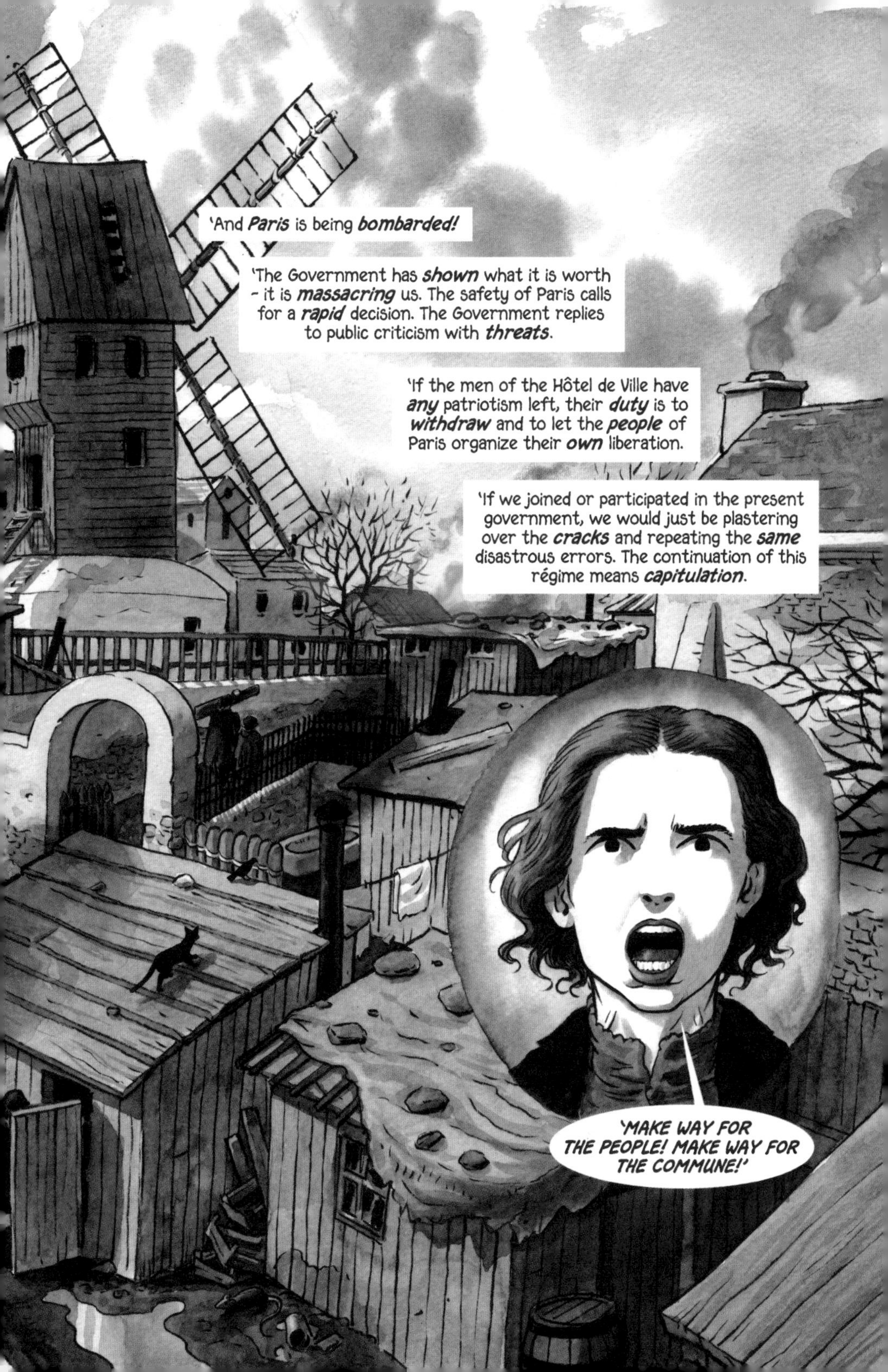
'And *Paris* is being *bombarded!*
'The Government has *shown* what it is worth – it is *massacring* us. The safety of Paris calls for a *rapid* decision. The Government replies to public criticism with *threats*.
'If the men of the Hôtel de Ville have *any* patriotism left, their *duty* is to *withdraw* and to let the *people* of Paris organize their *own* liberation.
'If we joined or participated in the present government, we would just be plastering over the *cracks* and repeating the *same* disastrous errors. The continuation of this régime means *capitulation*.
'MAKE WAY FOR THE PEOPLE! MAKE WAY FOR THE COMMUNE!'

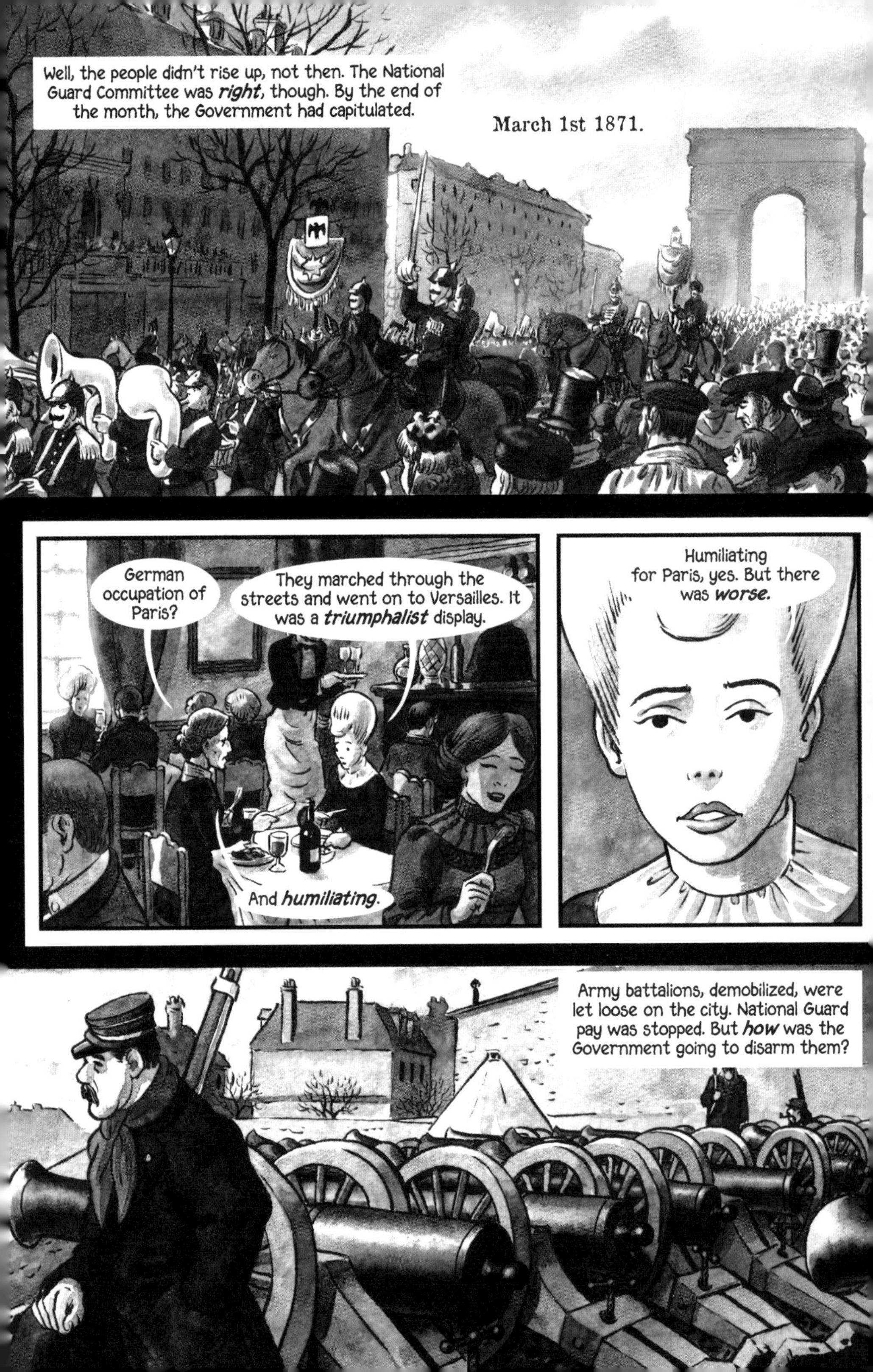
Well, the people didn't rise up, not then. The National Guard Committee was *right*, though. By the end of the month, the Government had capitulated.
March 1st 1871.
German occupation of Paris?
They marched through the streets and went on to Versailles. It was a *triumphalist* display.
And *humiliating*.
Humiliating for Paris, yes. But there was *worse*.
Army battalions, demobilized, were let loose on the city. National Guard pay was stopped. But *how* was the Government going to disarm them?

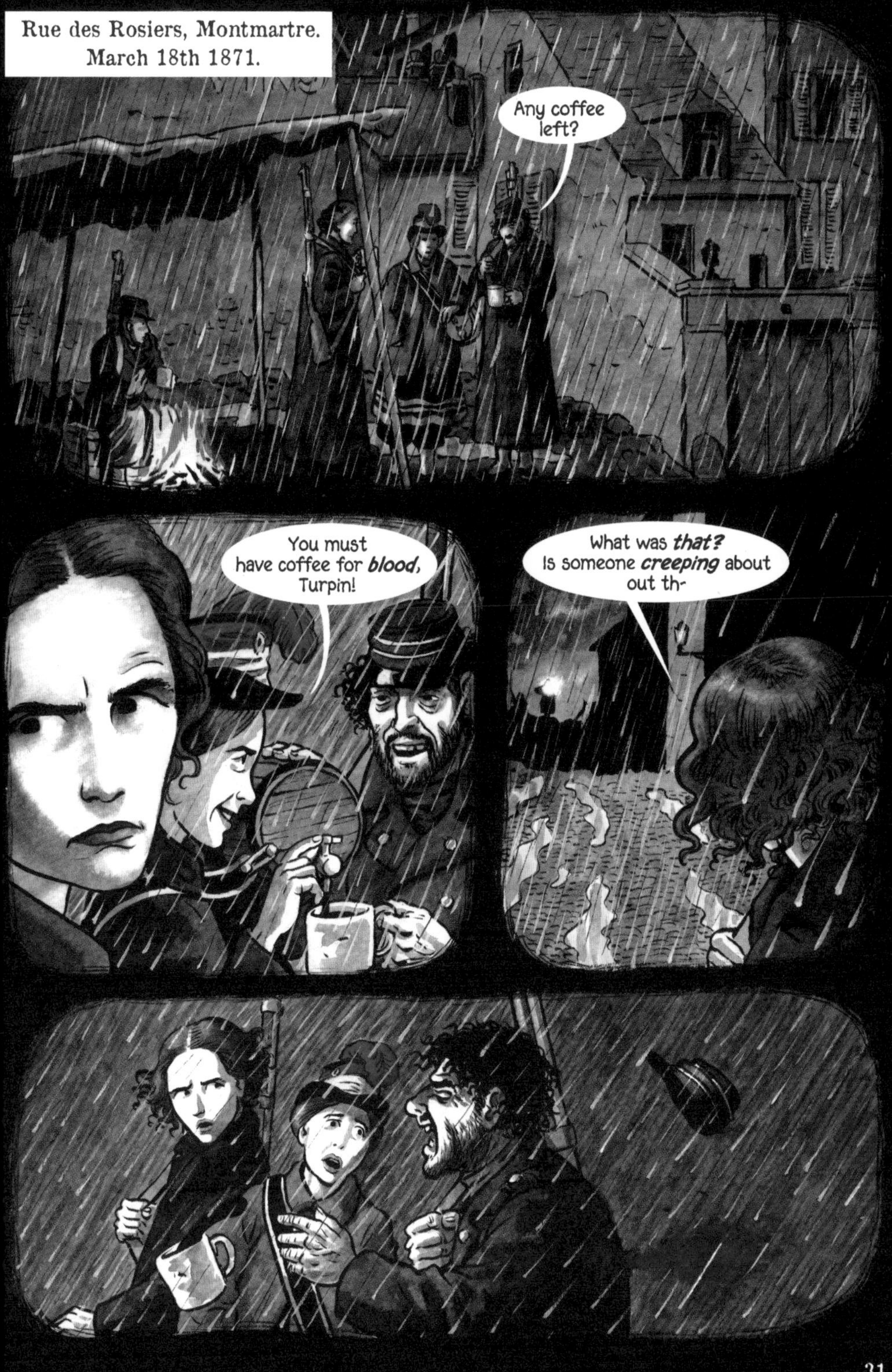
Rue des Rosiers, Montmartre.
March 18th 1871.
Any coffee left?
You must have coffee for *blood*, Turpin!
What was *that?* Is someone *creeping* about out th-

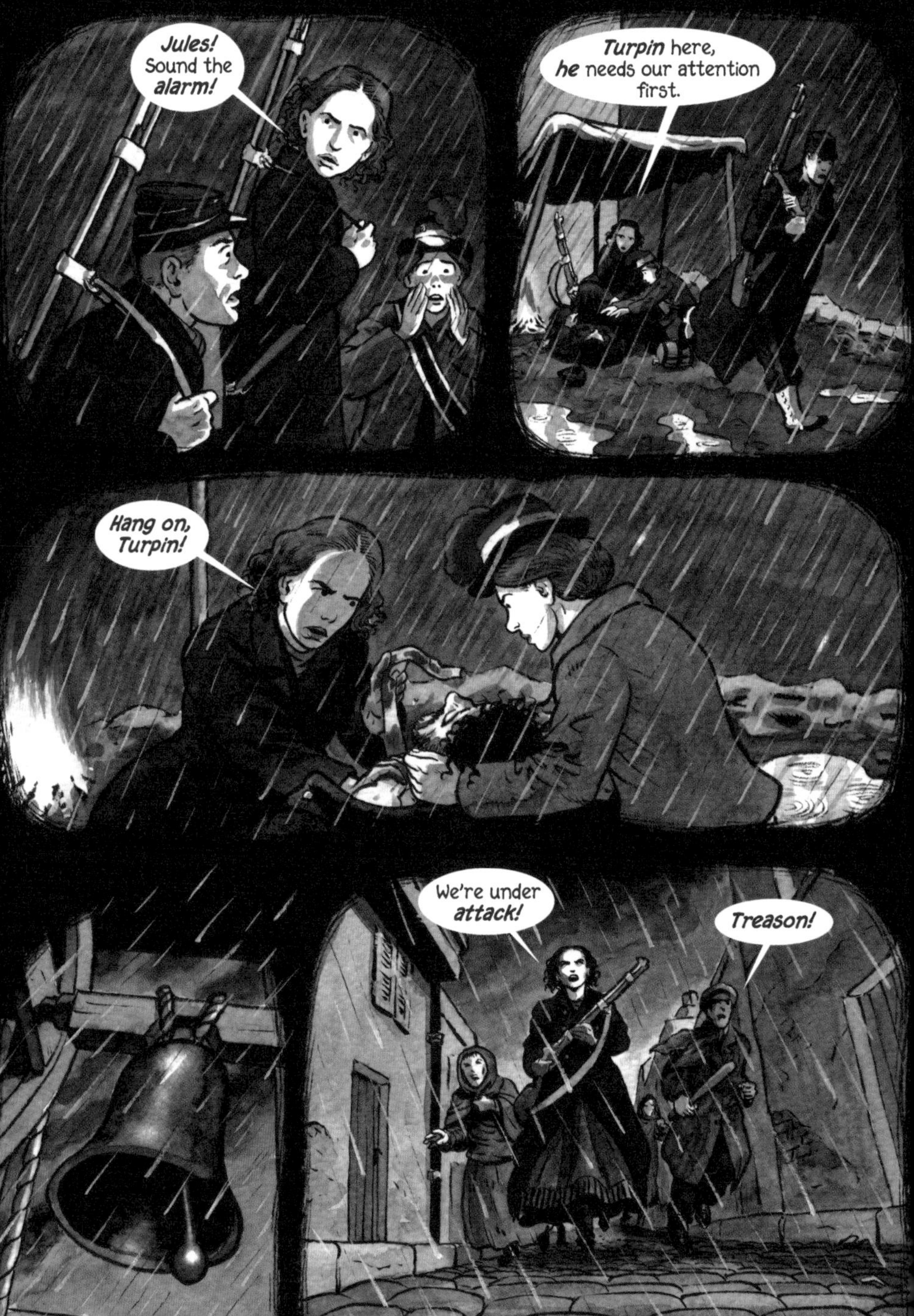
Jules! Sound the alarm!
Turpin here, he needs our attention first.
Hang on, Turpin!
We're under attack!
Treason!

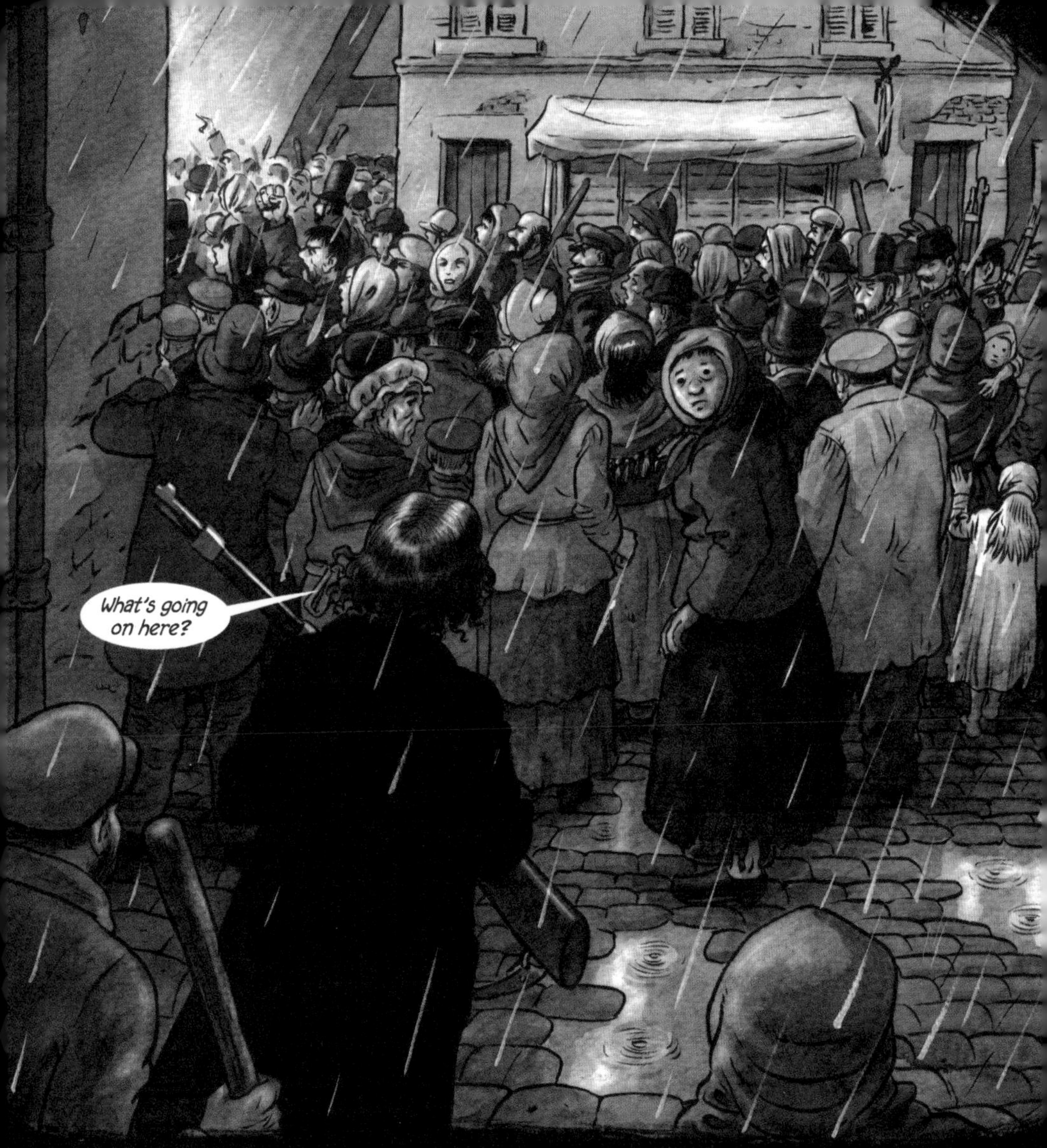
What's going on here?

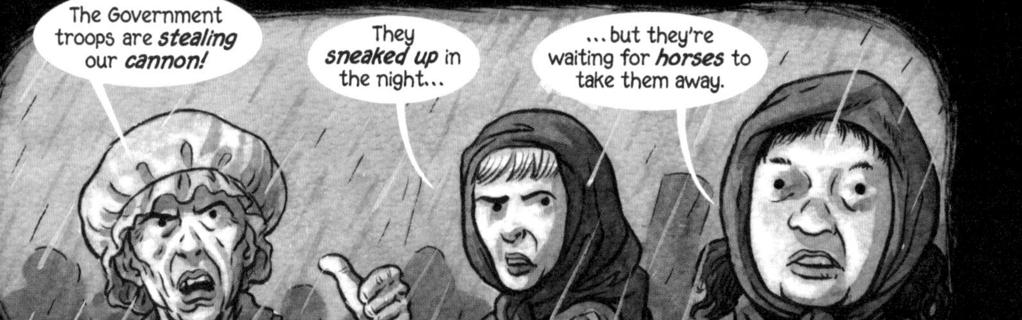
The Government troops are *stealing* our *cannon!*
They *sneaked up* in the night...
...but they're waiting for *horses* to take them away.

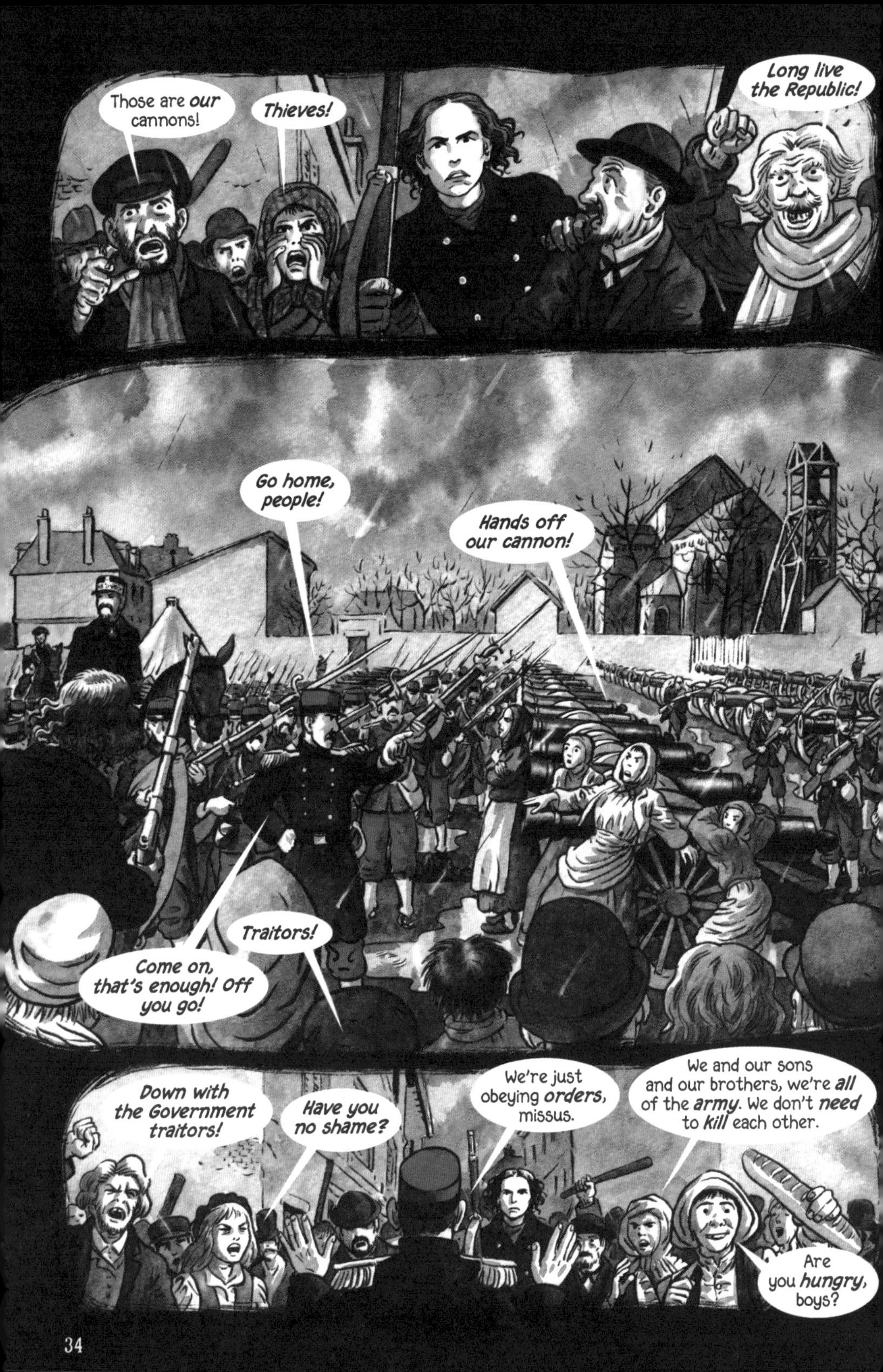

Those are our cannons!
Thieves!
Long live the Republic!
Go home, people!
Hands off our cannon!
Traitors!
Come on, that's enough! Off you go!
Down with the Government traitors!
Have you no shame?
We're just obeying orders, missus.
We and our sons and our brothers, we're all of the army. We don't need to kill each other.
Are you hungry, boys?

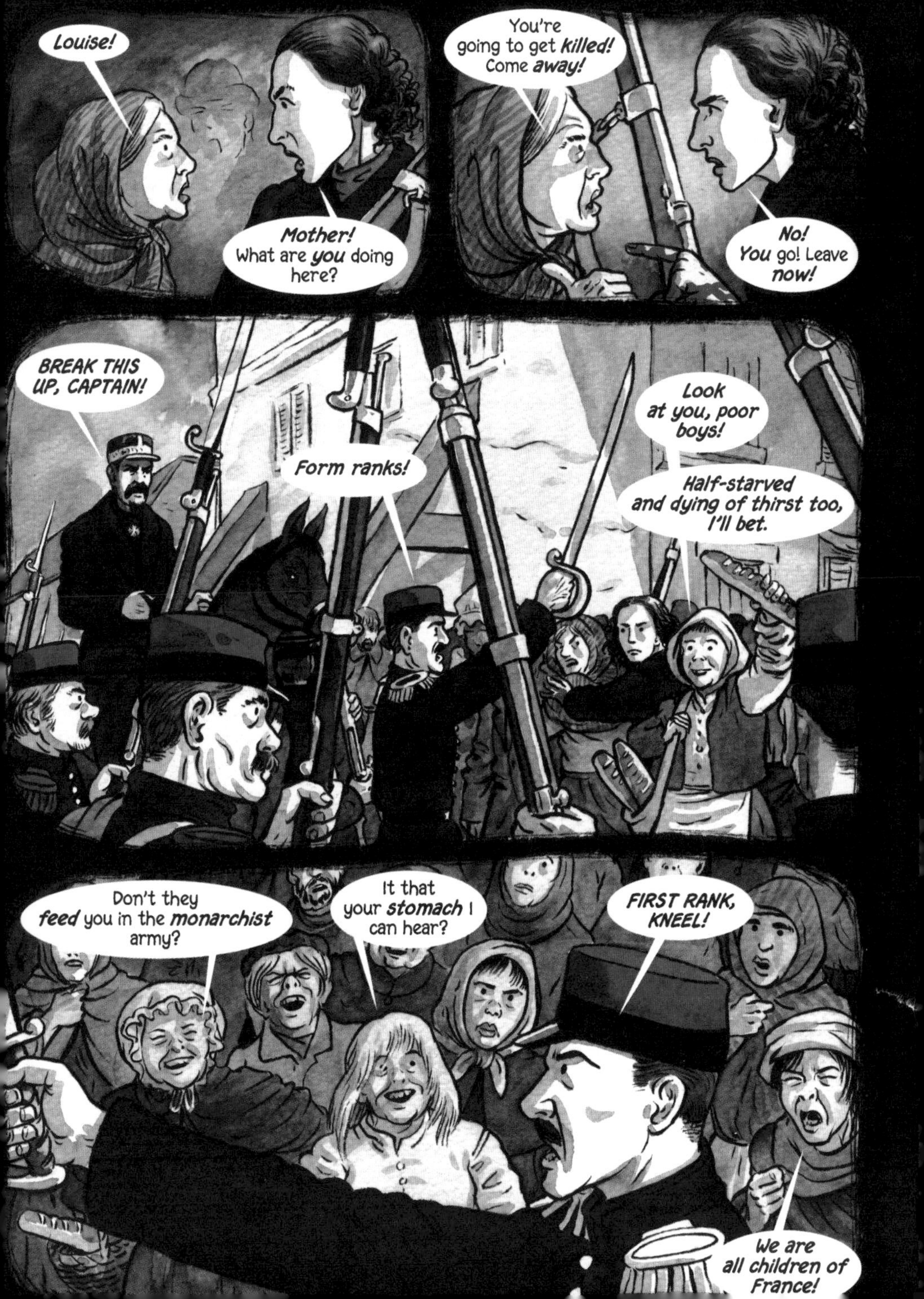
Louise!
Mother! What are you doing here?
You're going to get killed! Come away!
No! You go! Leave now!
BREAK THIS UP, CAPTAIN!
Form ranks!
Look at you, poor boys!
Half-starved and dying of thirst too, I'll bet.
Don't they feed you in the monarchist army?
It that your stomach I can hear?
FIRST RANK, KNEEL!
We are all children of France!

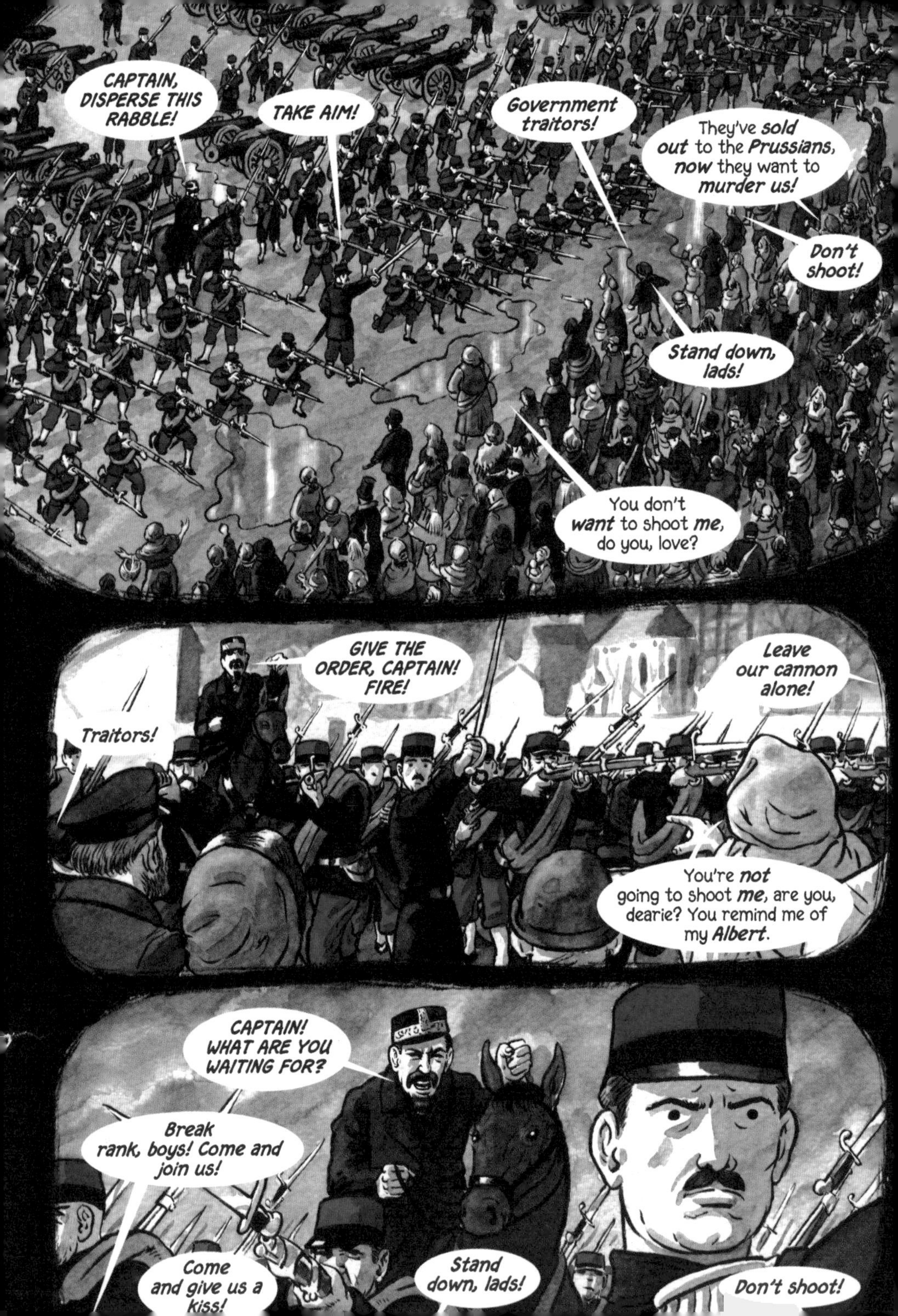

CAPTAIN, DISPERSE THIS RABBLE!
TAKE AIM!
Government traitors!
They've sold out to the Prussians, now they want to murder us!
Don't shoot!
Stand down, lads!
You don't want to shoot me, do you, love?
GIVE THE ORDER, CAPTAIN! FIRE!
Leave our cannon alone!
Traitors!
You're not going to shoot me, are you, dearie? You remind me of my Albert.
CAPTAIN! WHAT ARE YOU WAITING FOR?
Break rank, boys! Come and join us!
Come and give us a kiss!
Stand down, lads!
Don't shoot!

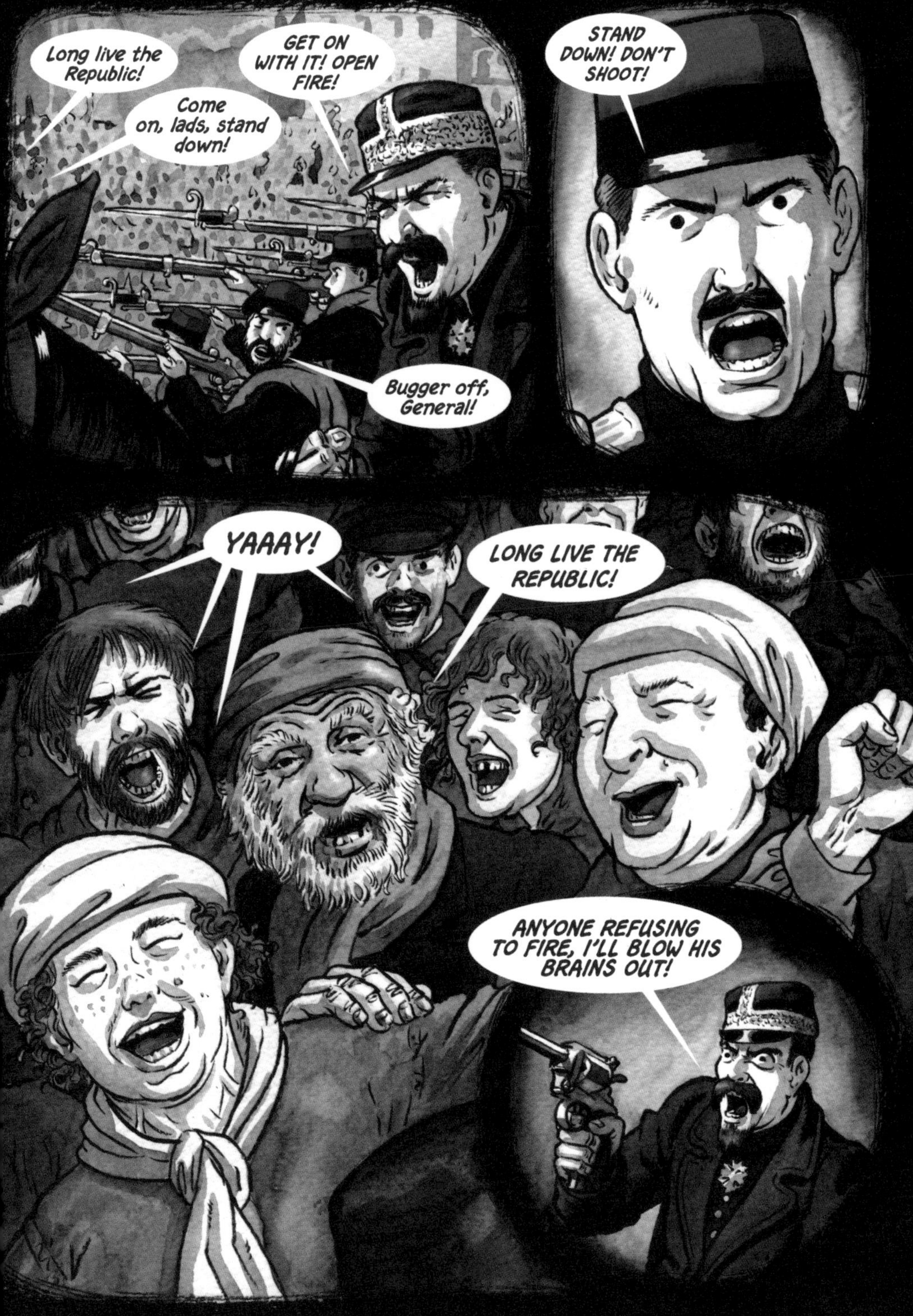
Long live the Republic!
Come on, lads, stand down!
GET ON WITH IT! OPEN FIRE!
Bugger off, General!
STAND DOWN! DON'T SHOOT!
YAAAY!
LONG LIVE THE REPUBLIC!
ANYONE REFUSING TO FIRE, I'LL BLOW HIS BRAINS OUT!

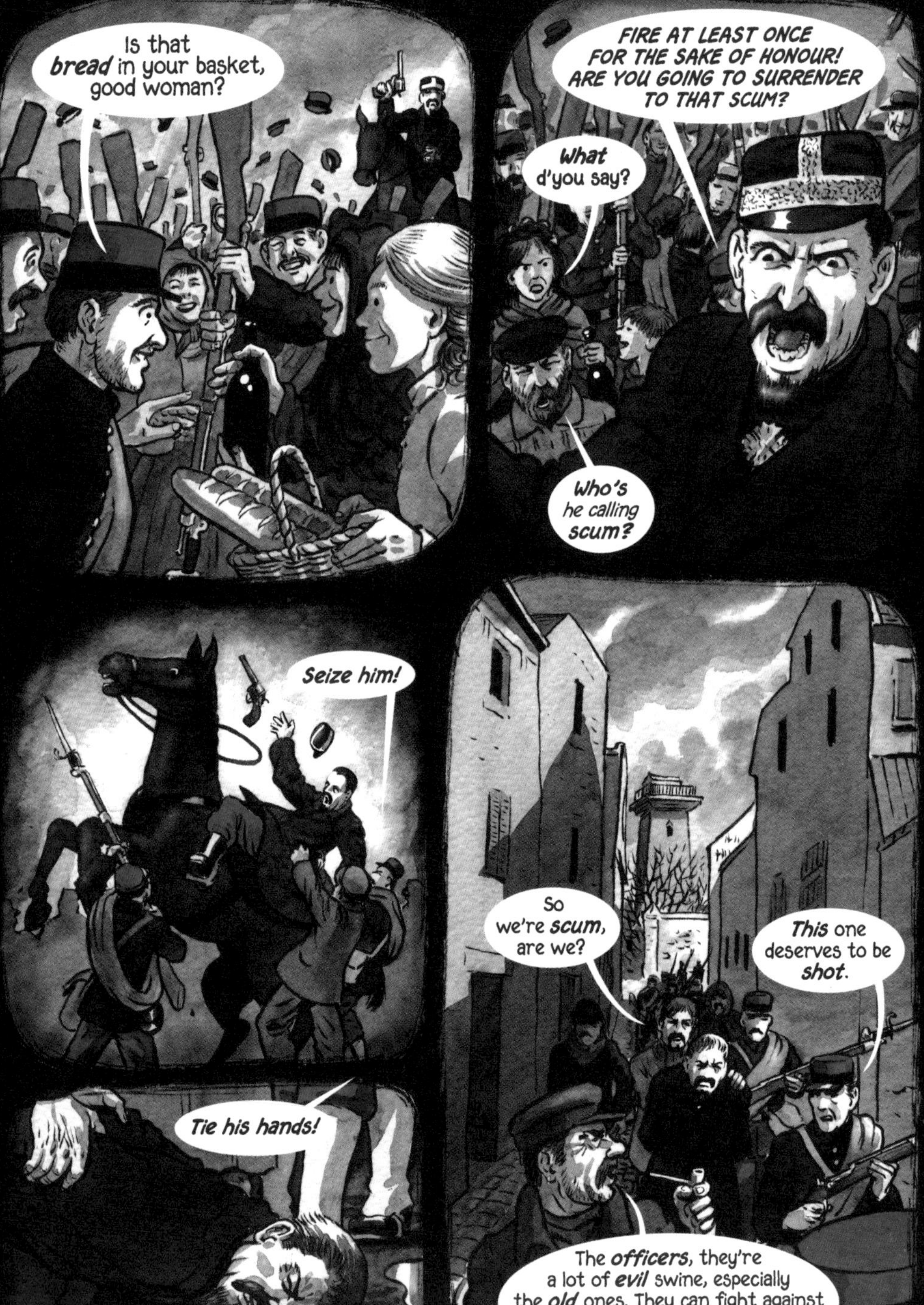
Is that bread in your basket, good woman?
FIRE AT LEAST ONCE FOR THE SAKE OF HONOUR! ARE YOU GOING TO SURRENDER TO THAT SCUM?
What d'you say?
Who's he calling scum?
Seize him!
Tie his hands!
So we're scum, are we?
This one deserves to be shot.
The officers, they're a lot of evil swine, especially the old ones. They can fight against French fathers of families, but not against Prussians.

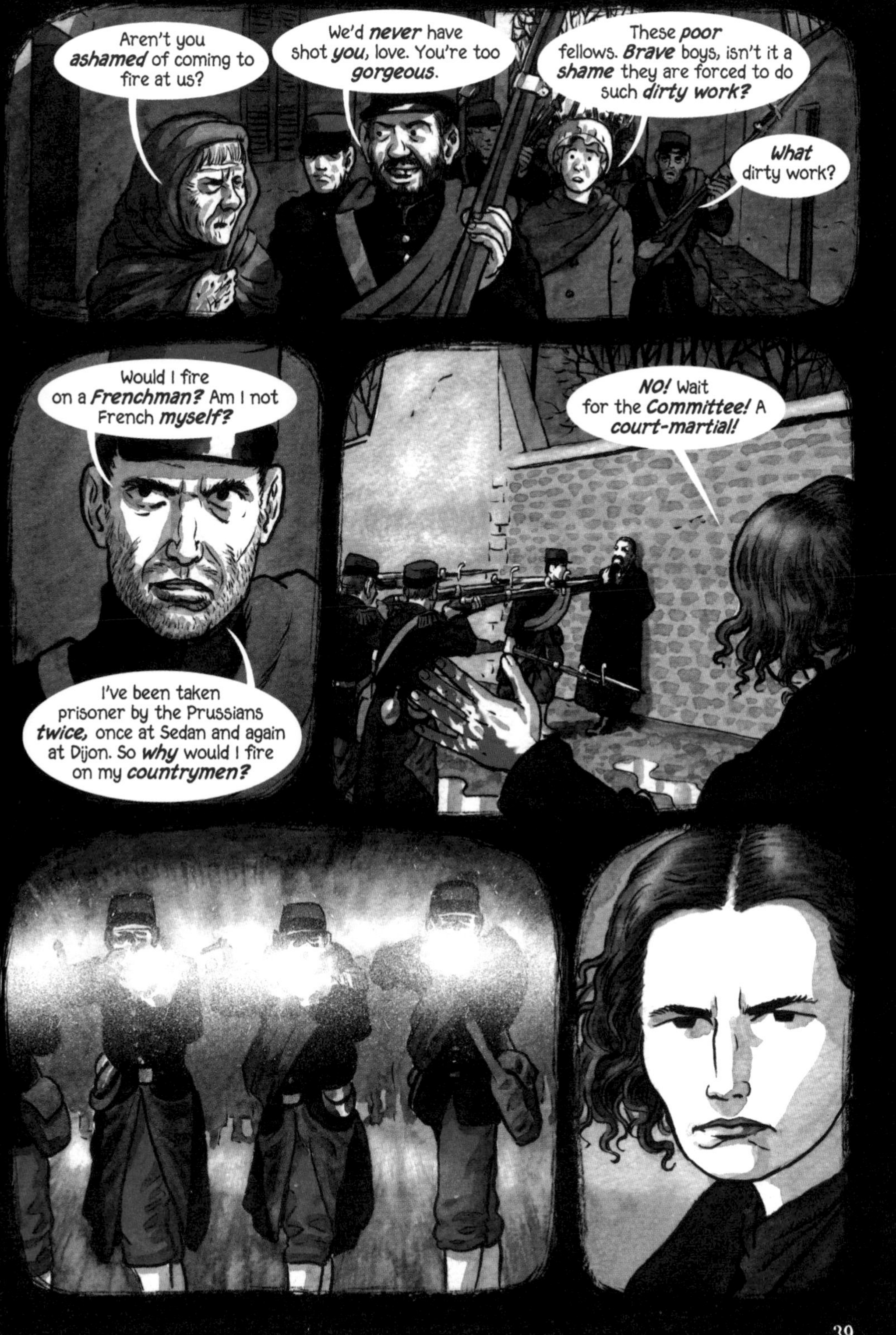
Aren't you ashamed of coming to fire at us?
We'd never have shot you, love. You're too gorgeous.
These poor fellows. Brave boys, isn't it a shame they are forced to do such dirty work?
What dirty work?
Would I fire on a Frenchman? Am I not French myself?
I've been taken prisoner by the Prussians twice, once at Sedan and again at Dijon. So why would I fire on my countrymen?
NO! Wait for the Committee! A court-martial!

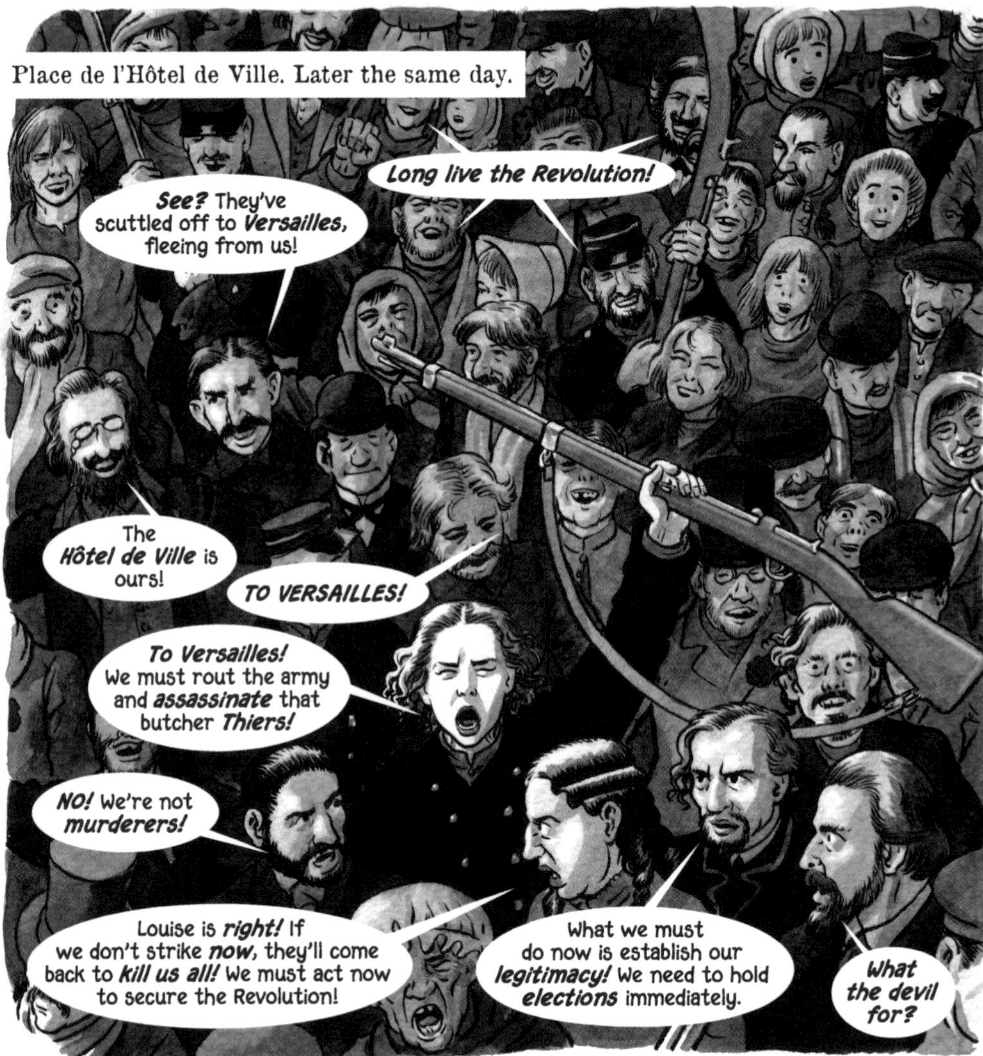
Place de l'Hôtel de Ville. Later the same day.
Long live the Revolution!
See? They've scuttled off to Versailles, fleeing from us!
The Hôtel de Ville is ours!
TO VERSAILLES!
To Versailles! We must rout the army and assassinate that butcher Thiers!
NO! We're not murderers!
Louise is right! If we don't strike now, they'll come back to kill us all! We must act now to secure the Revolution!
What we must do now is establish our legitimacy! We need to hold elections immediately.
What the devil for?

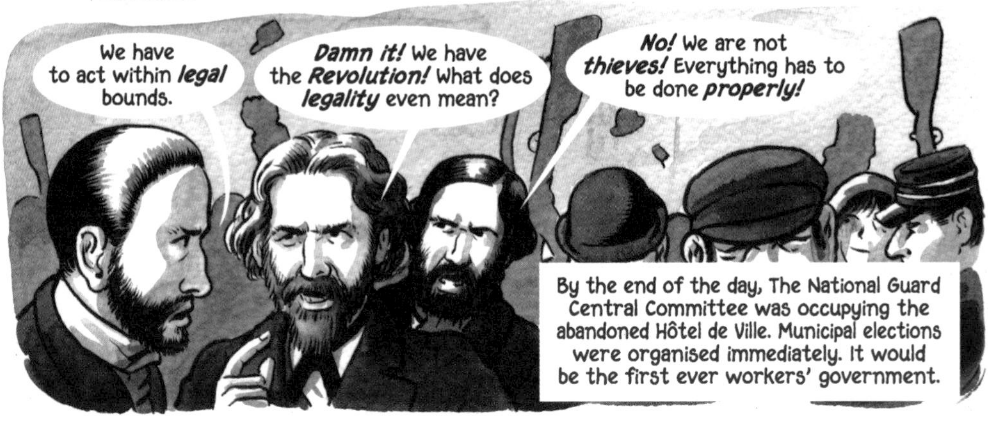
We have to act within legal bounds.
Damn it! We have the Revolution! What does legality even mean?
No! We are not thieves! Everything has to be done properly!
By the end of the day, The National Guard Central Committee was occupying the abandoned Hôtel de Ville. Municipal elections were organised immediately. It would be the first ever workers' government.

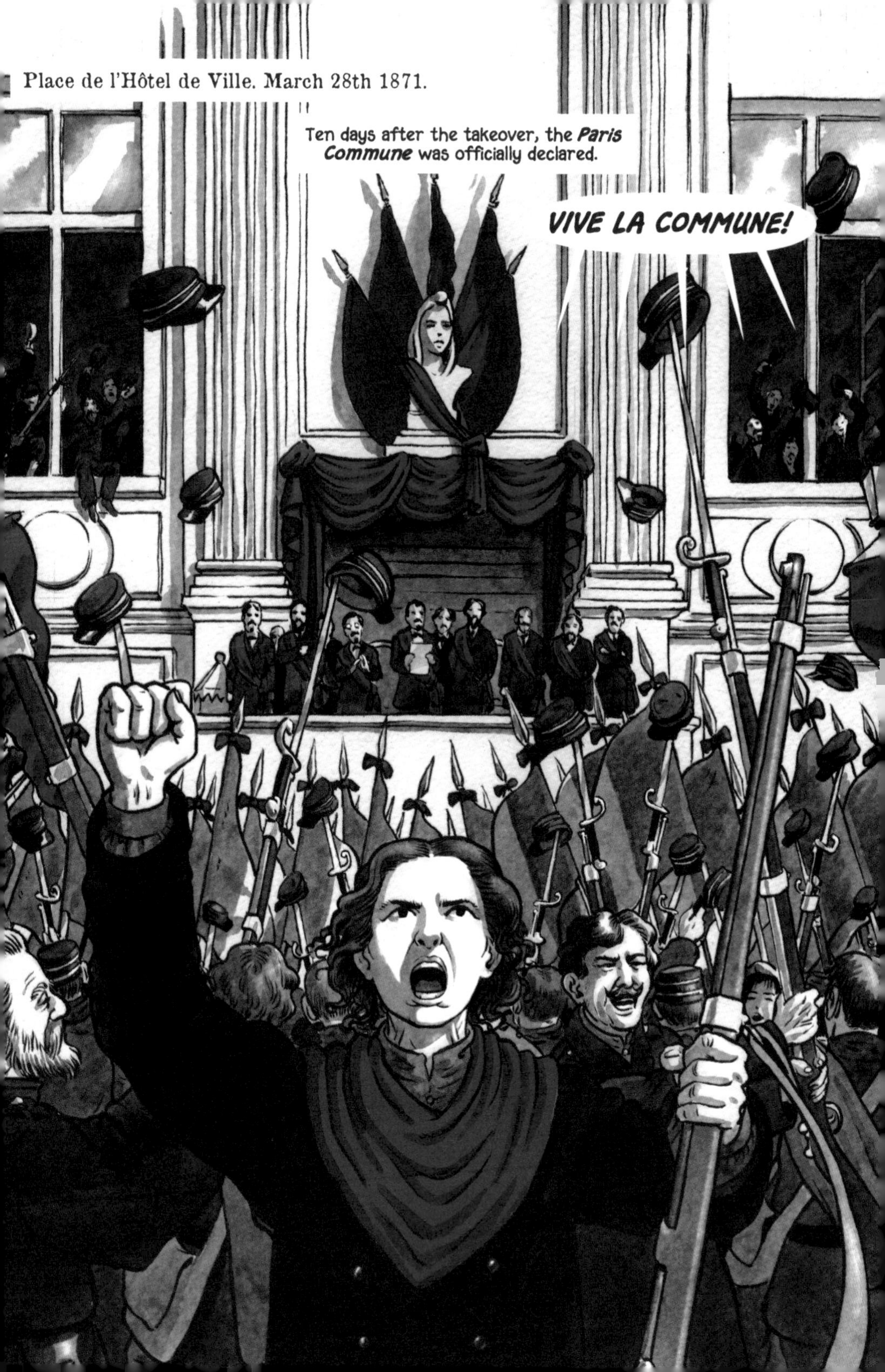
Place de l'Hôtel de Ville. March 28th 1871.
Ten days after the takeover, the *Paris Commune* was officially declared.
VIVE LA COMMUNE!

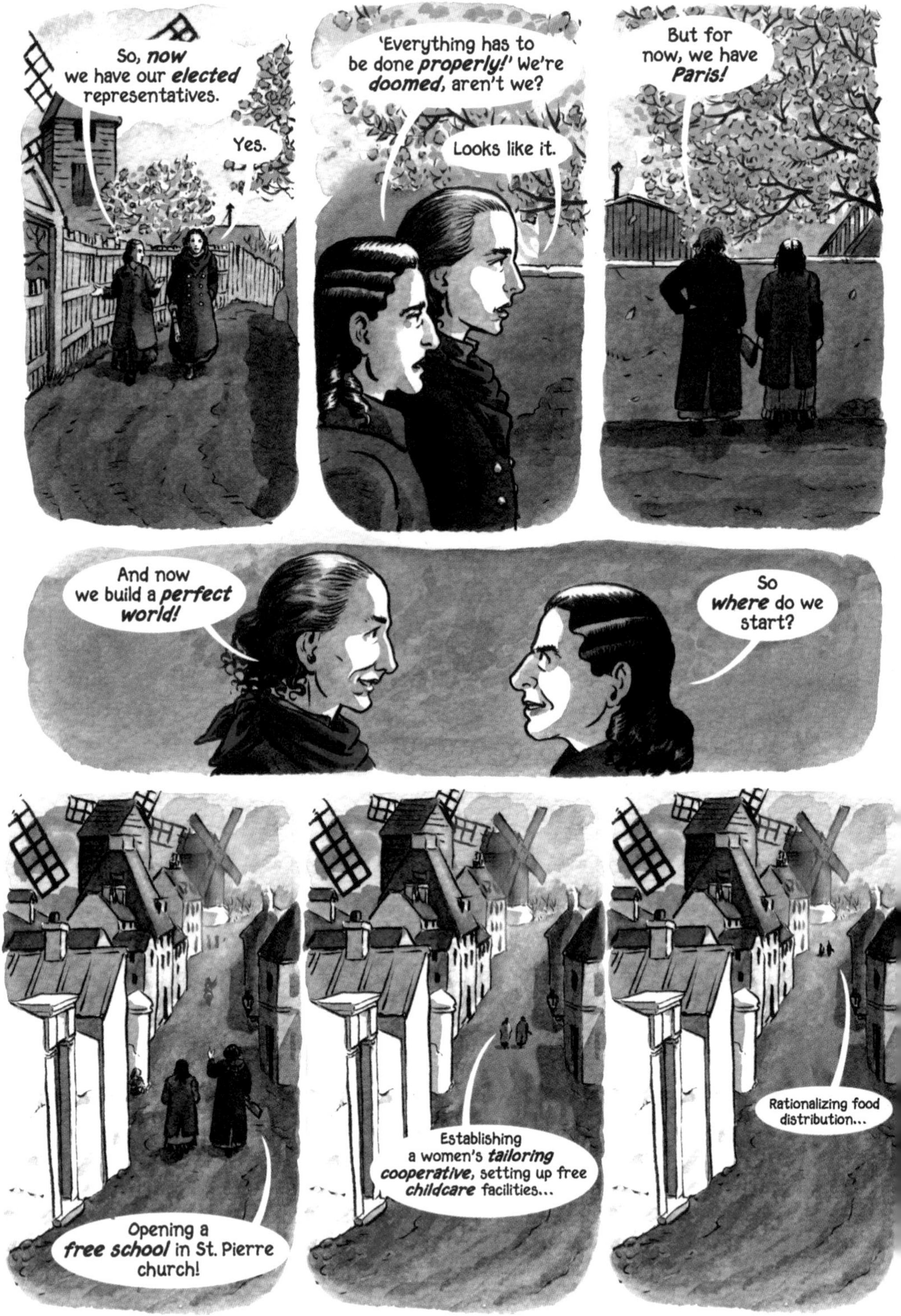

So, *now* we have our *elected* representatives.
Yes.
'Everything has to be done *properly!*' We're *doomed*, aren't we?
Looks like it.
But for now, we have *Paris!*
And now we build a *perfect world!*
So *where* do we start?
Opening a *free school* in St. Pierre church!
Establishing a women's *tailoring cooperative*, setting up free *childcare* facilities...
Rationalizing food distribution...

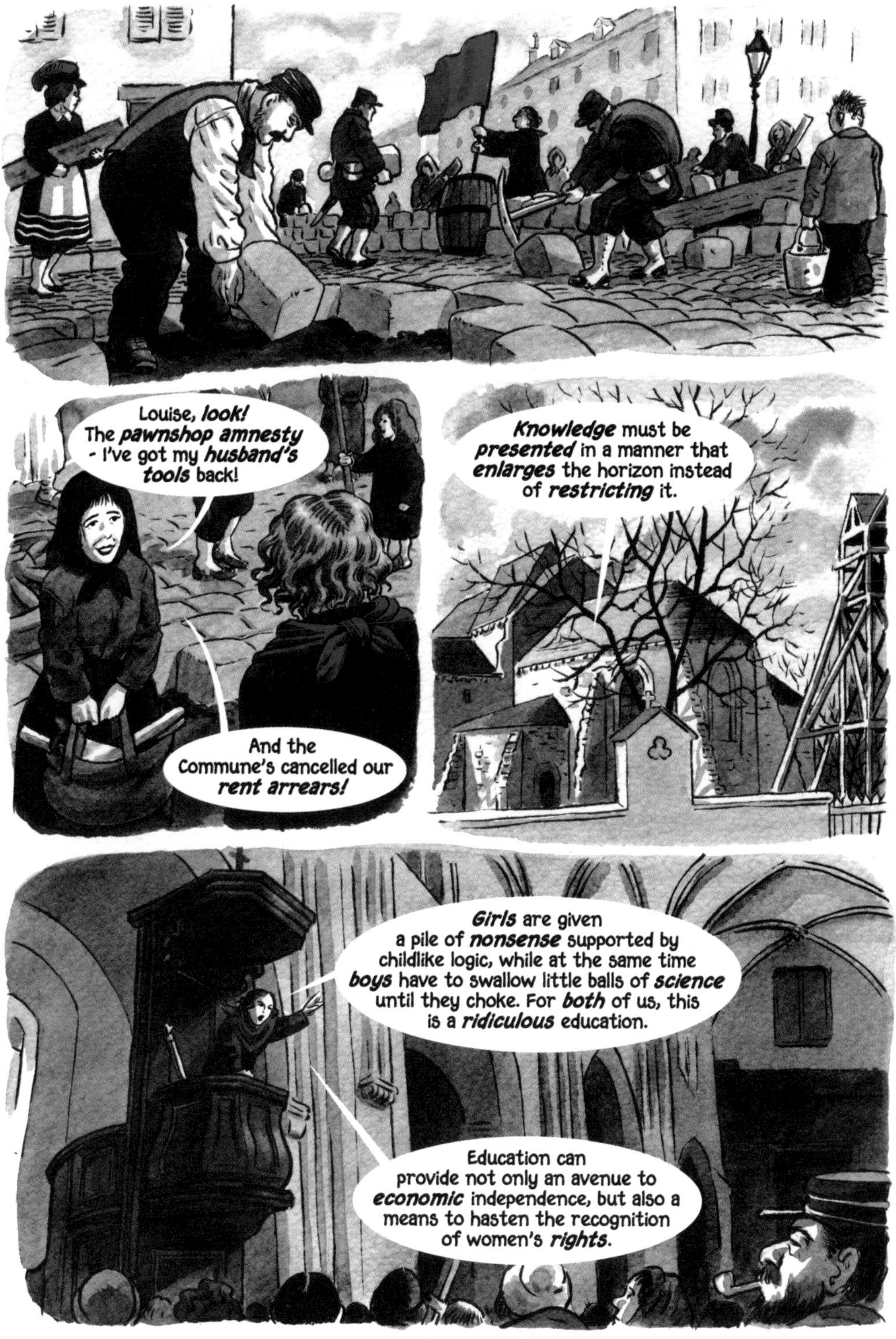
Louise, look! The pawnshop amnesty - I've got my husband's tools back!
And the Commune's cancelled our rent arrears!
Knowledge must be presented in a manner that enlarges the horizon instead of restricting it.
Girls are given a pile of nonsense supported by childlike logic, while at the same time boys have to swallow little balls of science until they choke. For both of us, this is a ridiculous education.
Education can provide not only an avenue to economic independence, but also a means to hasten the recognition of women's rights.

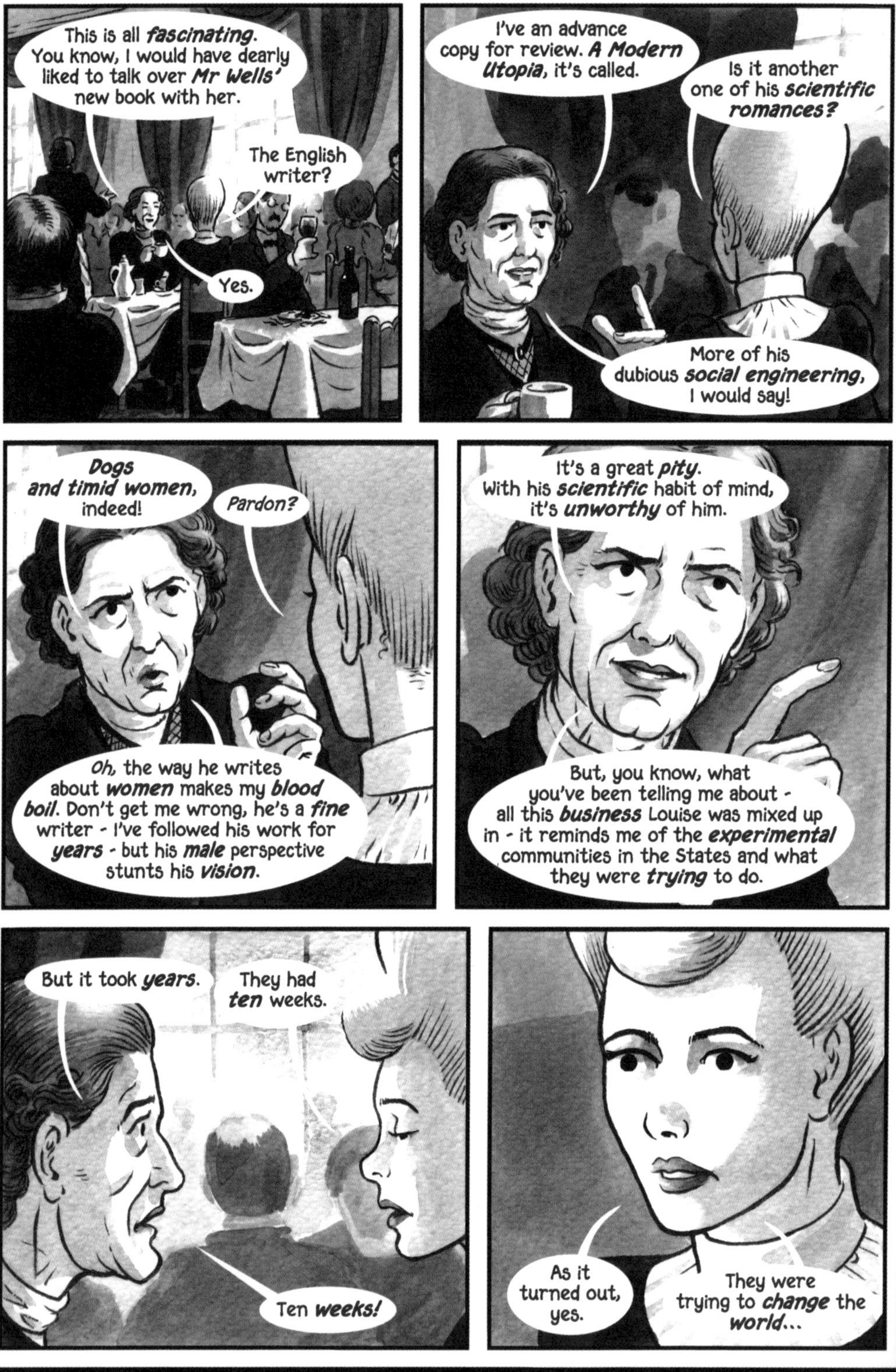
This is all fascinating. You know, I would have dearly liked to talk over Mr Wells' new book with her.
The English writer?
Yes.
I've an advance copy for review. A Modern Utopia, it's called.
Is it another one of his scientific romances?
More of his dubious social engineering, I would say!
Dogs and timid women, indeed!
Pardon?
Oh, the way he writes about women makes my blood boil. Don't get me wrong, he's a fine writer - I've followed his work for years - but his male perspective stunts his vision.
It's a great pity. With his scientific habit of mind, it's unworthy of him.
But, you know, what you've been telling me about - all this business Louise was mixed up in - it reminds me of the experimental communities in the States and what they were trying to do.
But it took years.
They had ten weeks.
Ten weeks!
As it turned out, yes.
They were trying to change the world...

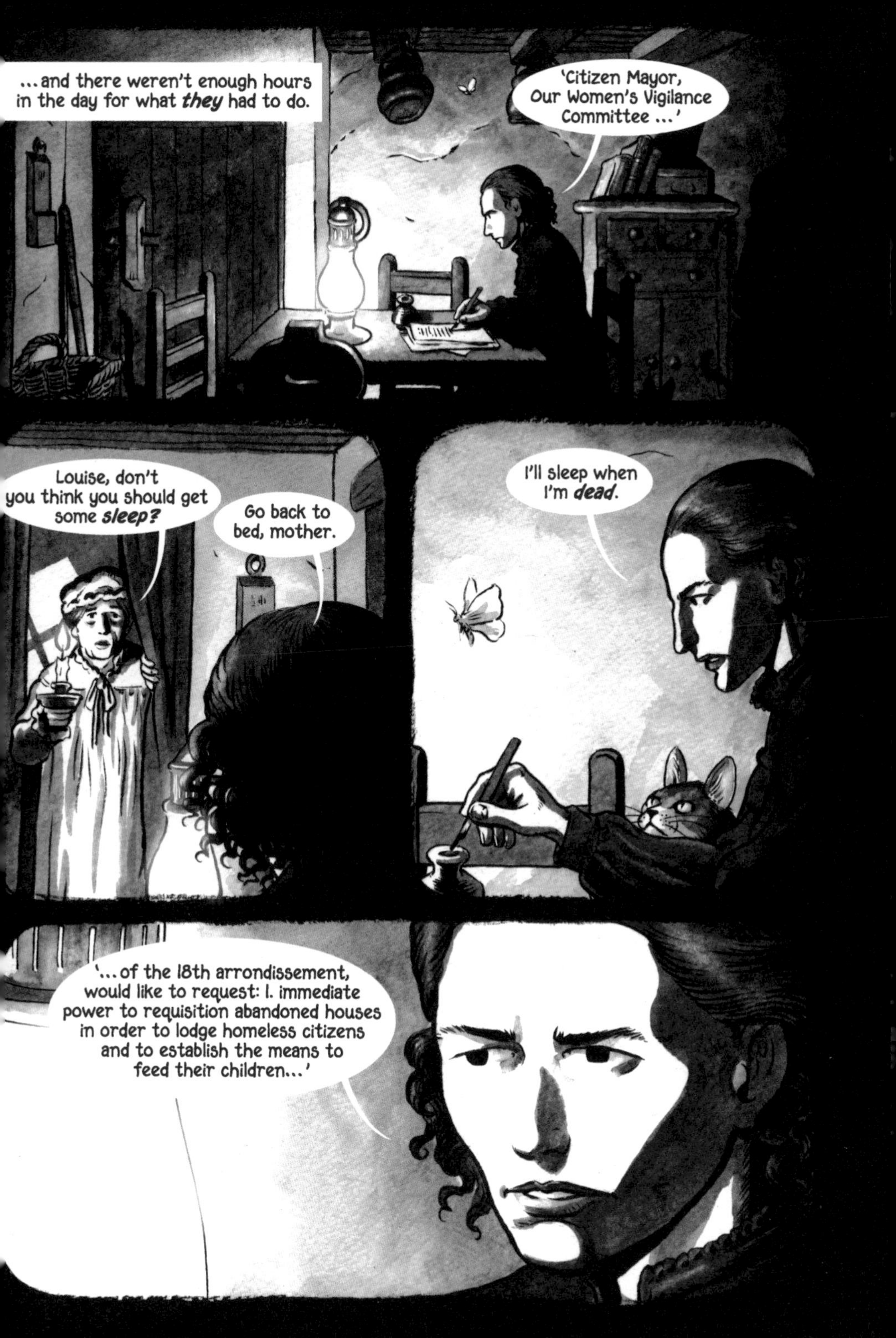
...and there weren't enough hours in the day for what *they* had to do.
'Citizen Mayor, Our Women's Vigilance Committee ...'
Louise, don't you think you should get some *sleep?*
Go back to bed, mother.
I'll sleep when I'm *dead*.
'...of the 18th arrondissement, would like to request: 1. immediate power to requisition abandoned houses in order to lodge homeless citizens and to establish the means to feed their children...'

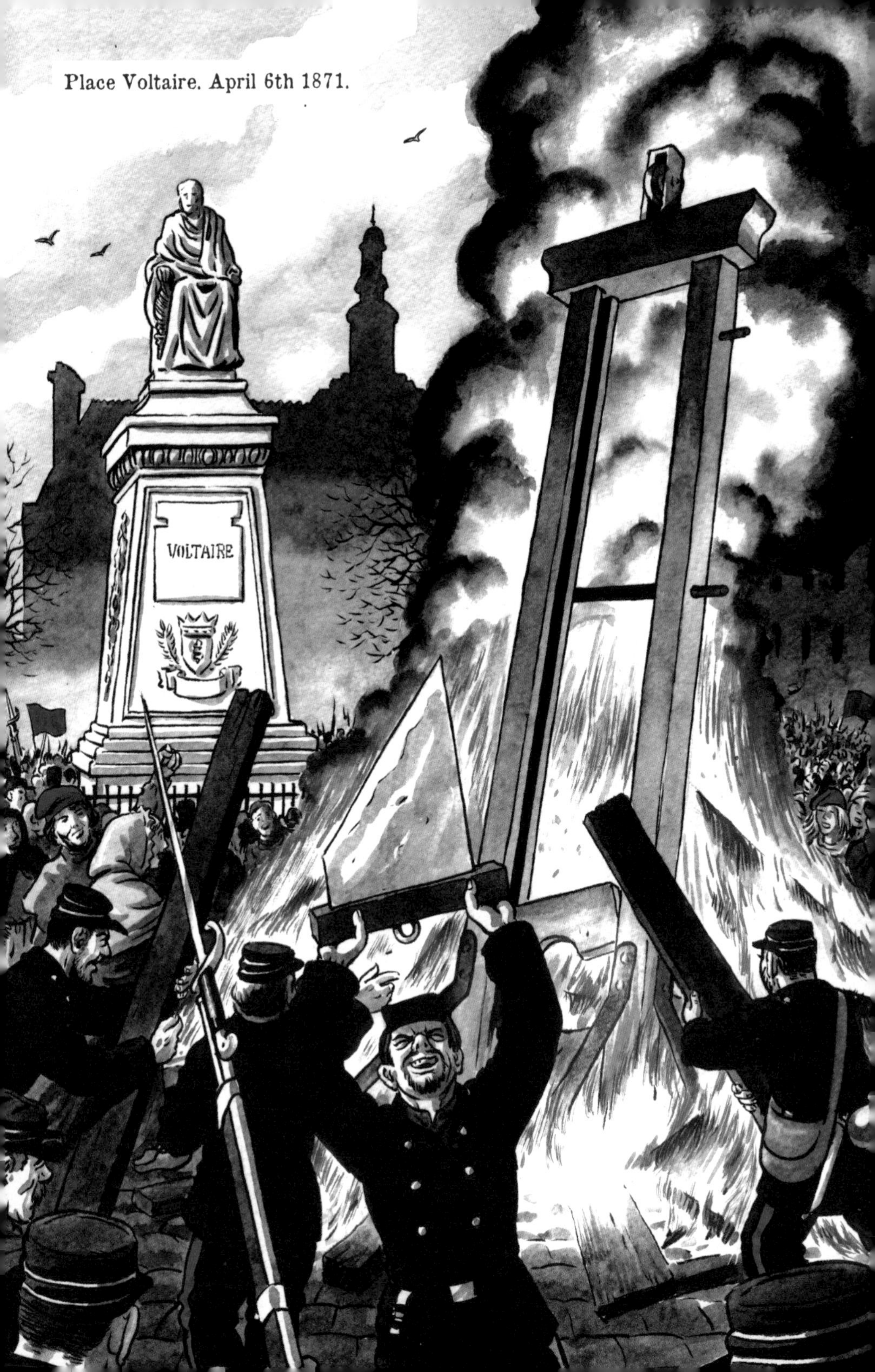
Place Voltaire. April 6th 1871.
VOLTAIRE

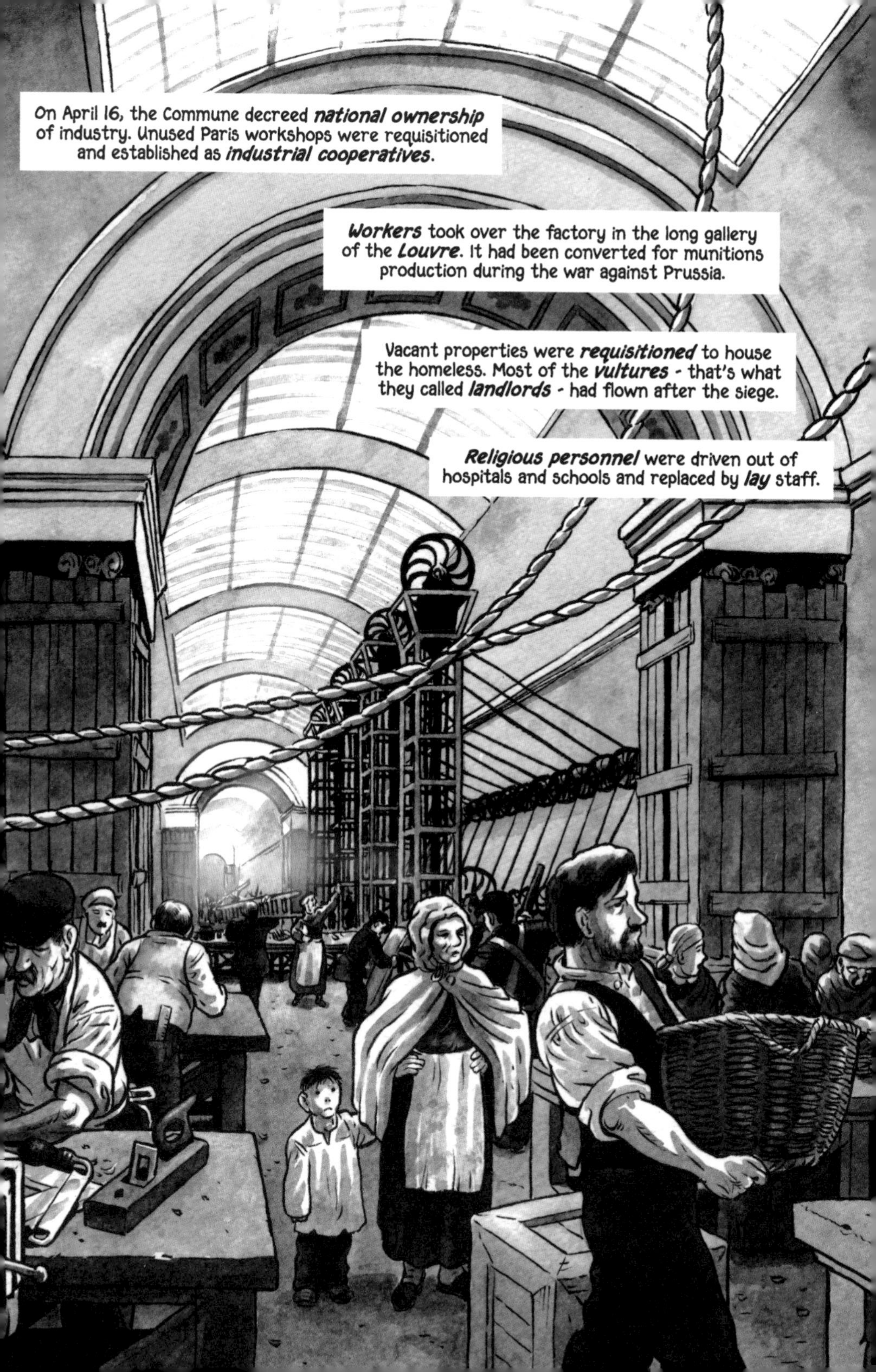

On April 16, the Commune decreed *national ownership* of industry. Unused Paris workshops were requisitioned and established as *industrial cooperatives*.
Workers took over the factory in the long gallery of the *Louvre*. It had been converted for munitions production during the war against Prussia.
Vacant properties were *requisitioned* to house the homeless. Most of the *vultures* - that's what they called *landlords* - had flown after the siege.
Religious personnel were driven out of hospitals and schools and replaced by *lay* staff.

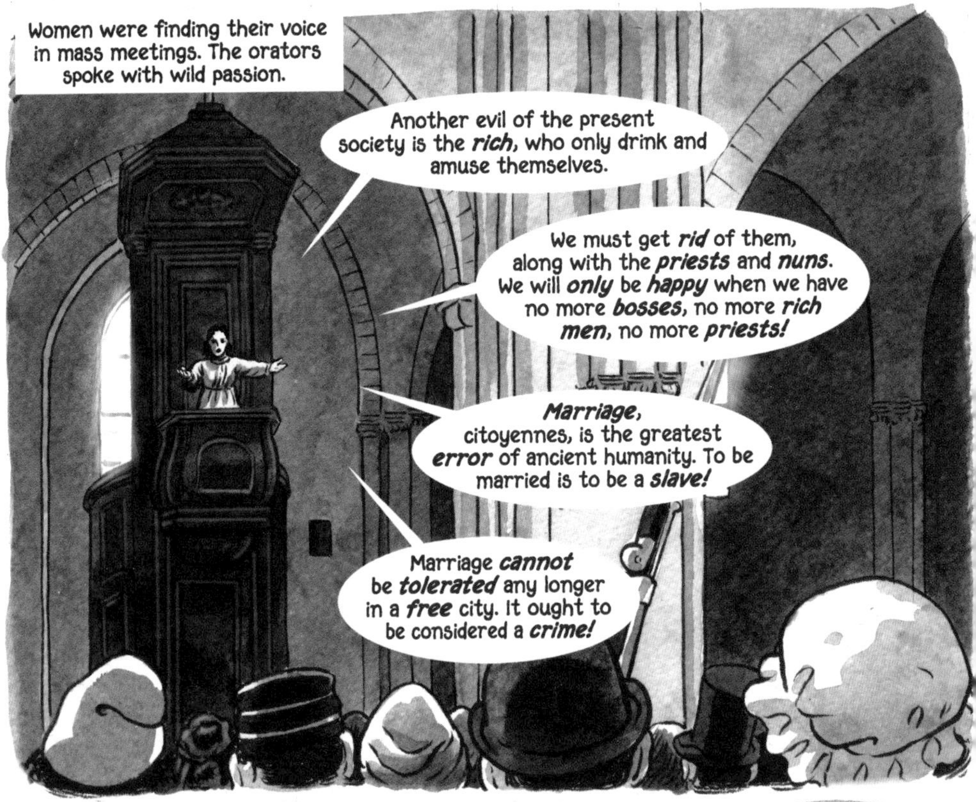
Women were finding their voice in mass meetings. The orators spoke with wild passion.
Another evil of the present society is the rich, who only drink and amuse themselves.
We must get rid of them, along with the priests and nuns. We will only be happy when we have no more bosses, no more rich men, no more priests!
Marriage, citoyennes, is the greatest error of ancient humanity. To be married is to be a slave!
Marriage cannot be tolerated any longer in a free city. It ought to be considered a crime!

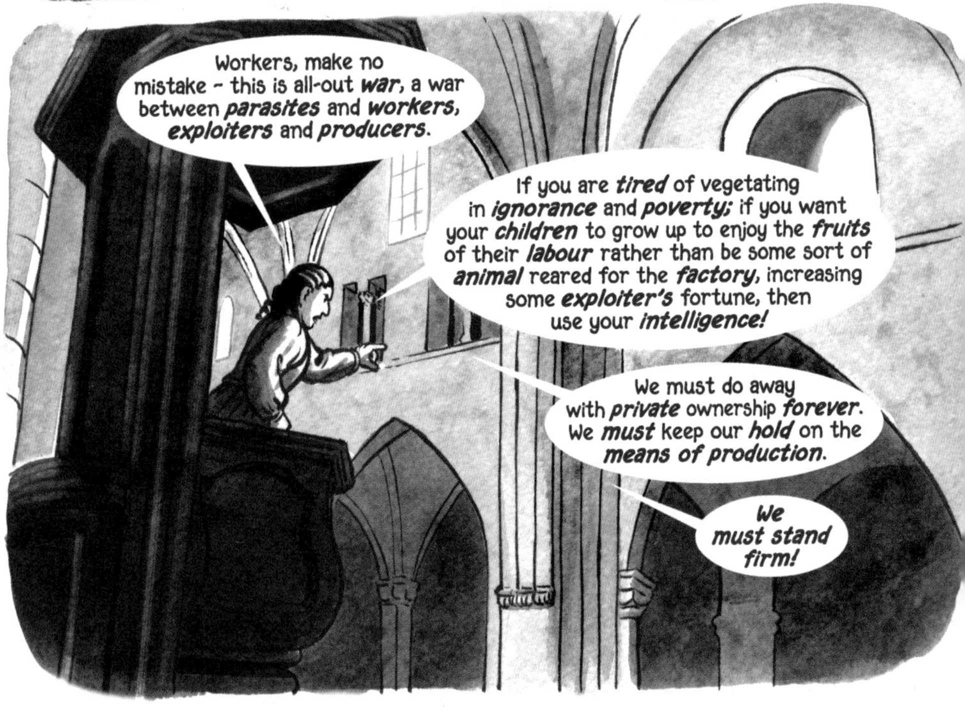
Workers, make no mistake - this is all-out war, a war between parasites and workers, exploiters and producers.
If you are tired of vegetating in ignorance and poverty; if you want your children to grow up to enjoy the fruits of their labour rather than be some sort of animal reared for the factory, increasing some exploiter's fortune, then use your intelligence!
We must do away with private ownership forever. We must keep our hold on the means of production.
We must stand firm!

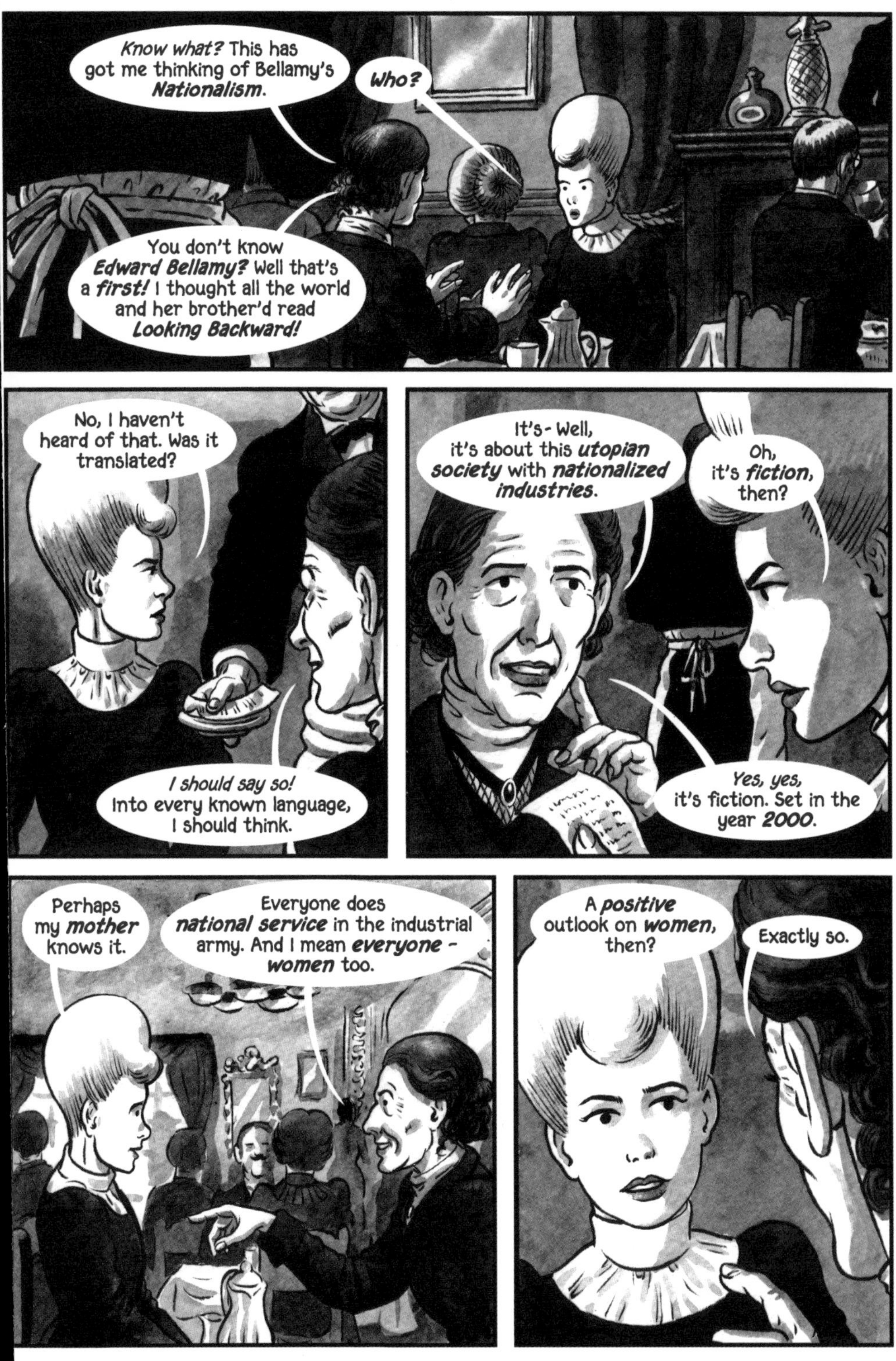
Know what? This has got me thinking of Bellamy's Nationalism.
Who?
You don't know Edward Bellamy? Well that's a first! I thought all the world and her brother'd read Looking Backward!
No, I haven't heard of that. Was it translated?
I should say so! Into every known language, I should think.
It's- Well, it's about this utopian society with nationalized industries.
Oh, it's fiction, then?
Yes, yes, it's fiction. Set in the year 2000.
Perhaps my mother knows it.
Everyone does national service in the industrial army. And I mean everyone - women too.
A positive outlook on women, then?
Exactly so.

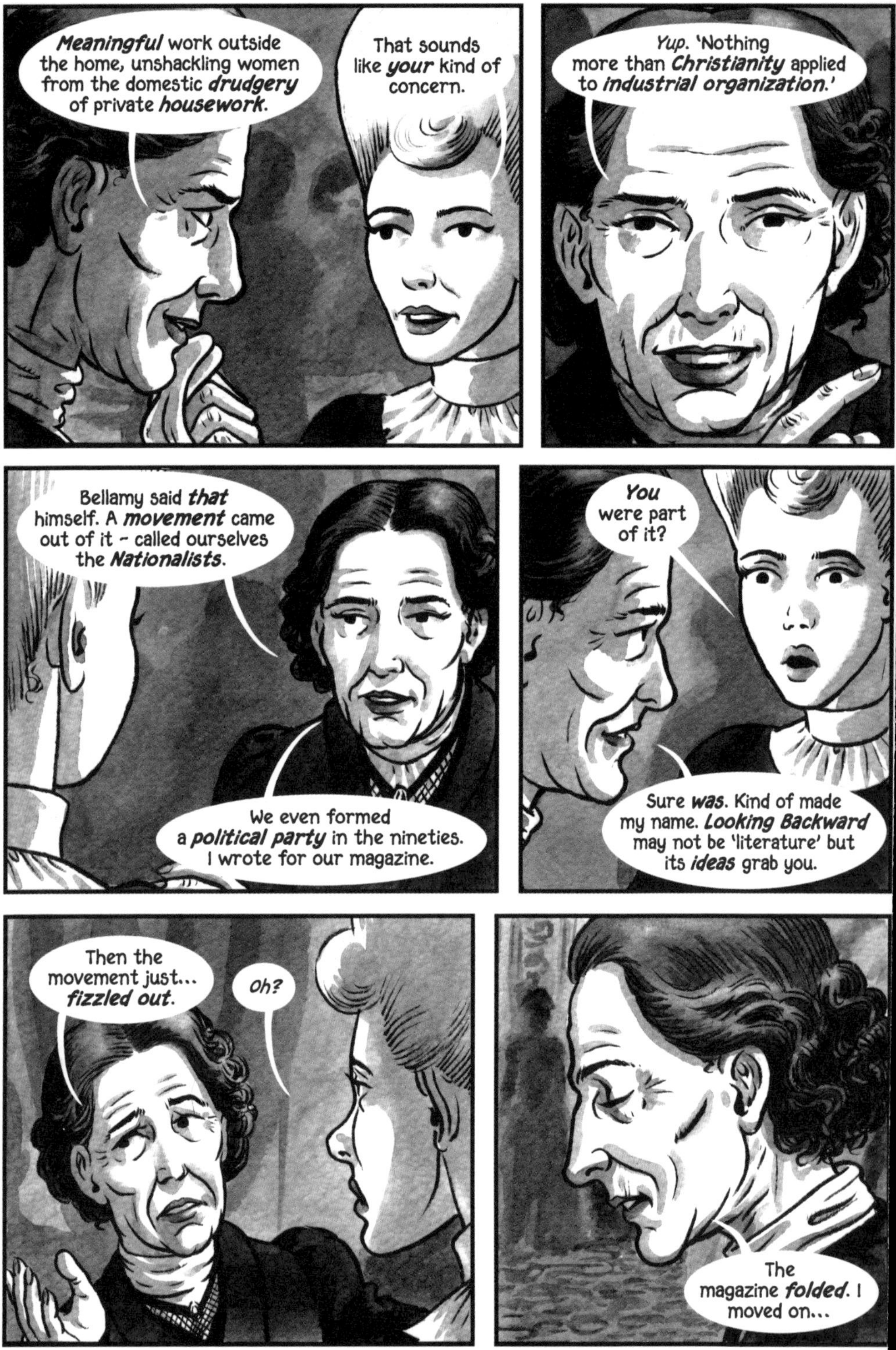
Meaningful work outside the home, unshackling women from the domestic *drudgery* of private *housework*.
That sounds like *your* kind of concern.
Yup. 'Nothing more than *Christianity* applied to *industrial organization*.'
Bellamy said *that* himself. A *movement* came out of it - called ourselves the *Nationalists*.
We even formed a *political party* in the nineties. I wrote for our magazine.
You were part of it?
Sure *was*. Kind of made my name. *Looking Backward* may not be 'literature' but its *ideas* grab you.
Then the movement just... *fizzled out*.
Oh?
The magazine *folded*. I moved on...

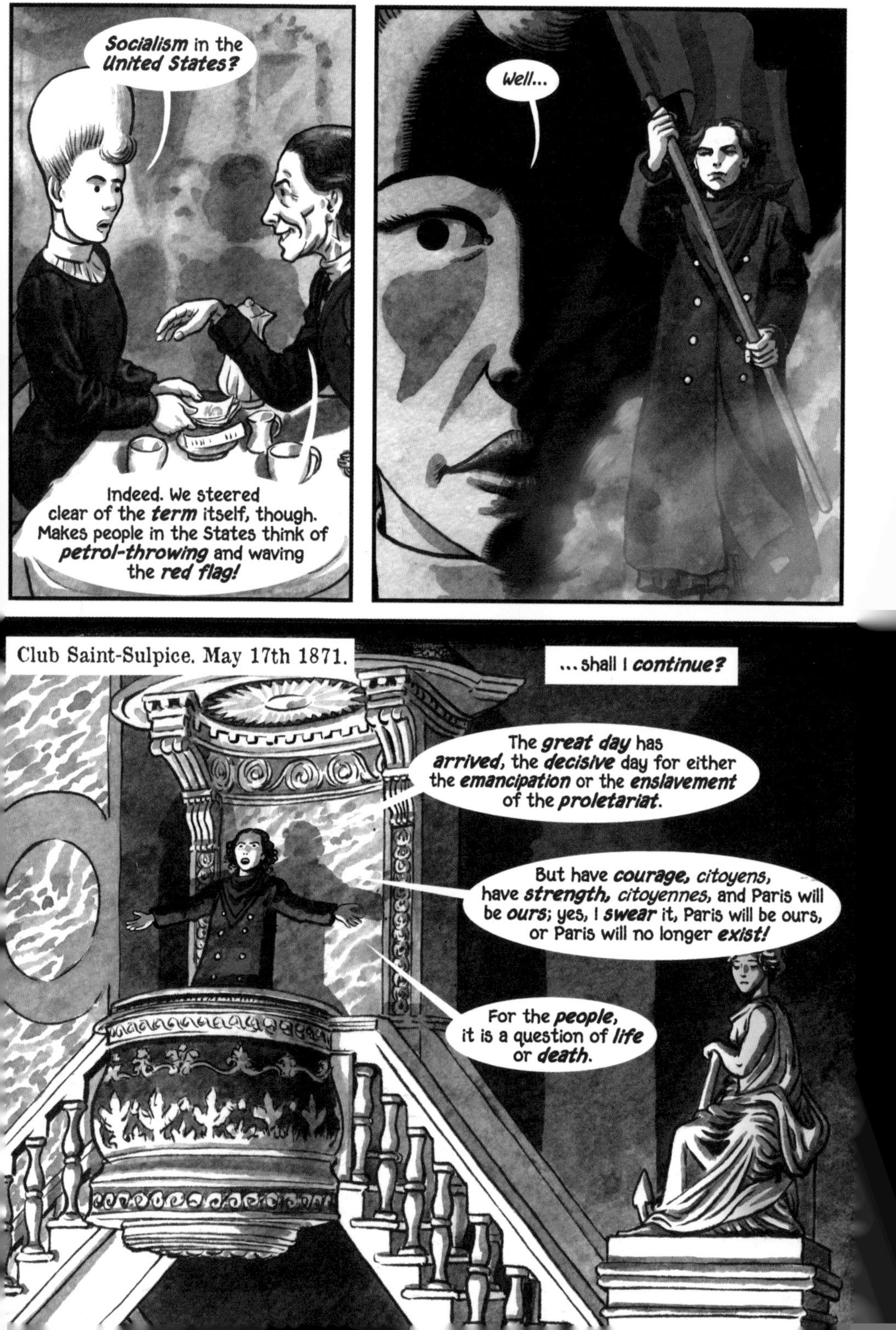
Socialism in the United States?
Indeed. We steered clear of the term itself, though. Makes people in the States think of petrol-throwing and waving the red flag!
Well...
Club Saint-Sulpice. May 17th 1871.
...shall I continue?
The great day has arrived, the decisive day for either the emancipation or the enslavement of the proletariat.
But have courage, citoyens, have strength, citoyennes, and Paris will be ours; yes, I swear it, Paris will be ours, or Paris will no longer exist!
For the people, it is a question of life or death.

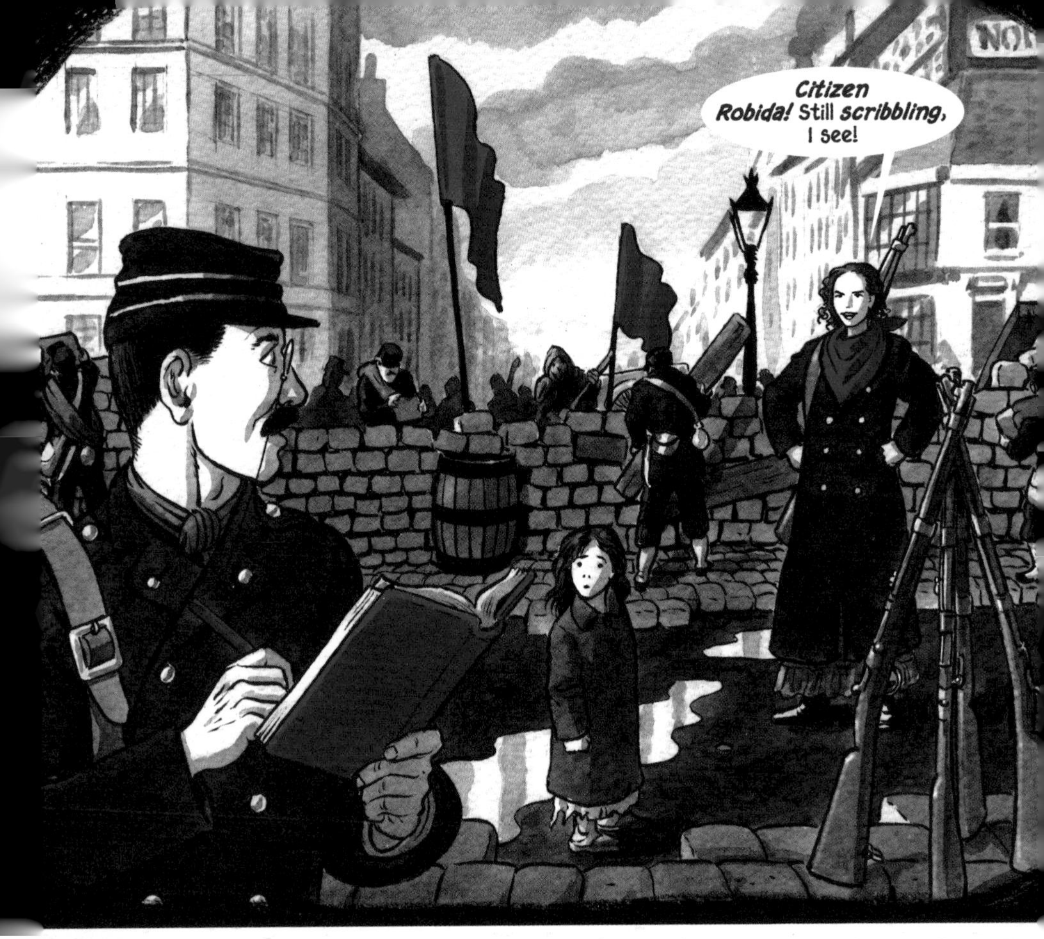
Citizen Robida! Still scribbling, I see!

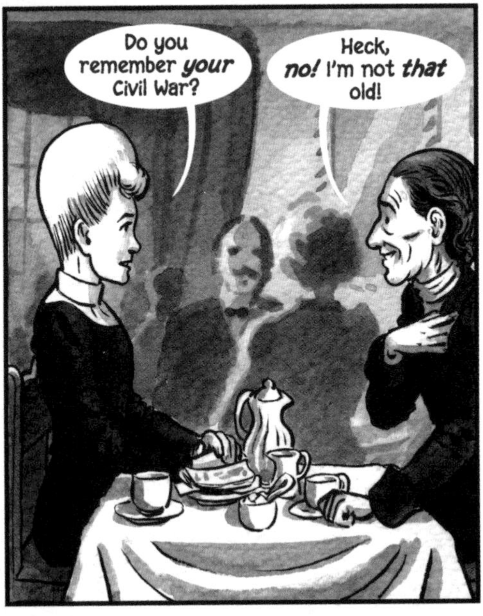
Do you remember your Civil War?
Heck, no! I'm not that old!

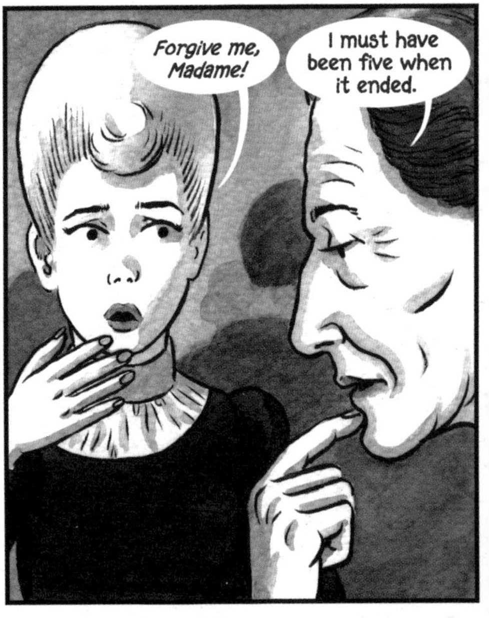
Forgive me, Madame!
I must have been five when it ended.

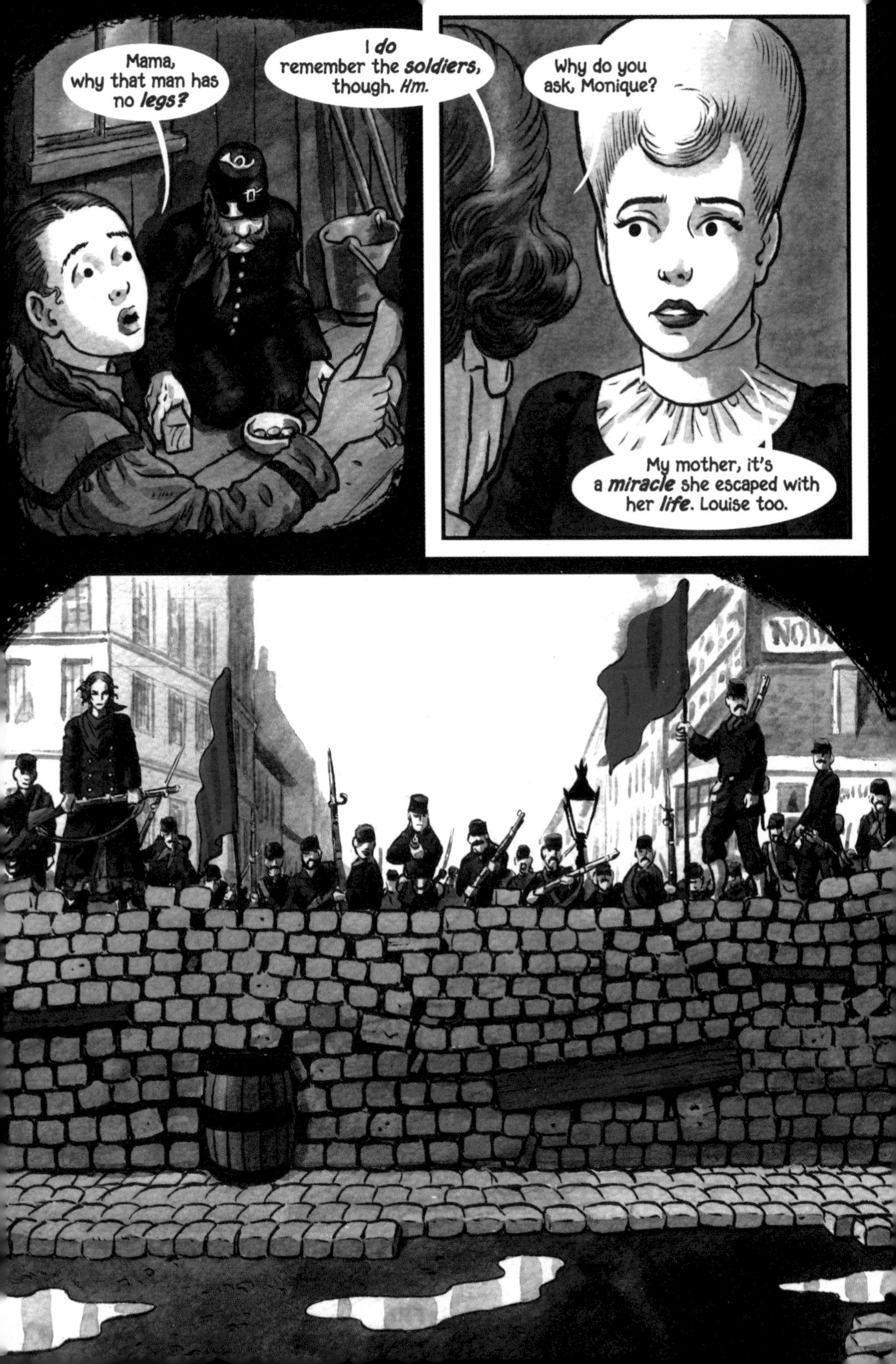
Mama, why that man has no legs?
I do remember the soldiers, though. Hm.
Why do you ask, Monique?
My mother, it's a miracle she escaped with her life. Louise too.

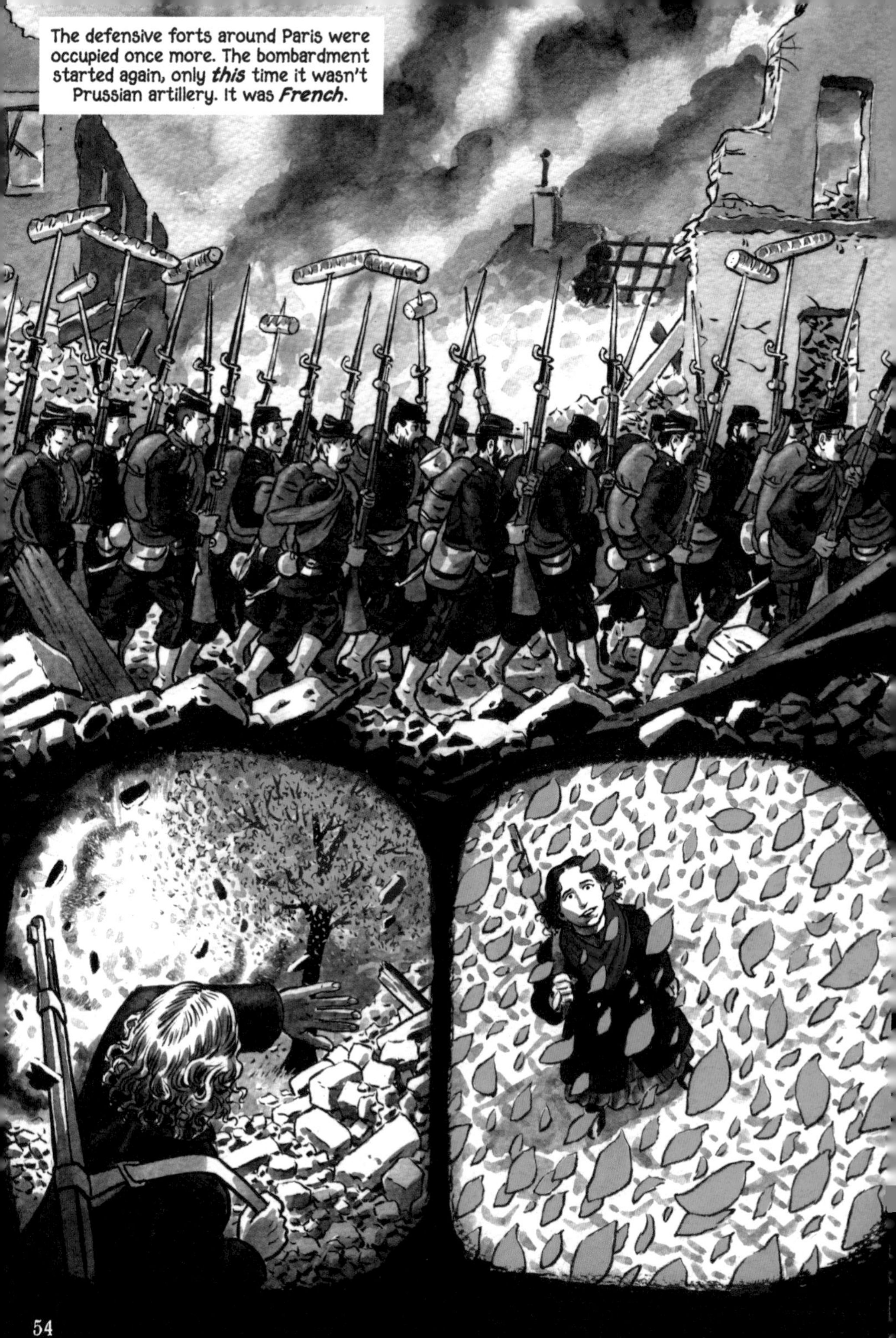
The defensive forts around Paris were occupied once more. The bombardment started again, only *this* time it wasn't Prussian artillery. It was *French*.

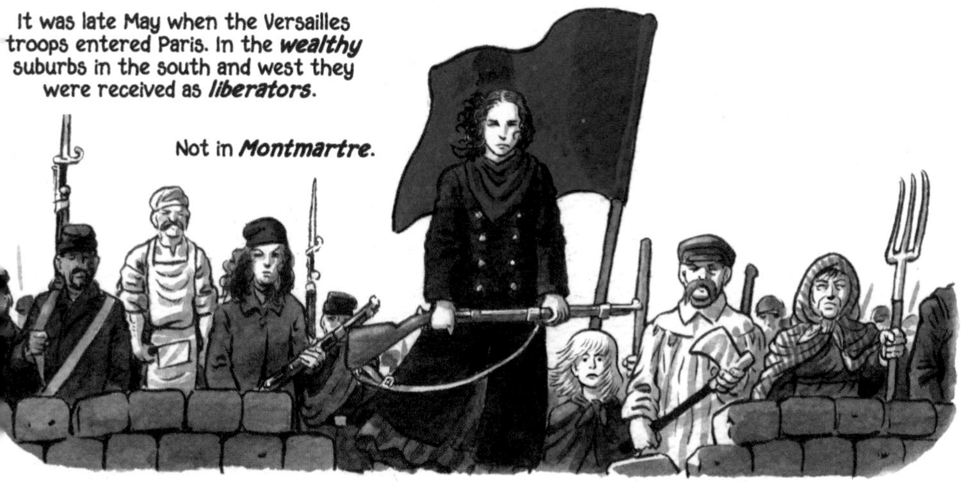
It was late May when the Versailles troops entered Paris. In the *wealthy* suburbs in the south and west they were received as *liberators*.
Not in *Montmartre*.

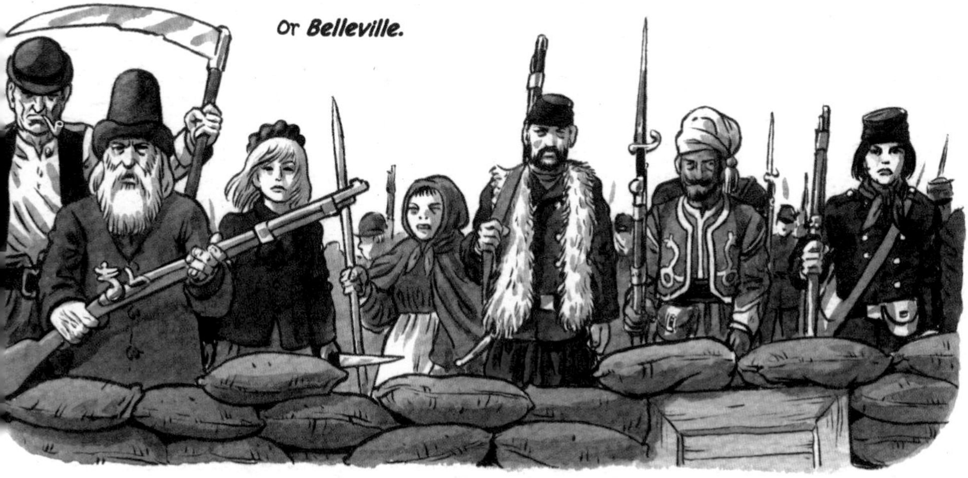
Or *Belleville*.

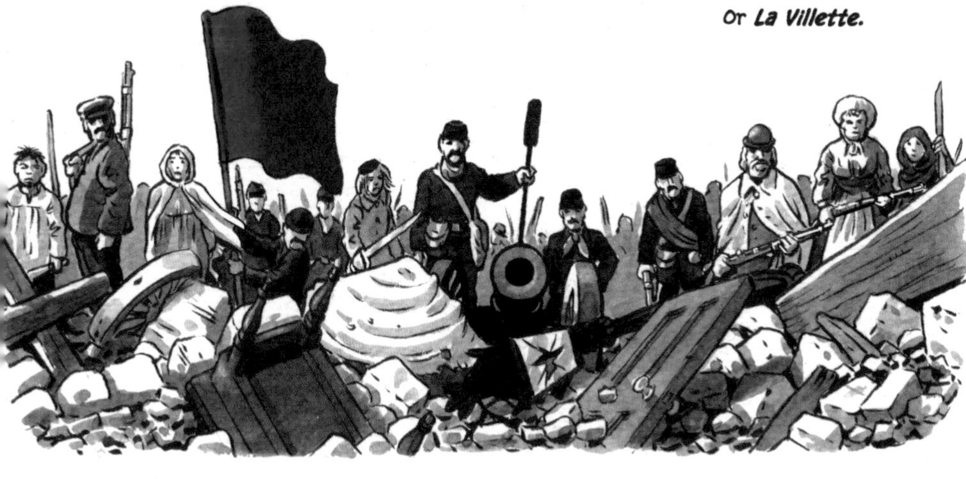
Or *La Villette*.

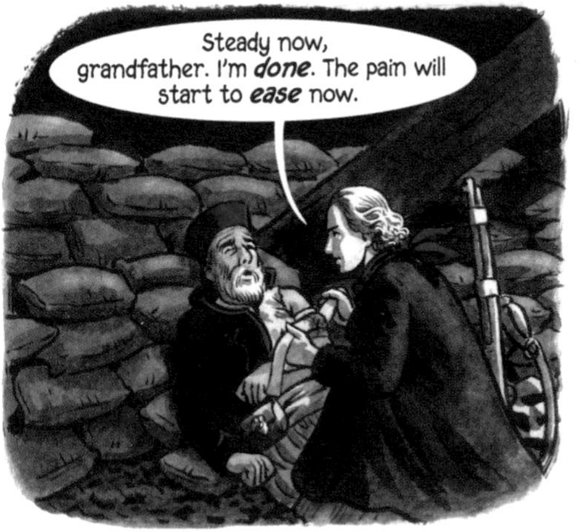
Steady now, grandfather. I'm *done*. The pain will start to *ease* now.

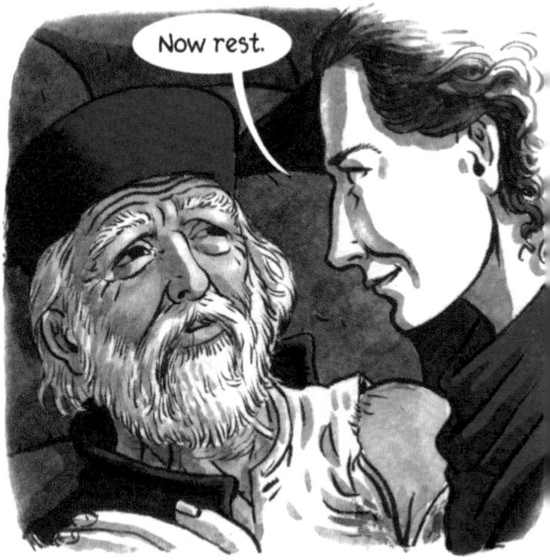
Now rest.

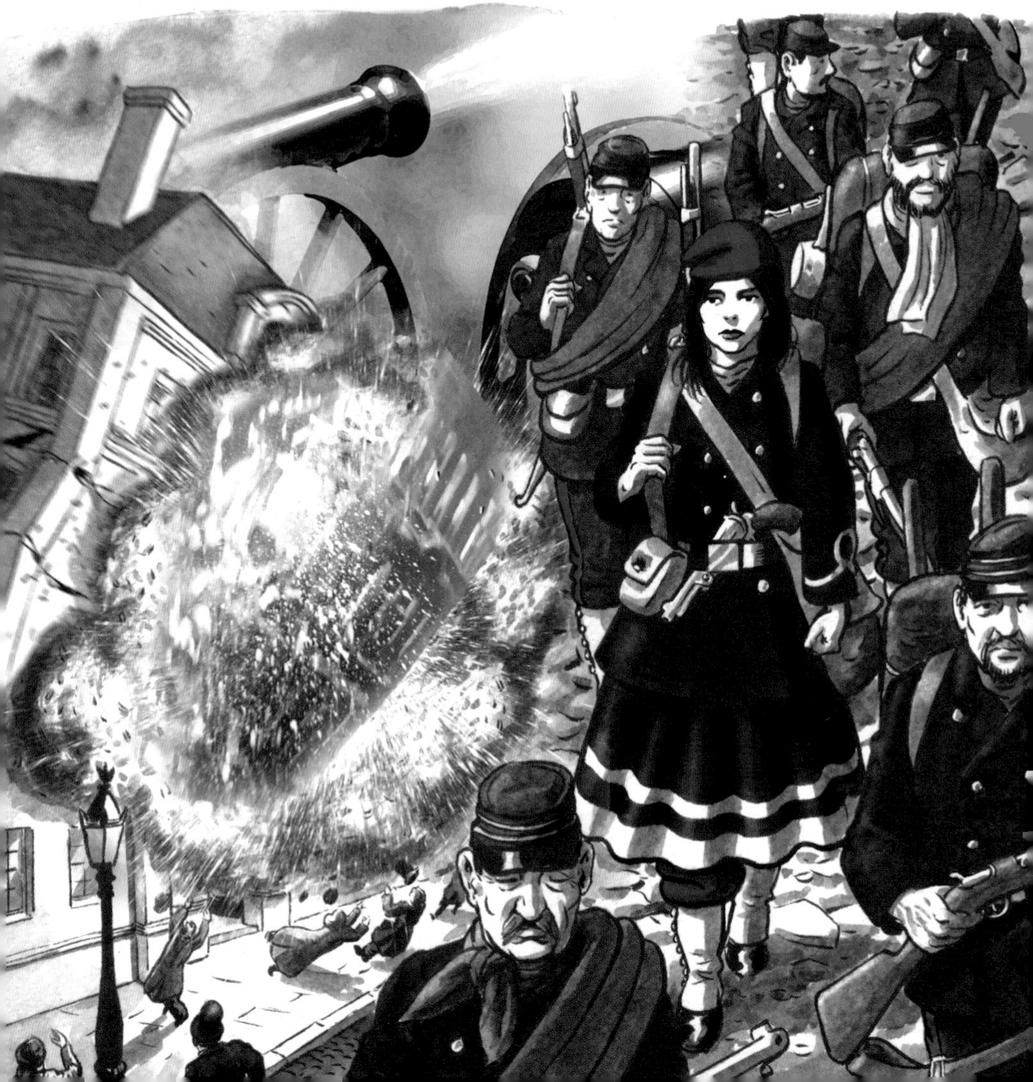

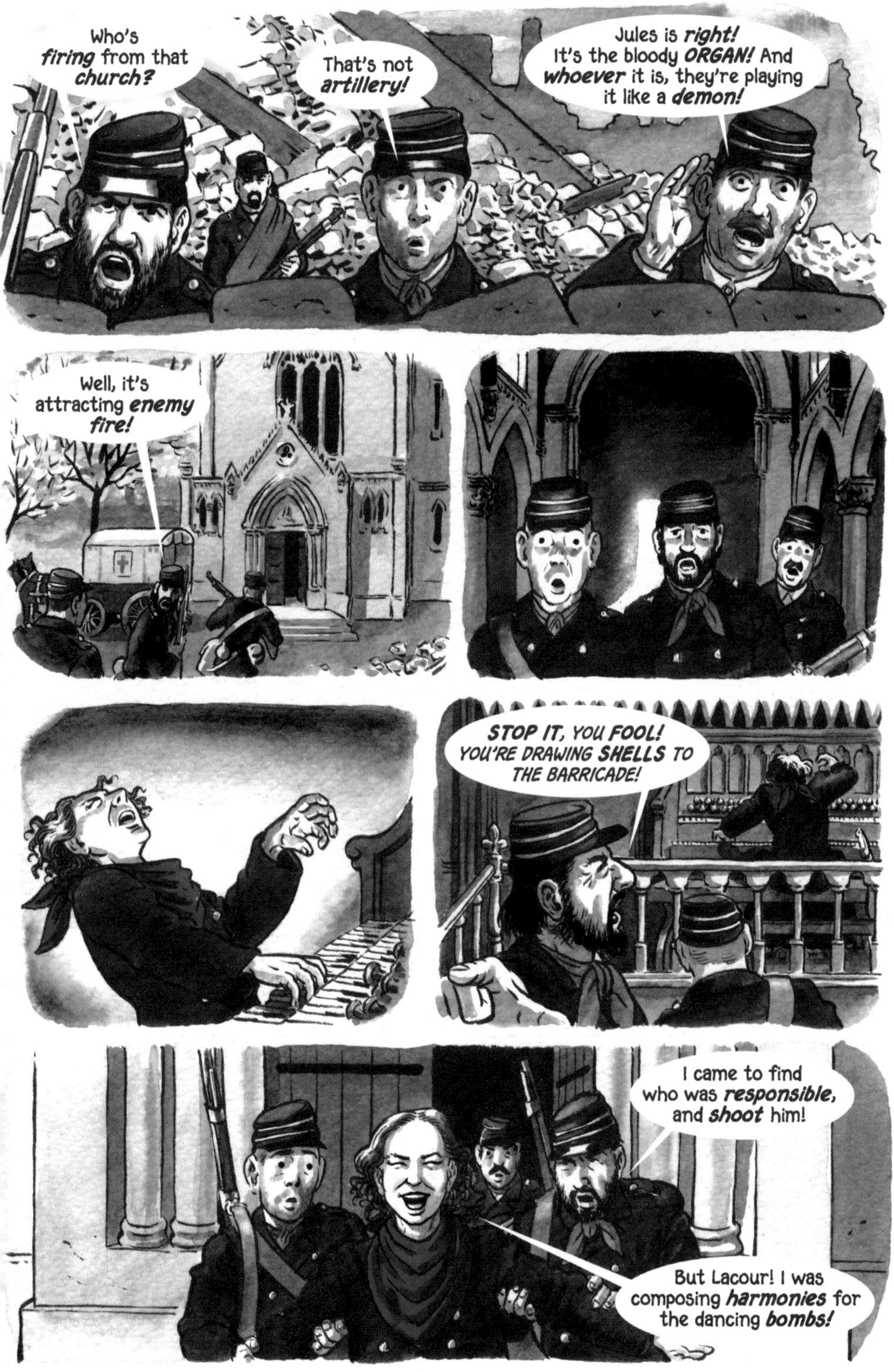
Who's firing from that church?
That's not artillery!
Jules is right! It's the bloody ORGAN! And whoever it is, they're playing it like a demon!
Well, it's attracting enemy fire!
STOP IT, YOU FOOL! YOU'RE DRAWING SHELLS TO THE BARRICADE!
I came to find who was responsible, and shoot him!
But Lacour! I was composing harmonies for the dancing bombs!

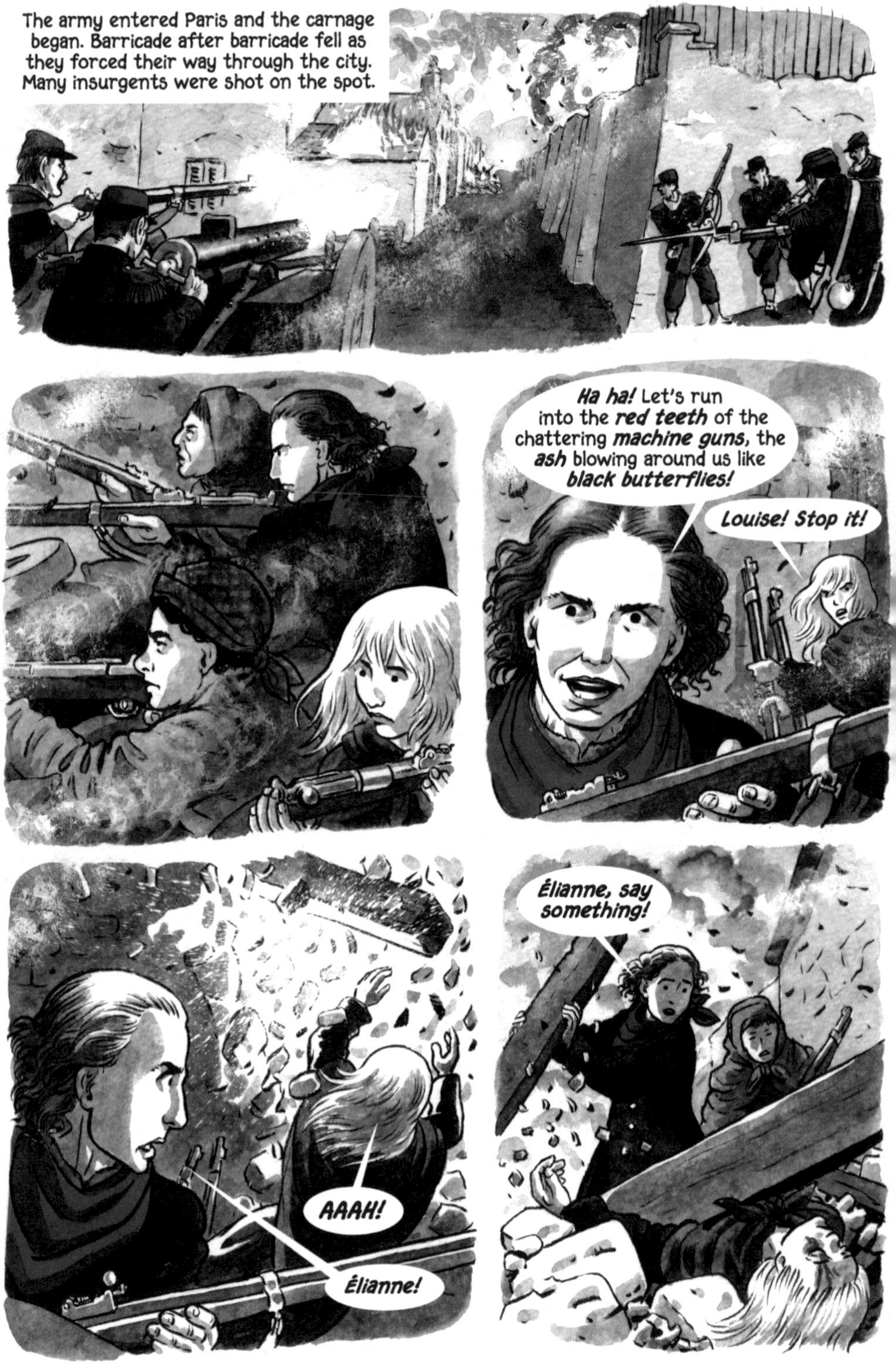
The army entered Paris and the carnage began. Barricade after barricade fell as they forced their way through the city. Many insurgents were shot on the spot.
Ha ha! Let's run into the red teeth of the chattering machine guns, the ash blowing around us like black butterflies!
Louise! Stop it!
AAAH!
Élianne!
Élianne, say something!

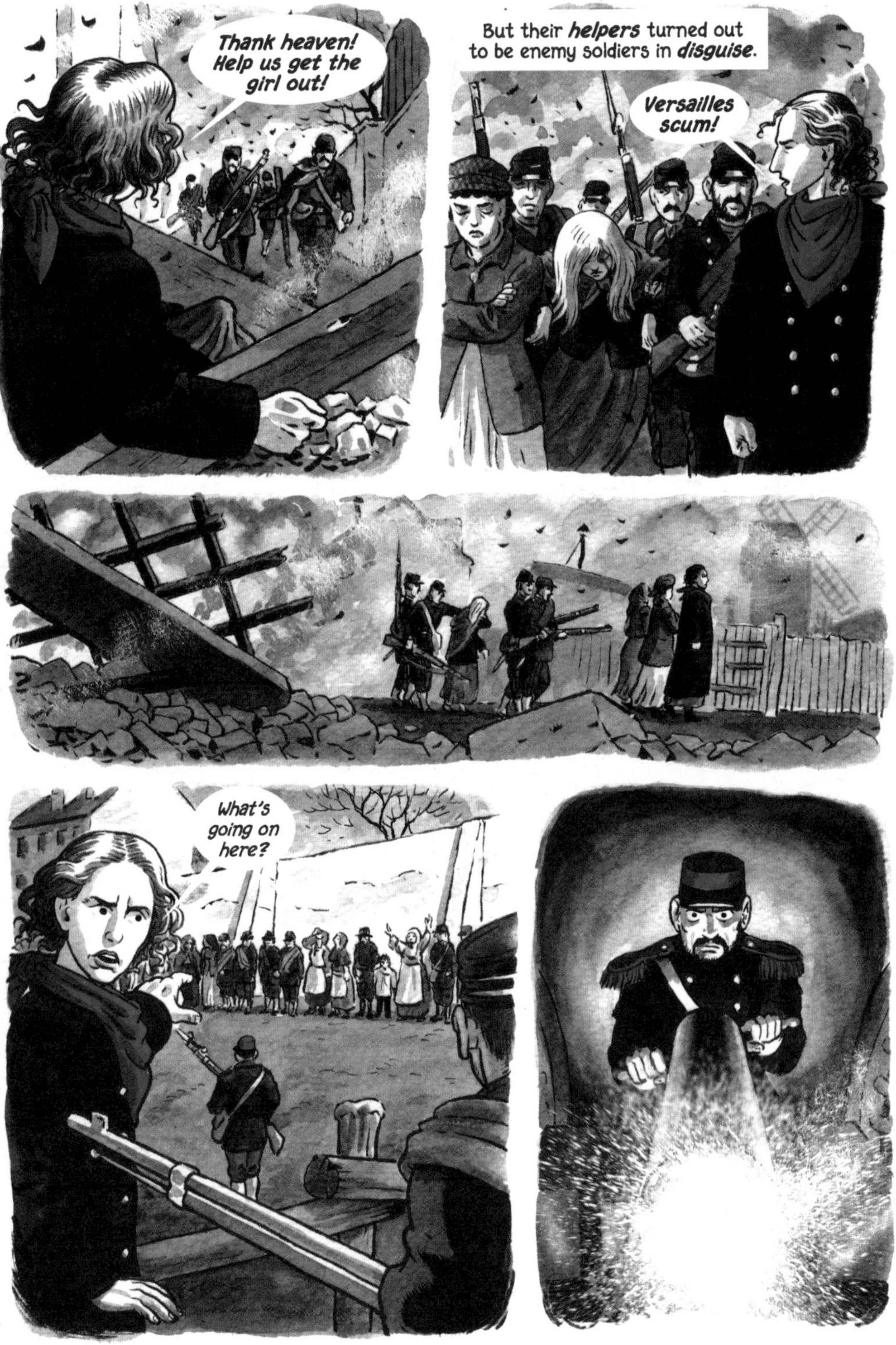
Thank heaven! Help us get the girl out!
But their helpers turned out to be enemy soldiers in disguise.
Versailles scum!
What's going on here?

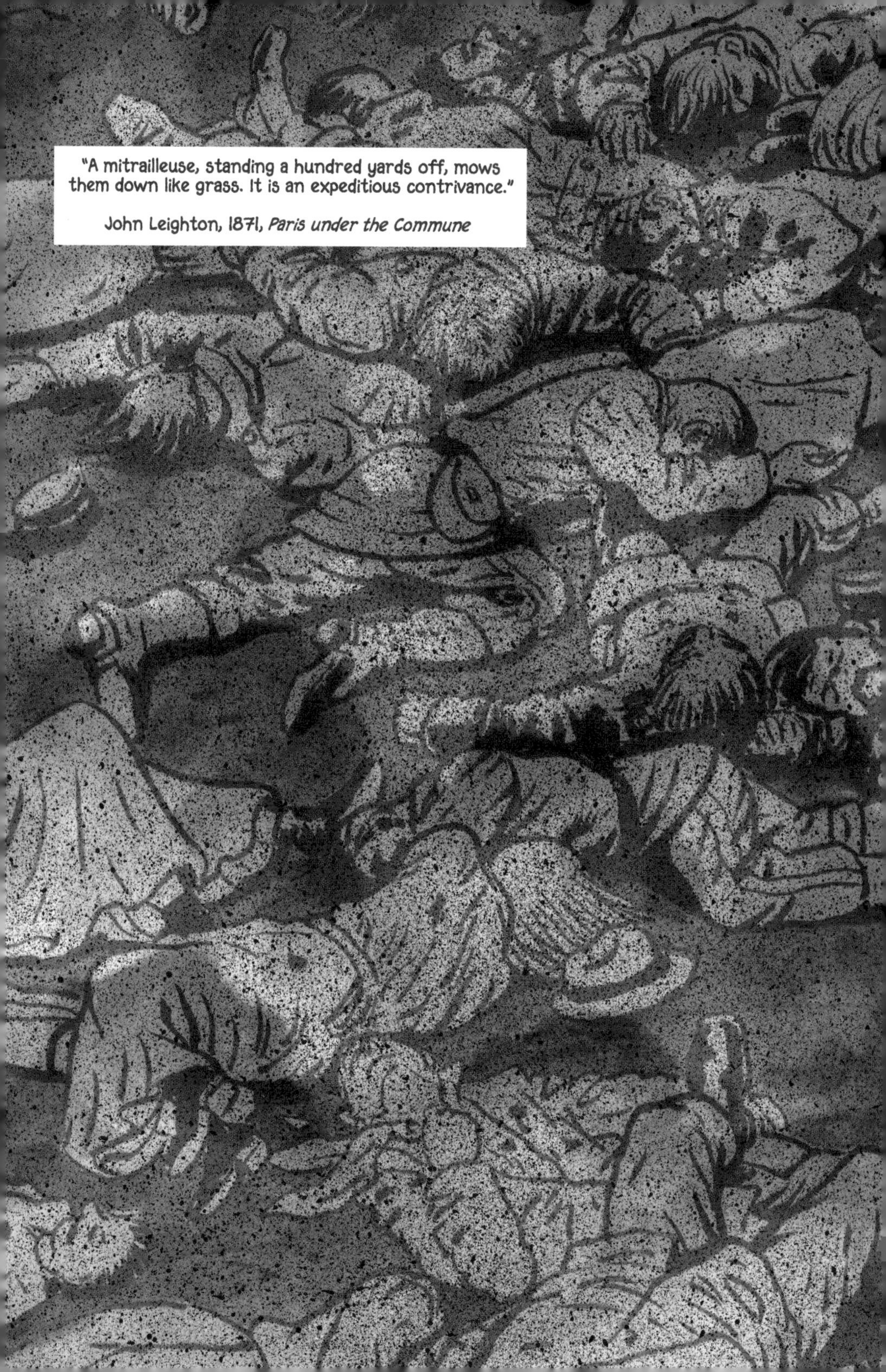
"A mitrailleuse, standing a hundred yards off, mows them down like grass. It is an expeditious contrivance."
John Leighton, 1871, *Paris under the Commune*

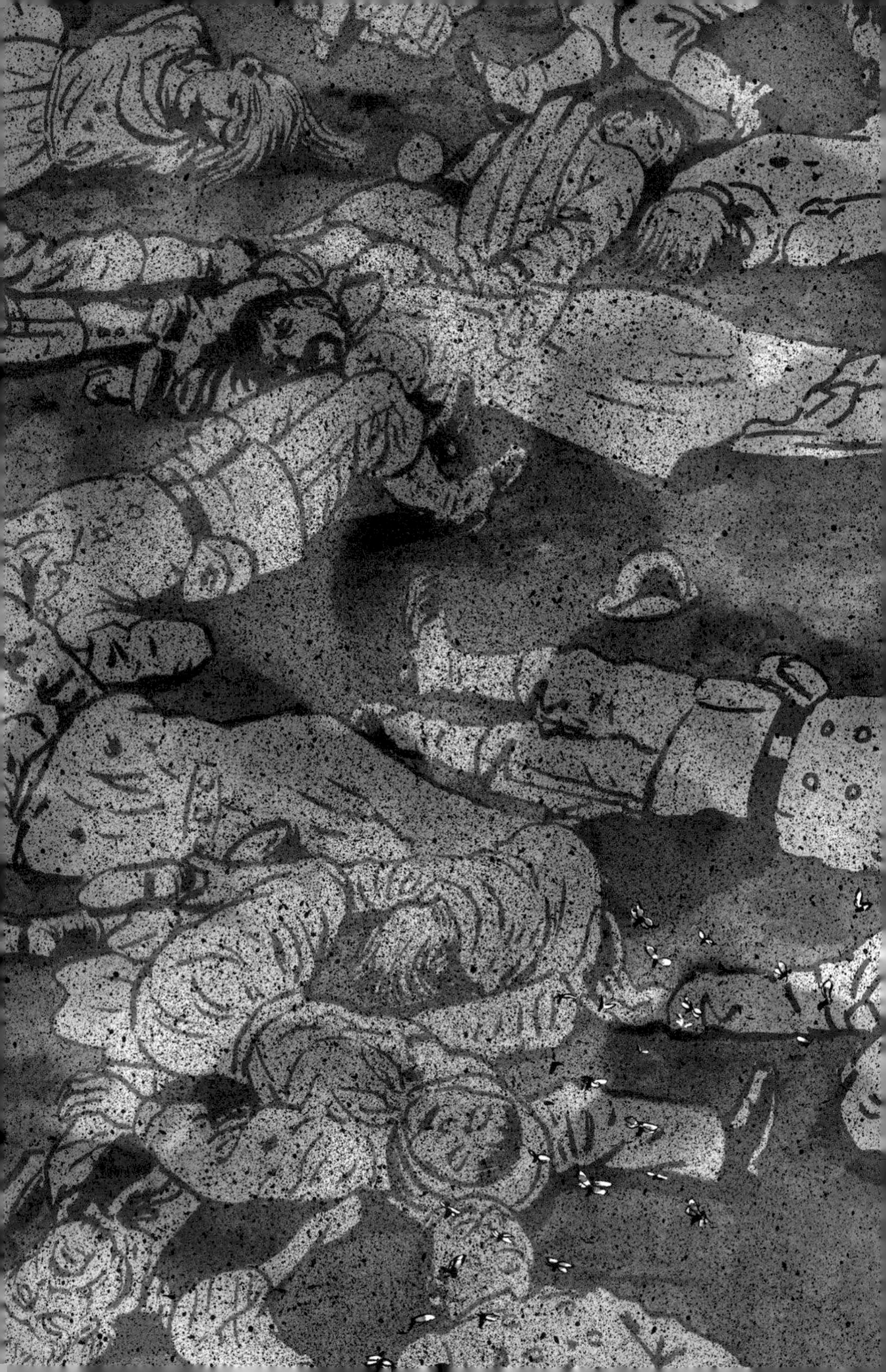

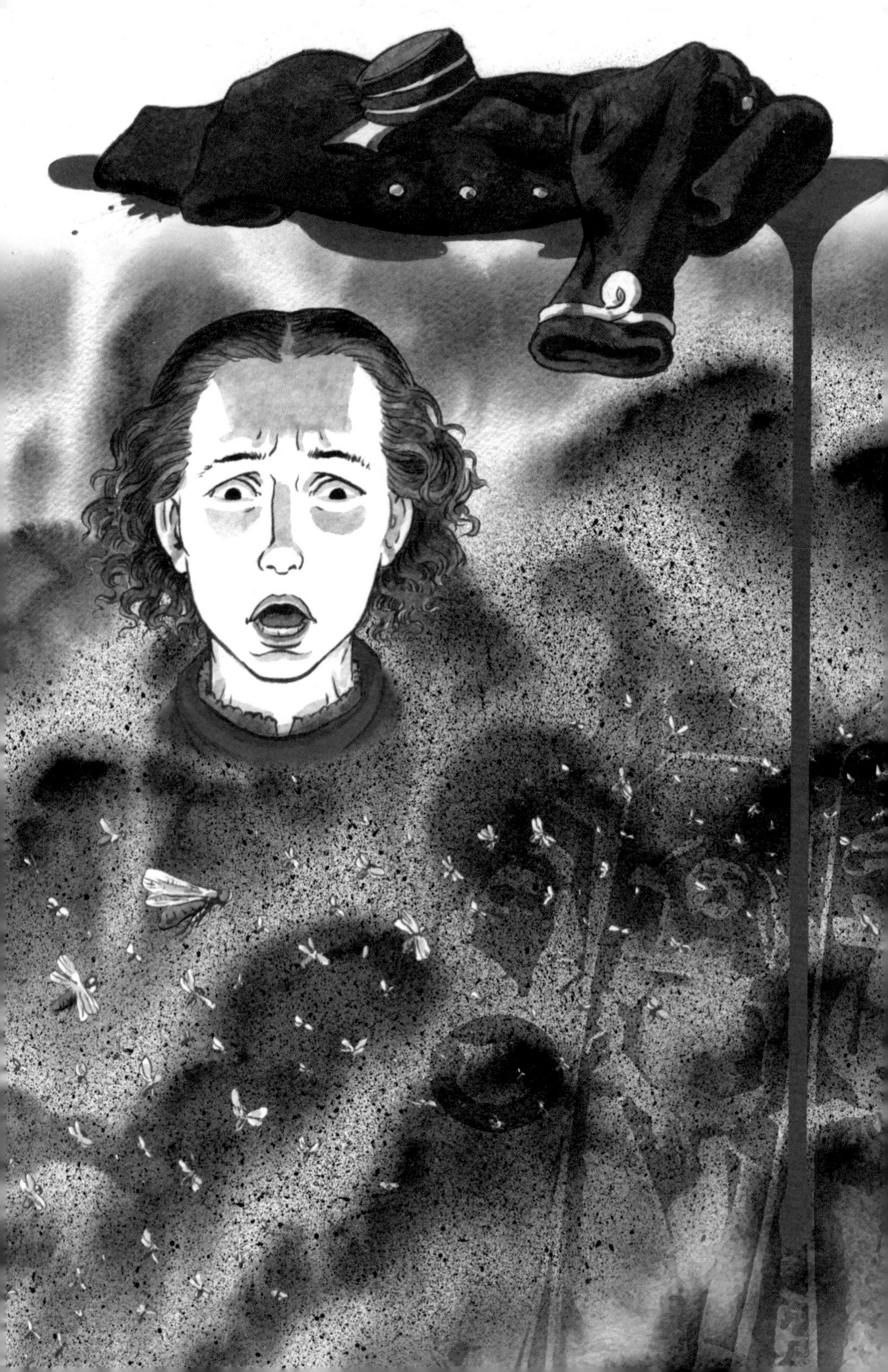

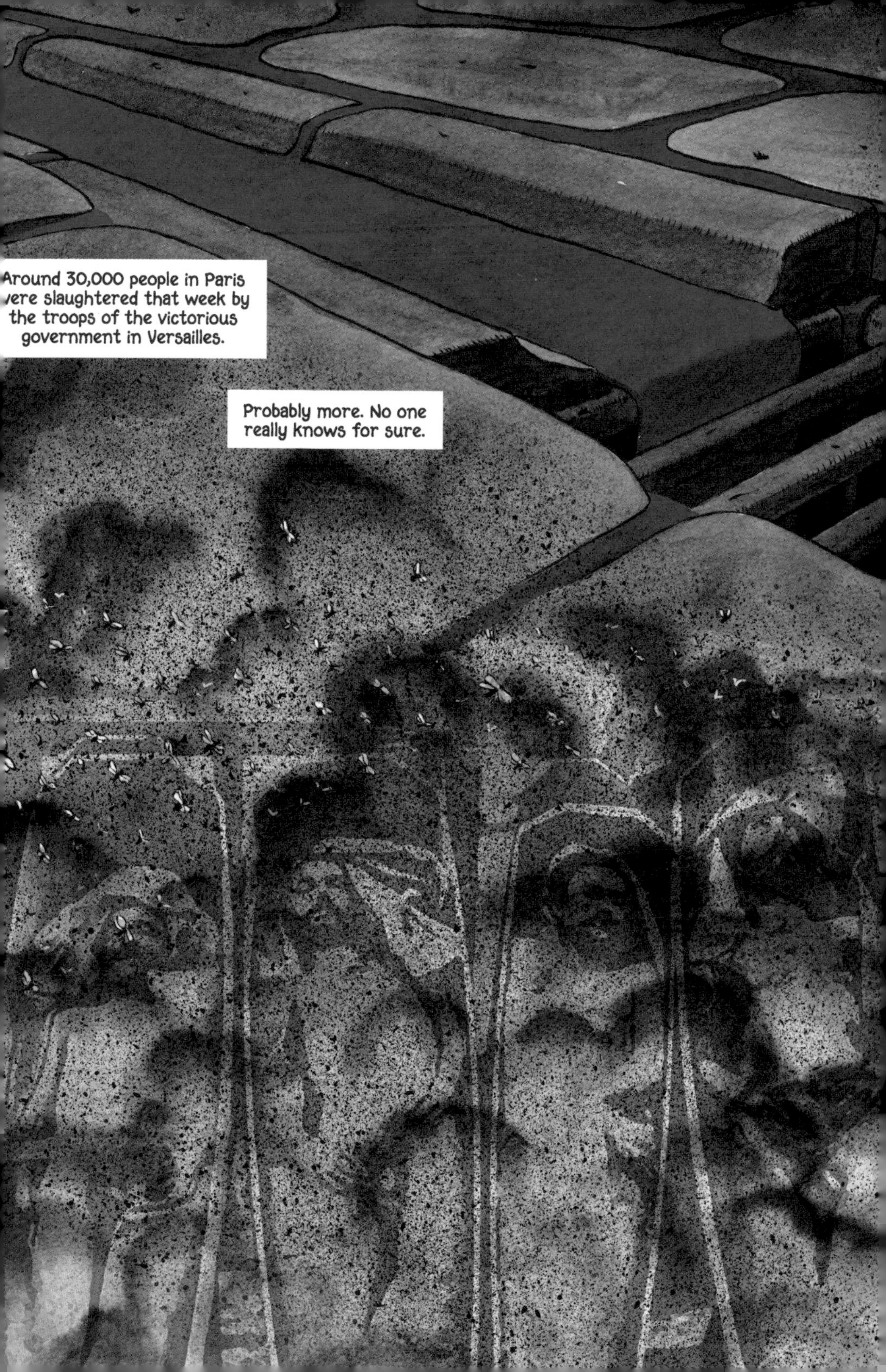
Around 30,000 people in Paris were slaughtered that week by the troops of the victorious government in Versailles.
Probably more. No one really knows for sure.

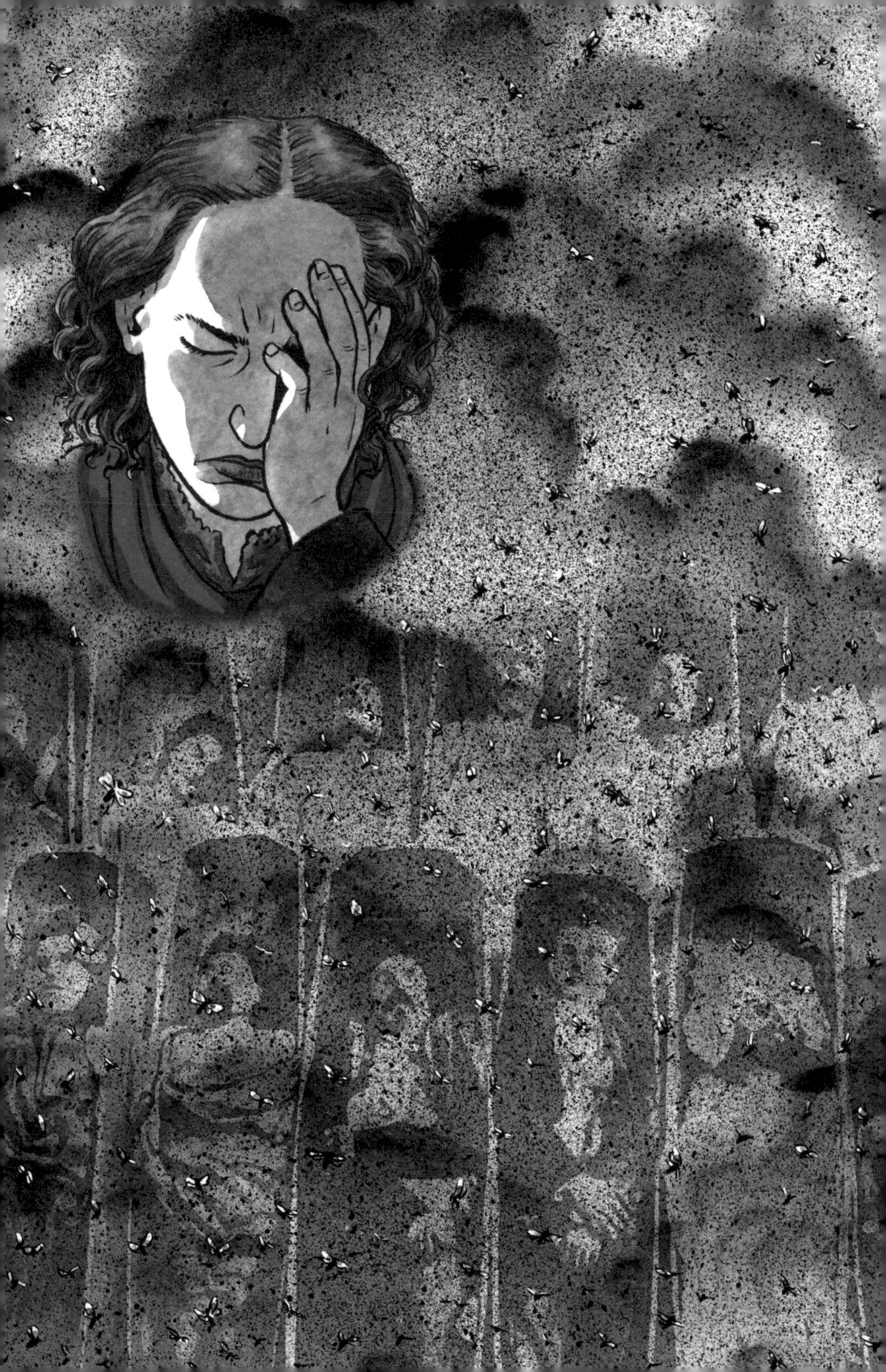

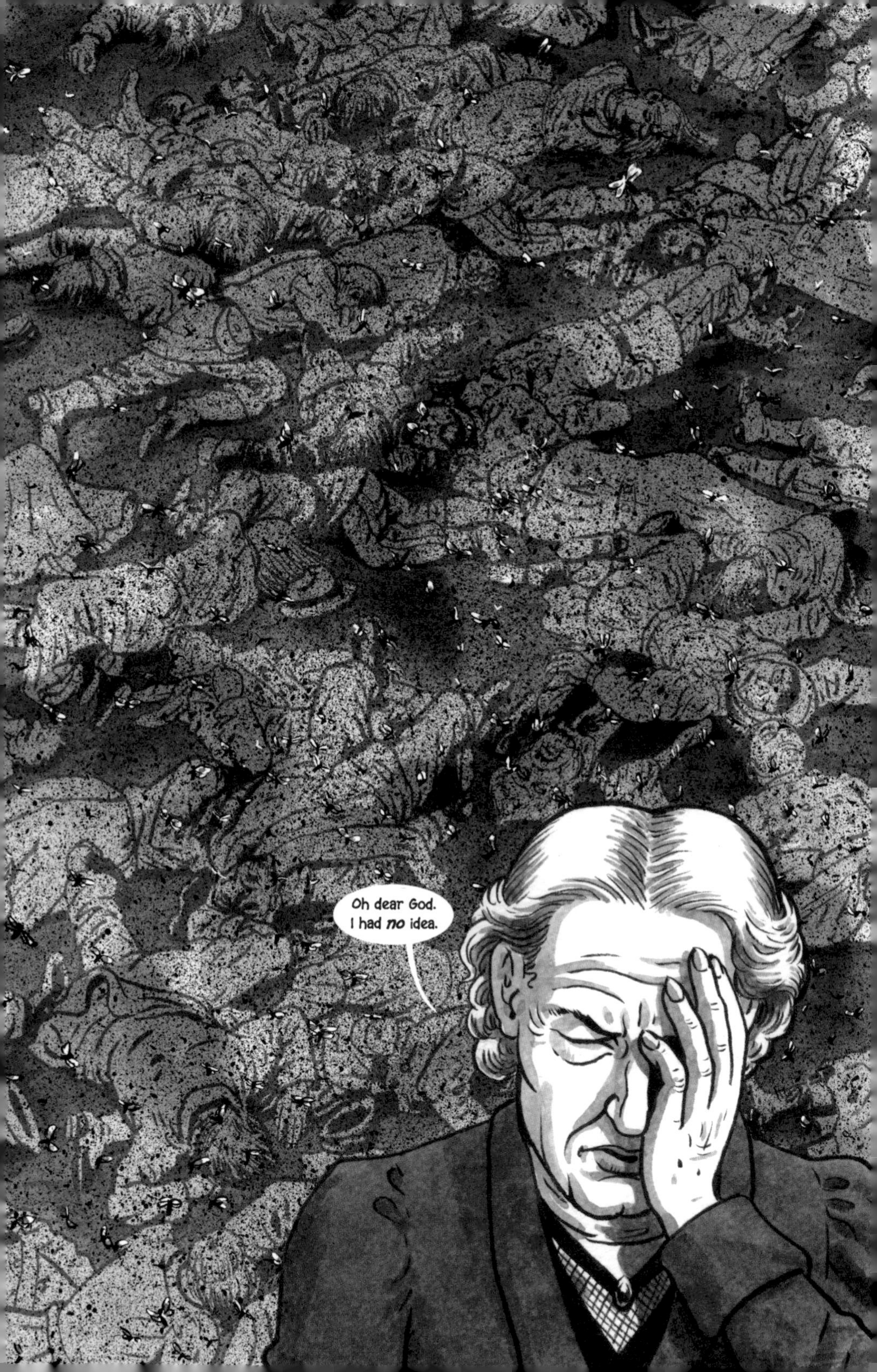
Oh dear God. I had *no* idea.

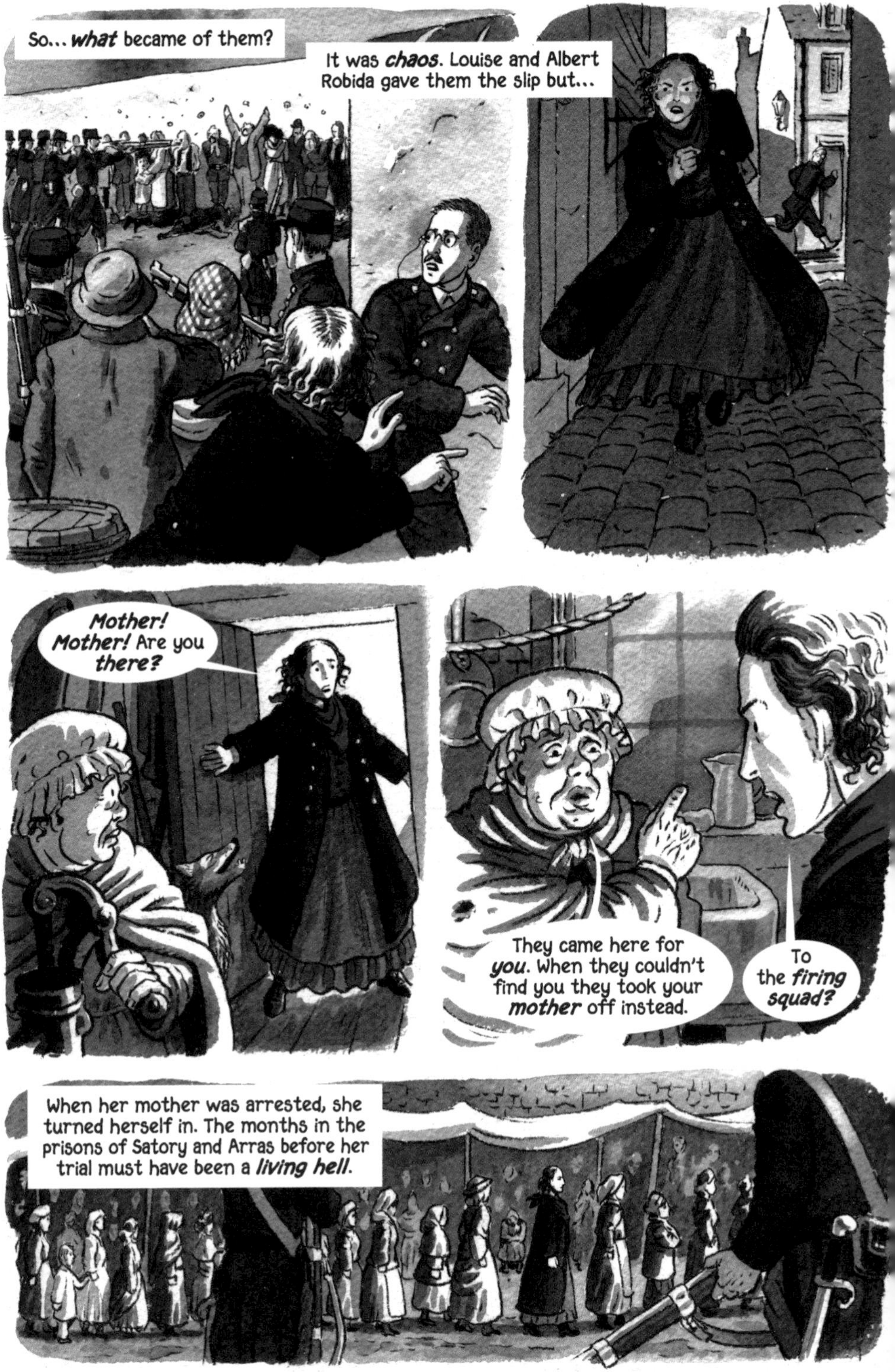

So... *what* became of them?
It was *chaos*. Louise and Albert Robida gave them the slip but...
Mother! Mother! Are you *there?*
They came here for *you*. When they couldn't find you they took your *mother* off instead.
To the *firing squad?*
When her mother was arrested, she turned herself in. The months in the prisons of Satory and Arras before her trial must have been a *living hell*.

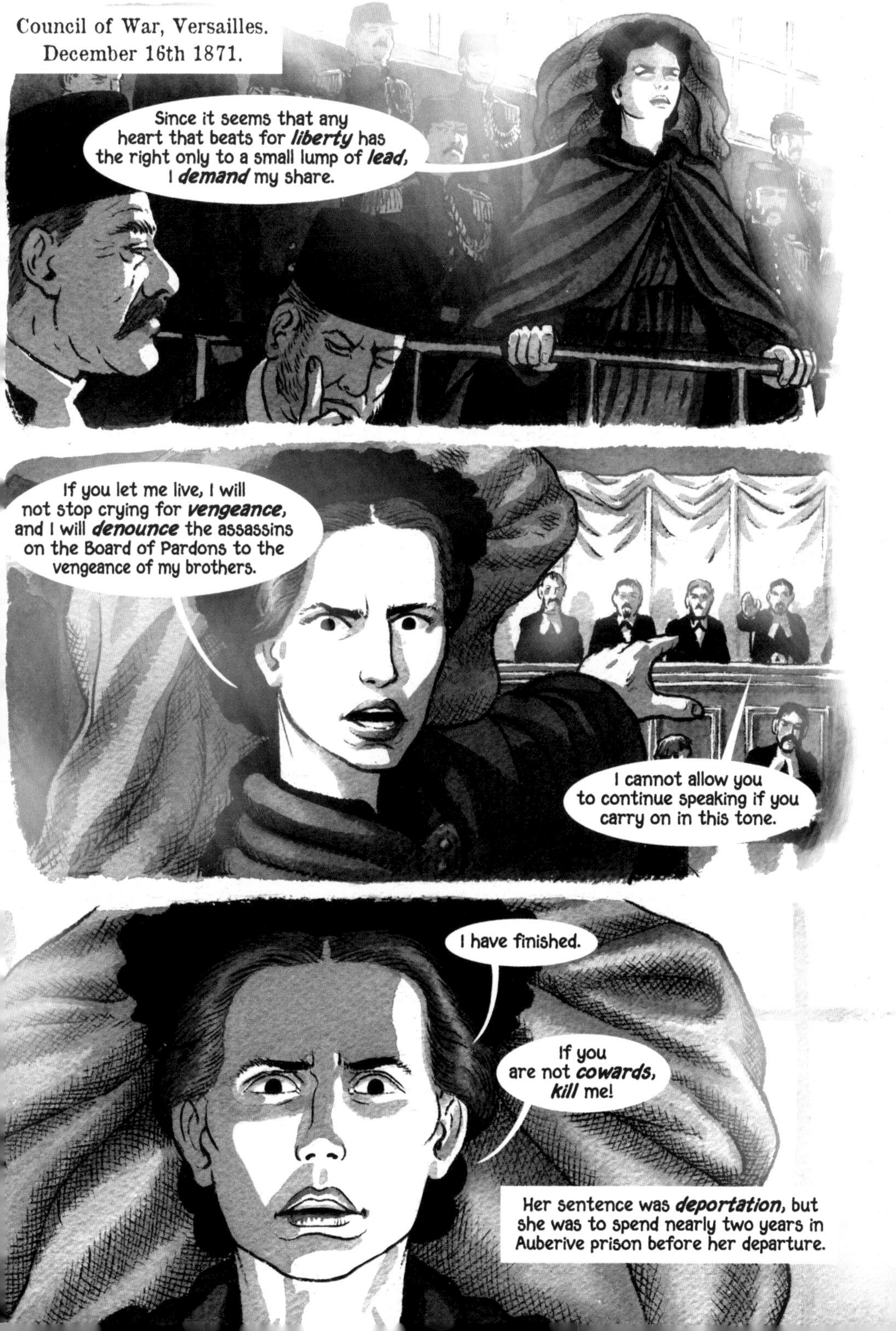
Council of War, Versailles.
December 16th 1871.
Since it seems that any heart that beats for *liberty* has the right only to a small lump of *lead*, I *demand* my share.
If you let me live, I will not stop crying for *vengeance*, and I will *denounce* the assassins on the Board of Pardons to the vengeance of my brothers.
I cannot allow you to continue speaking if you carry on in this tone.
I have finished.
If you are not *cowards*, *kill* me!
Her sentence was *deportation*, but she was to spend nearly two years in Auberive prison before her departure.

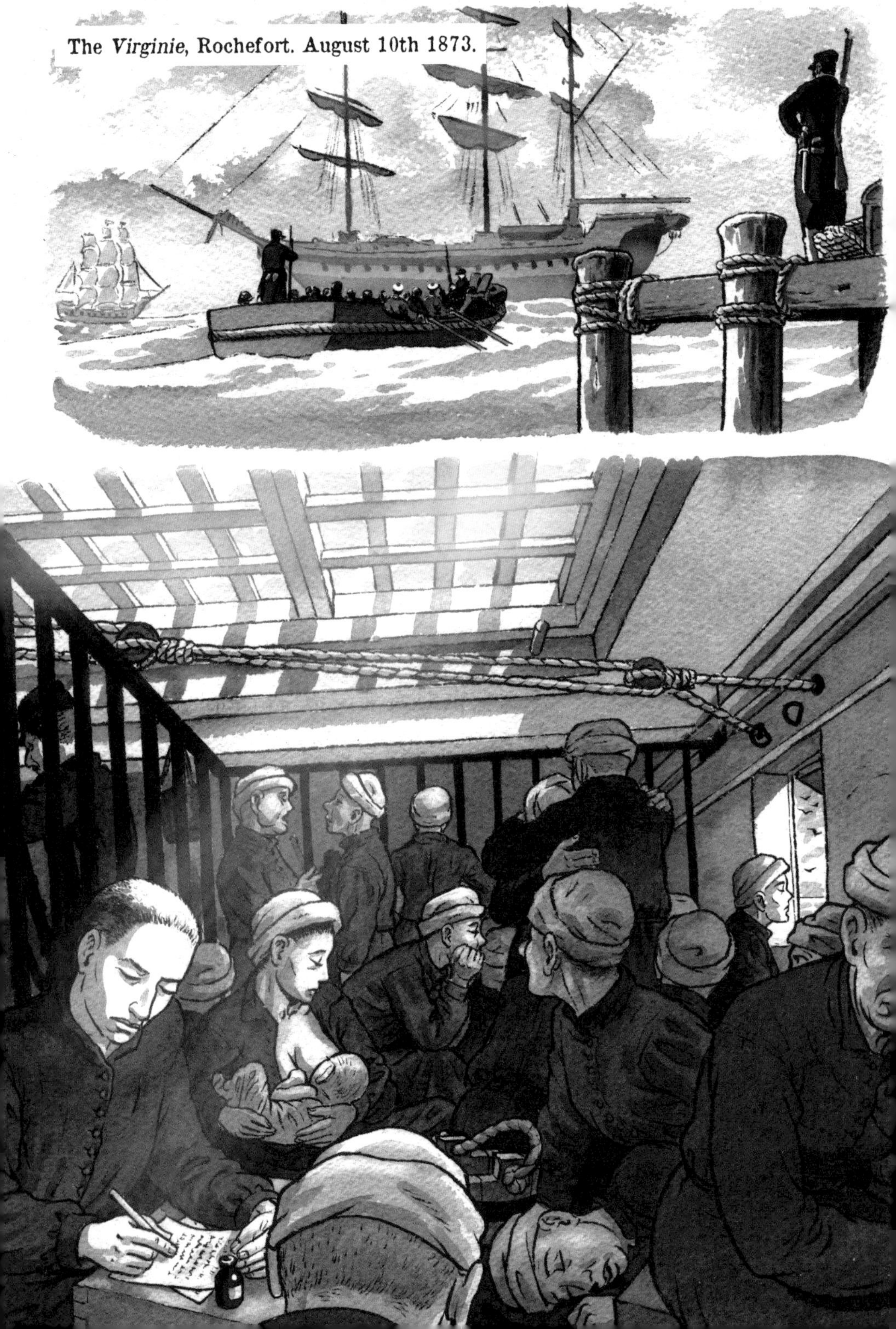
The *Virginie*, Rochefort. August 10th 1873.

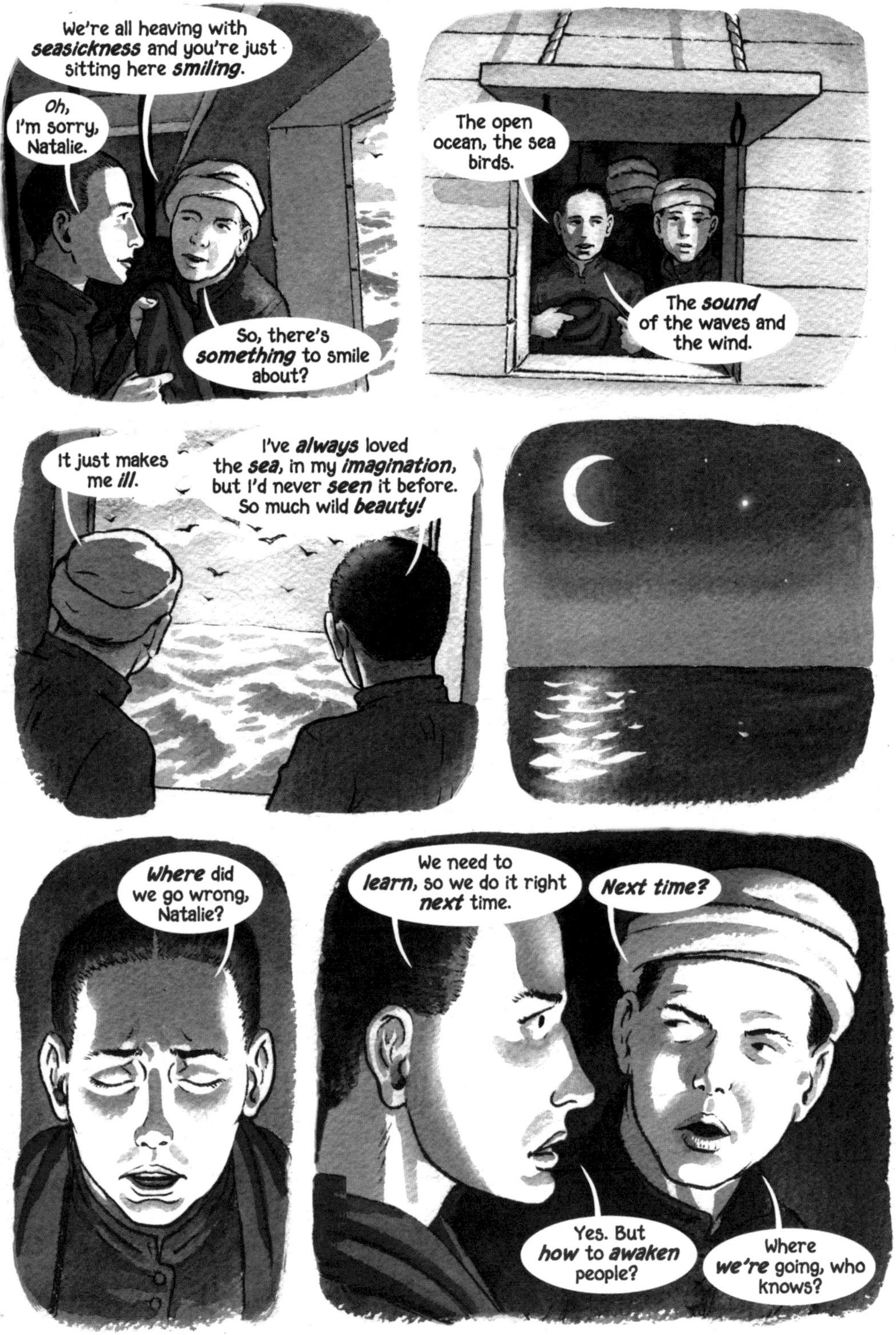

We're all heaving with *seasickness* and you're just sitting here *smiling*.
Oh, I'm sorry, Natalie.
So, there's *something* to smile about?
The open ocean, the sea birds.
The *sound* of the waves and the wind.
It just makes me *ill*.
I've *always* loved the *sea*, in my *imagination*, but I'd never *seen* it before. So much wild *beauty!*
Where did we go wrong, Natalie?
We need to *learn*, so we do it right *next* time.
Next time?
Yes. But *how* to *awaken* people?
Where *we're* going, who knows?

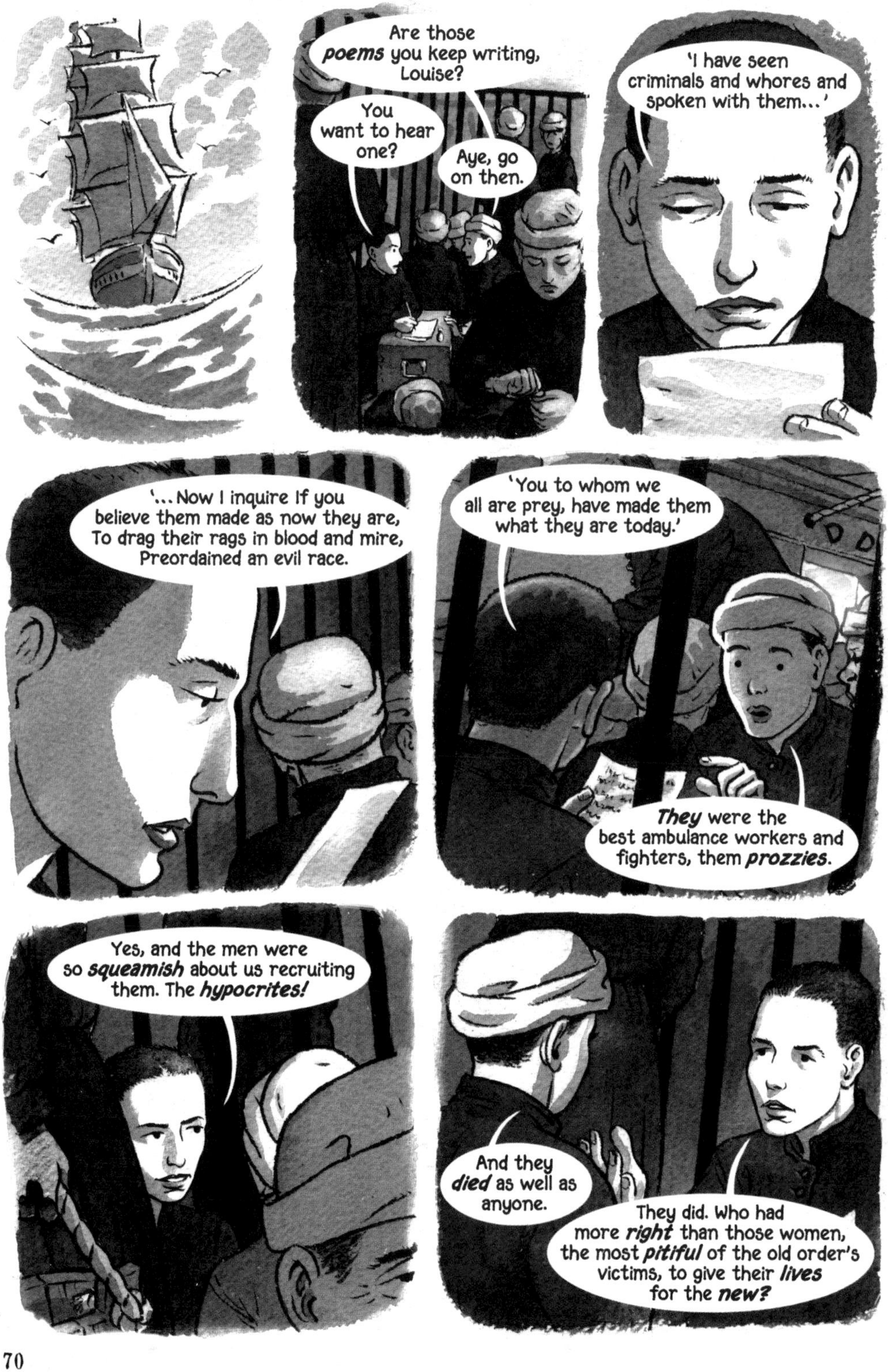

Are those *poems* you keep writing, Louise?
You want to hear one?
Aye, go on then.
'I have seen criminals and whores and spoken with them...'
'...Now I inquire If you believe them made as now they are, To drag their rags in blood and mire, Preordained an evil race.
'You to whom we all are prey, have made them what they are today.'
They were the best ambulance workers and fighters, them *prozzies*.
Yes, and the men were so *squeamish* about us recruiting them. The *hypocrites!*
And they *died* as well as anyone.
They did. Who had more *right* than those women, the most *pitiful* of the old order's victims, to give their *lives* for the *new?*

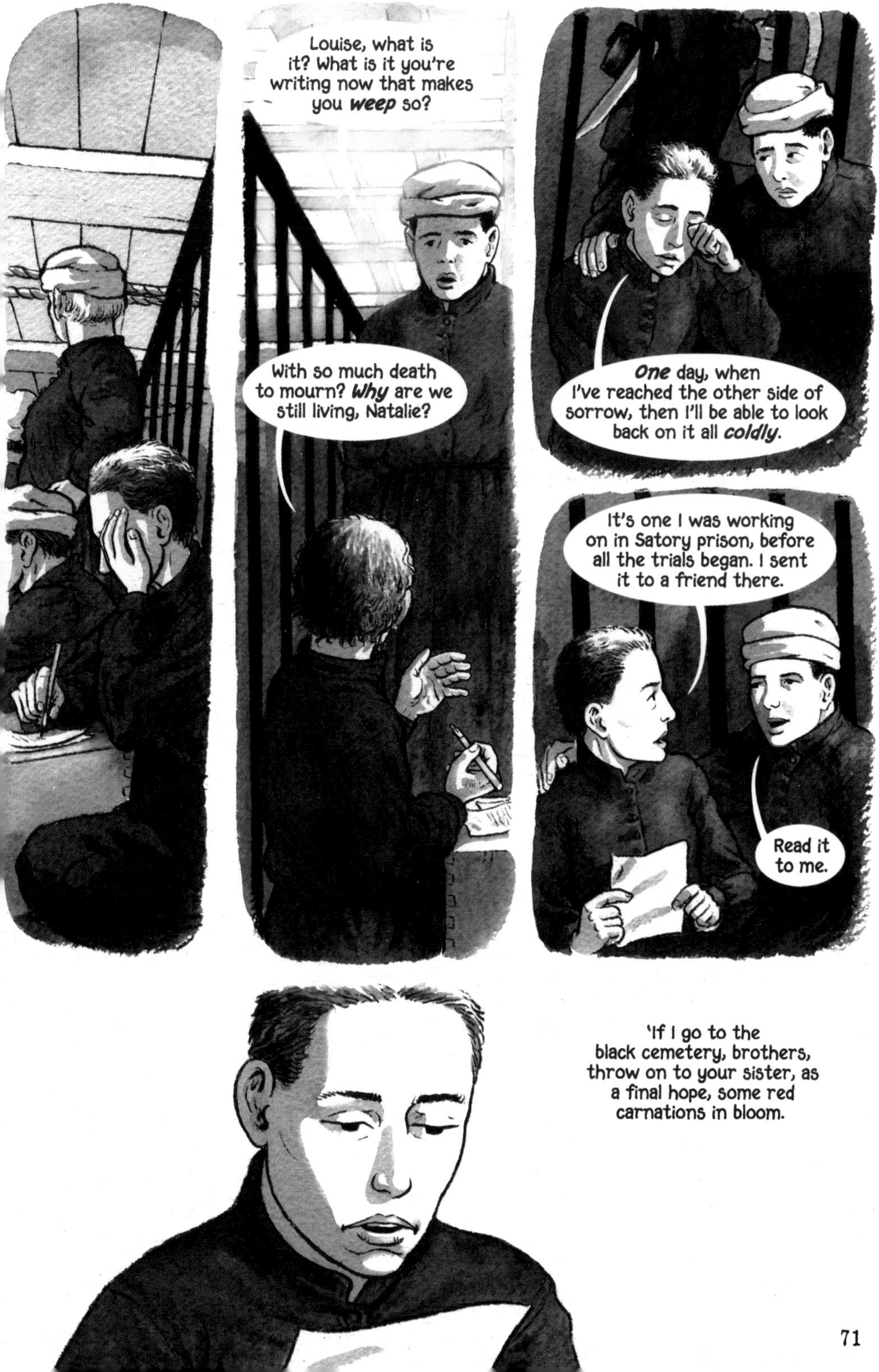
Louise, what is it? What is it you're writing now that makes you *weep* so?
With so much death to mourn? *Why* are we still living, Natalie?
One day, when I've reached the other side of sorrow, then I'll be able to look back on it all *coldly*.
It's one I was working on in Satory prison, before all the trials began. I sent it to a friend there.
Read it to me.
'If I go to the black cemetery, brothers, throw on to your sister, as a final hope, some red carnations in bloom.

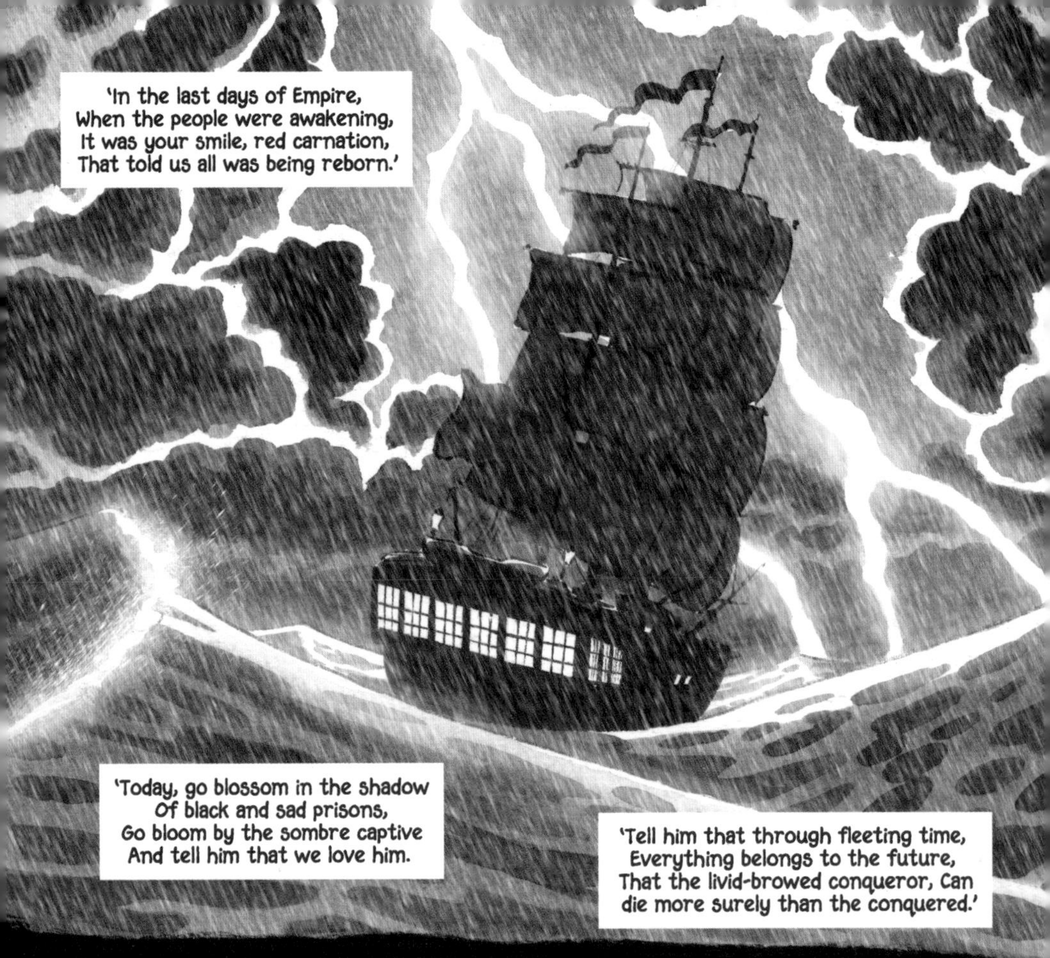
'In the last days of Empire,
When the people were awakening,
It was your smile, red carnation,
That told us all was being reborn.'
'Today, go blossom in the shadow
Of black and sad prisons,
Go bloom by the sombre captive
And tell him that we love him.
'Tell him that through fleeting time,
Everything belongs to the future,
That the livid-browed conqueror, Can
die more surely than the conquered.'

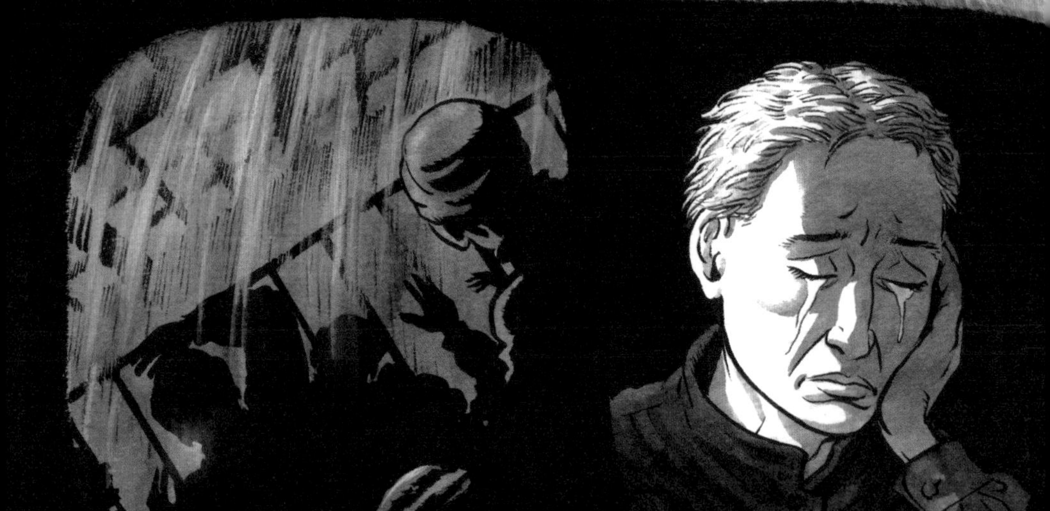

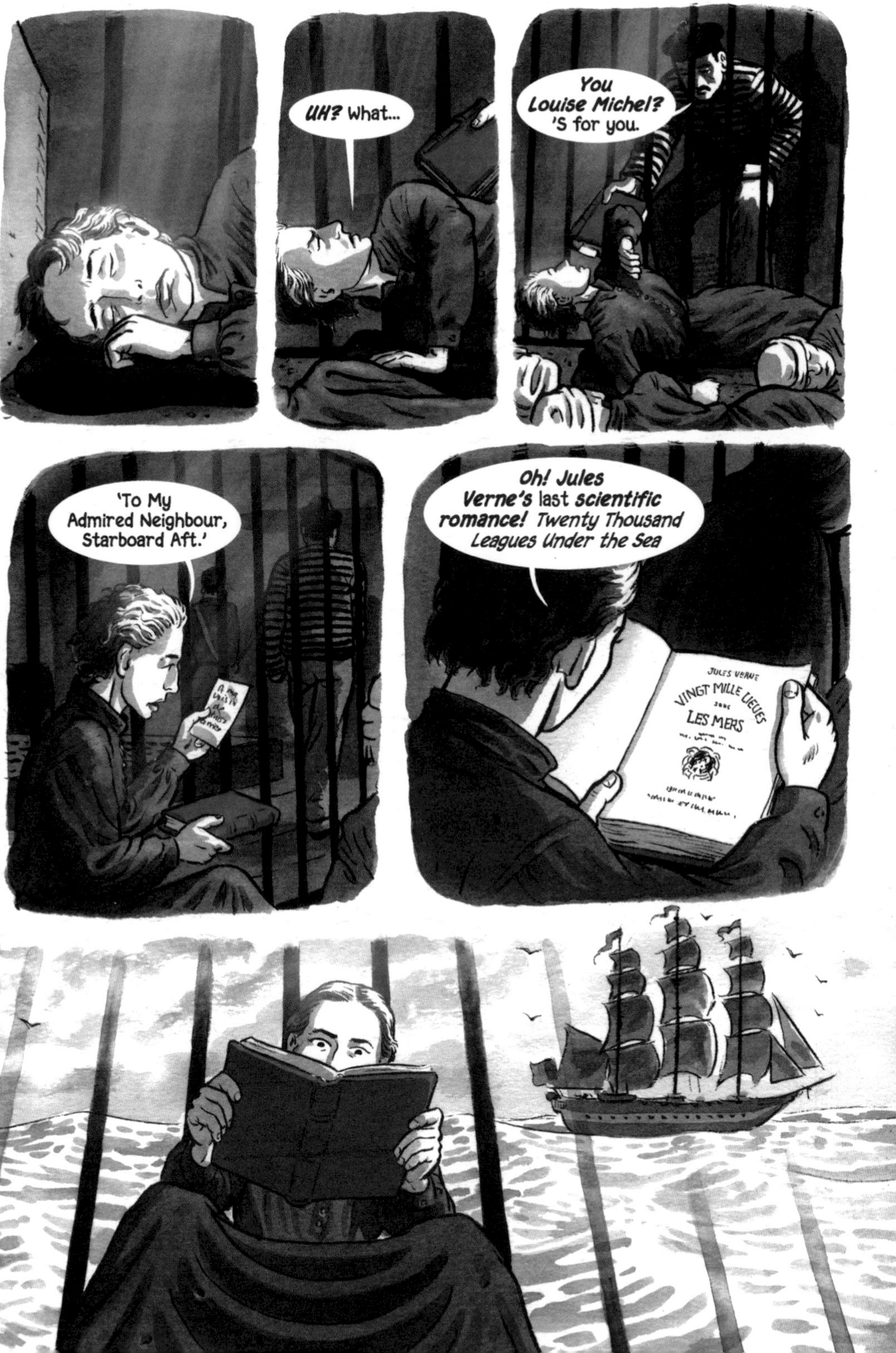
UH? What...
You Louise Michel? 'S for you.
'To My Admired Neighbour, Starboard Aft.'
Oh! Jules Verne's last scientific romance! Twenty Thousand Leagues Under the Sea
JULES VERNE
VINGT MILLE LIEUES SOUS LES MERS

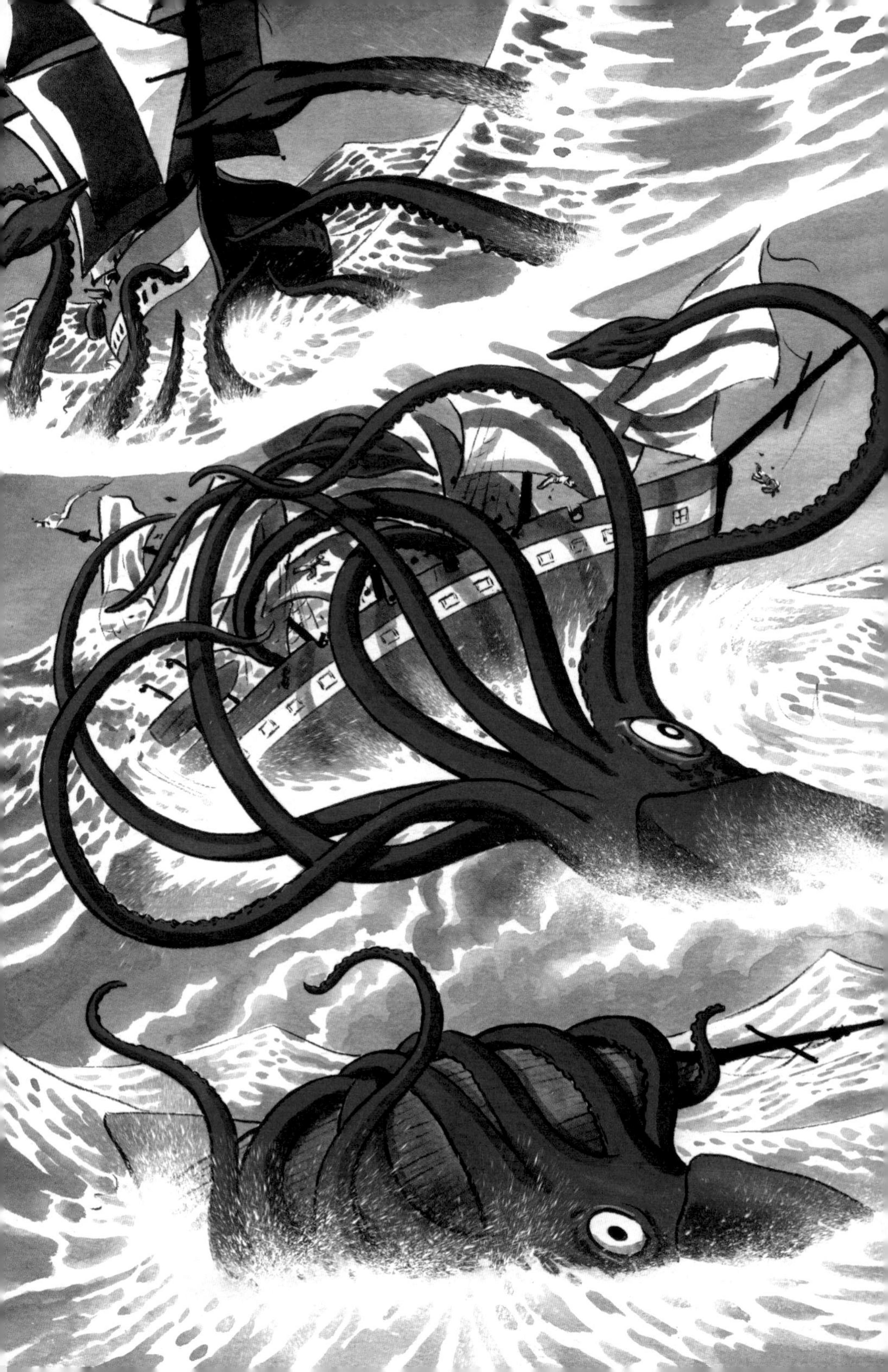

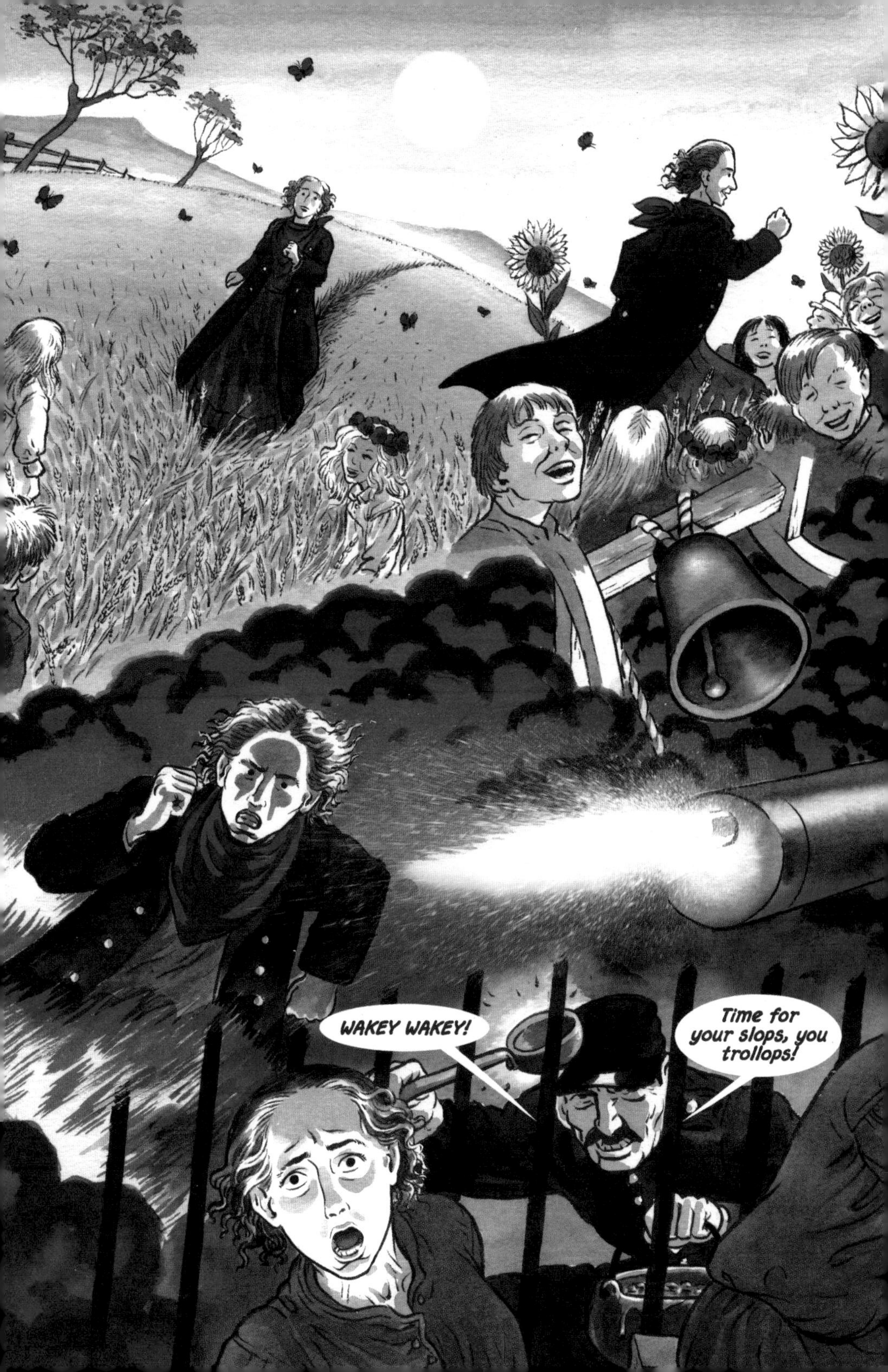
WAKEY WAKEY!
Time for your slops, you trollops!

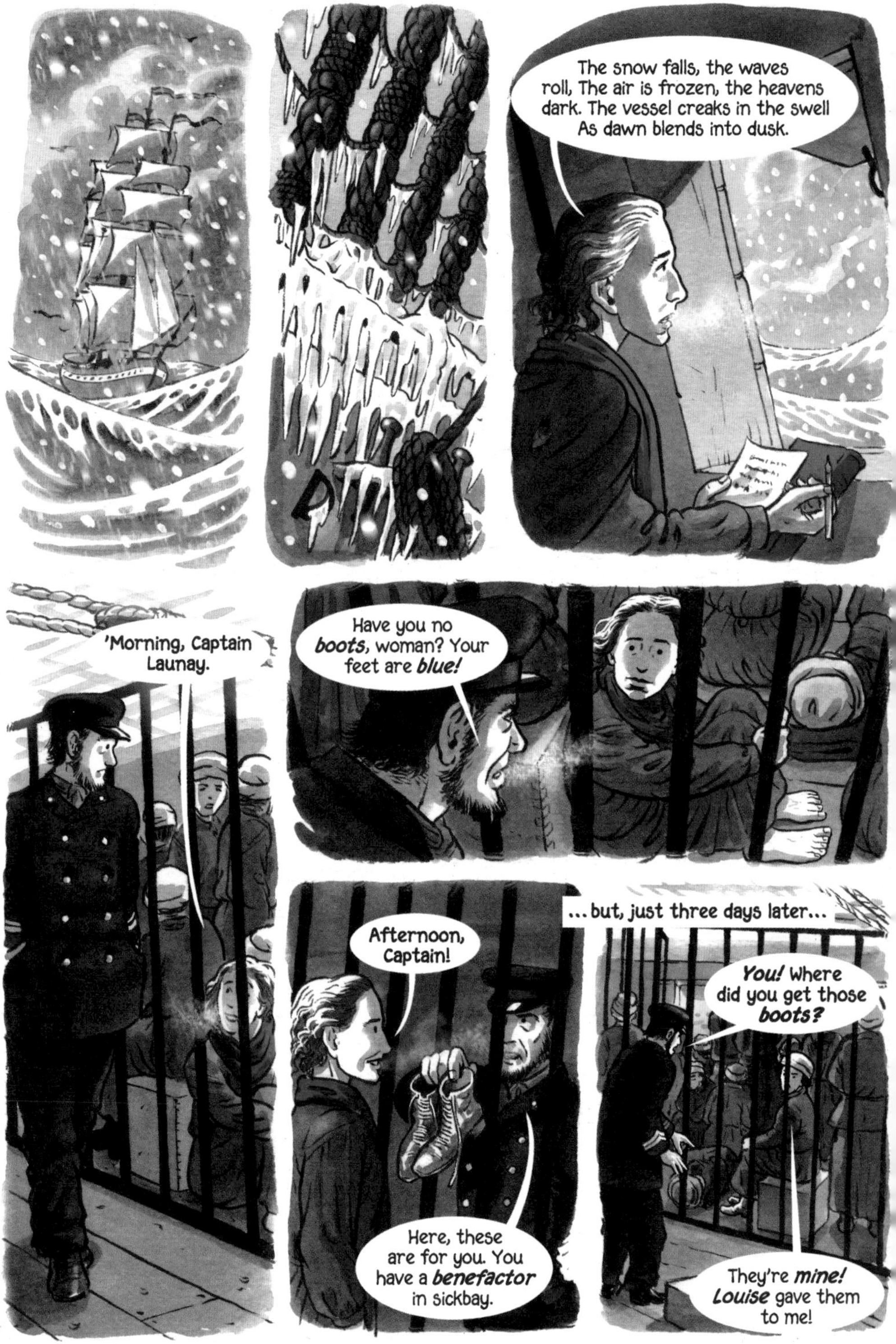

The snow falls, the waves roll, The air is frozen, the heavens dark. The vessel creaks in the swell As dawn blends into dusk.
'Morning, Captain Launay.
Have you no *boots*, woman? Your feet are *blue!*
Afternoon, Captain!
Here, these are for you. You have a *benefactor* in sickbay.
... but, just three days later...
You! Where did you get those *boots?*
They're *mine! Louise* gave them to me!

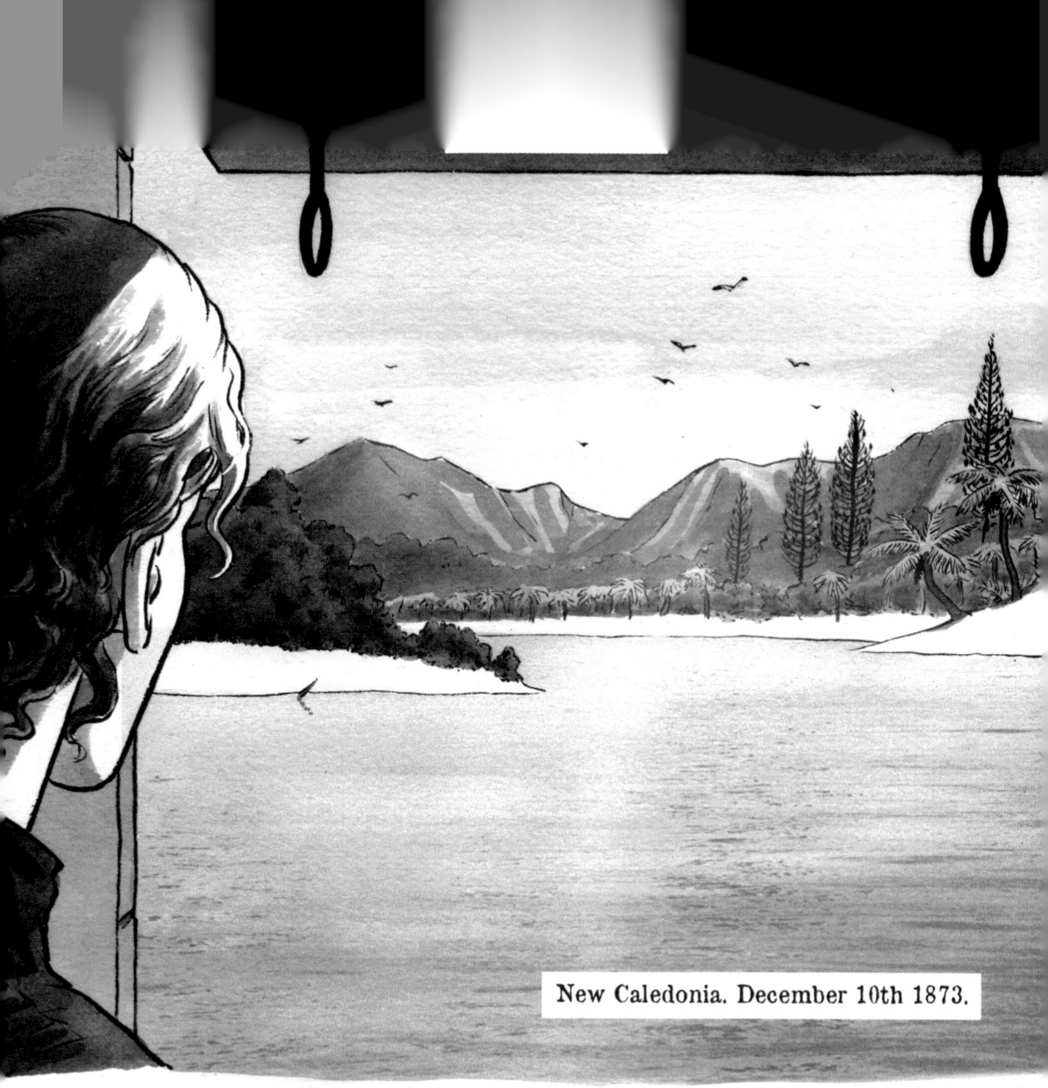
New Caledonia. December 10th 1873.

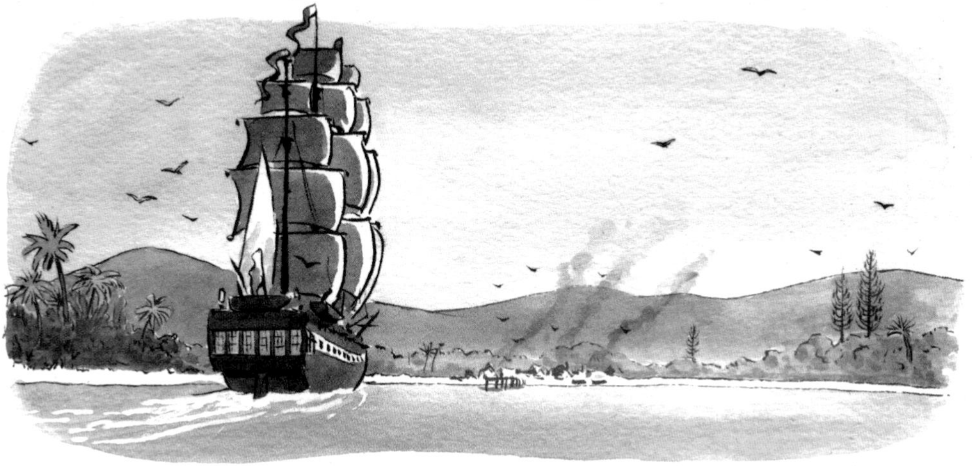

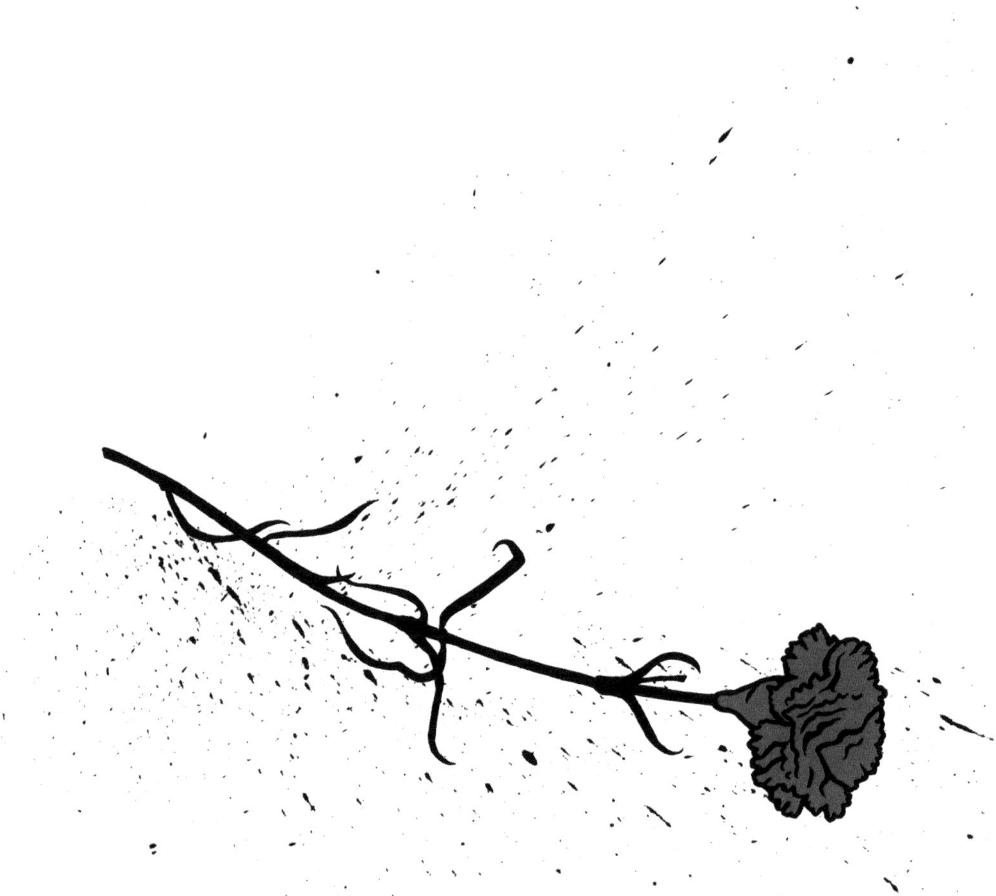

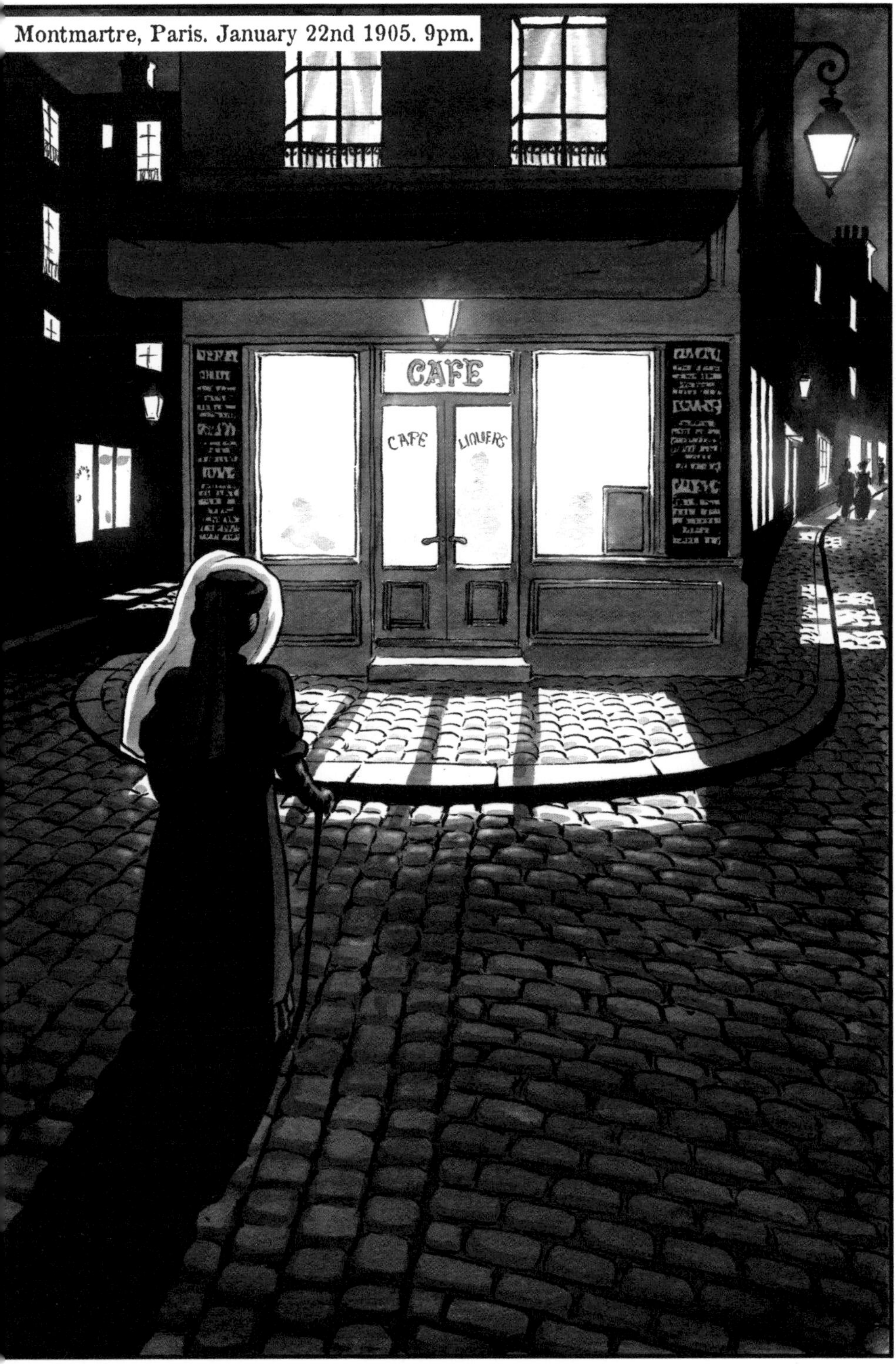
Montmartre, Paris. January 22nd 1905. 9pm.
CAFE
CAFE
LIQUERS

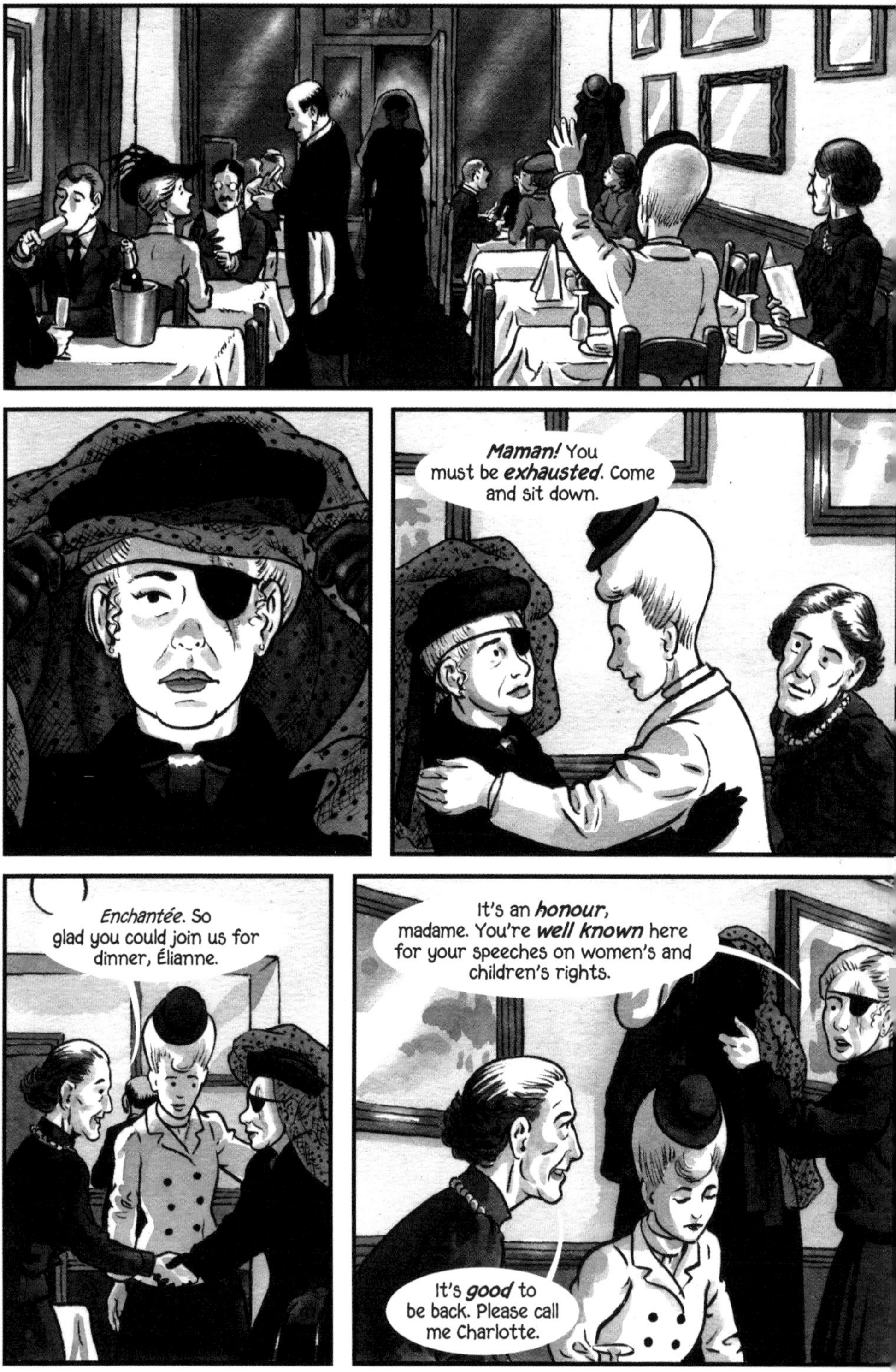
Maman! You must be exhausted. Come and sit down.
Enchantée. So glad you could join us for dinner, Élianne.
It's an honour, madame. You're well known here for your speeches on women's and children's rights.
It's good to be back. Please call me Charlotte.

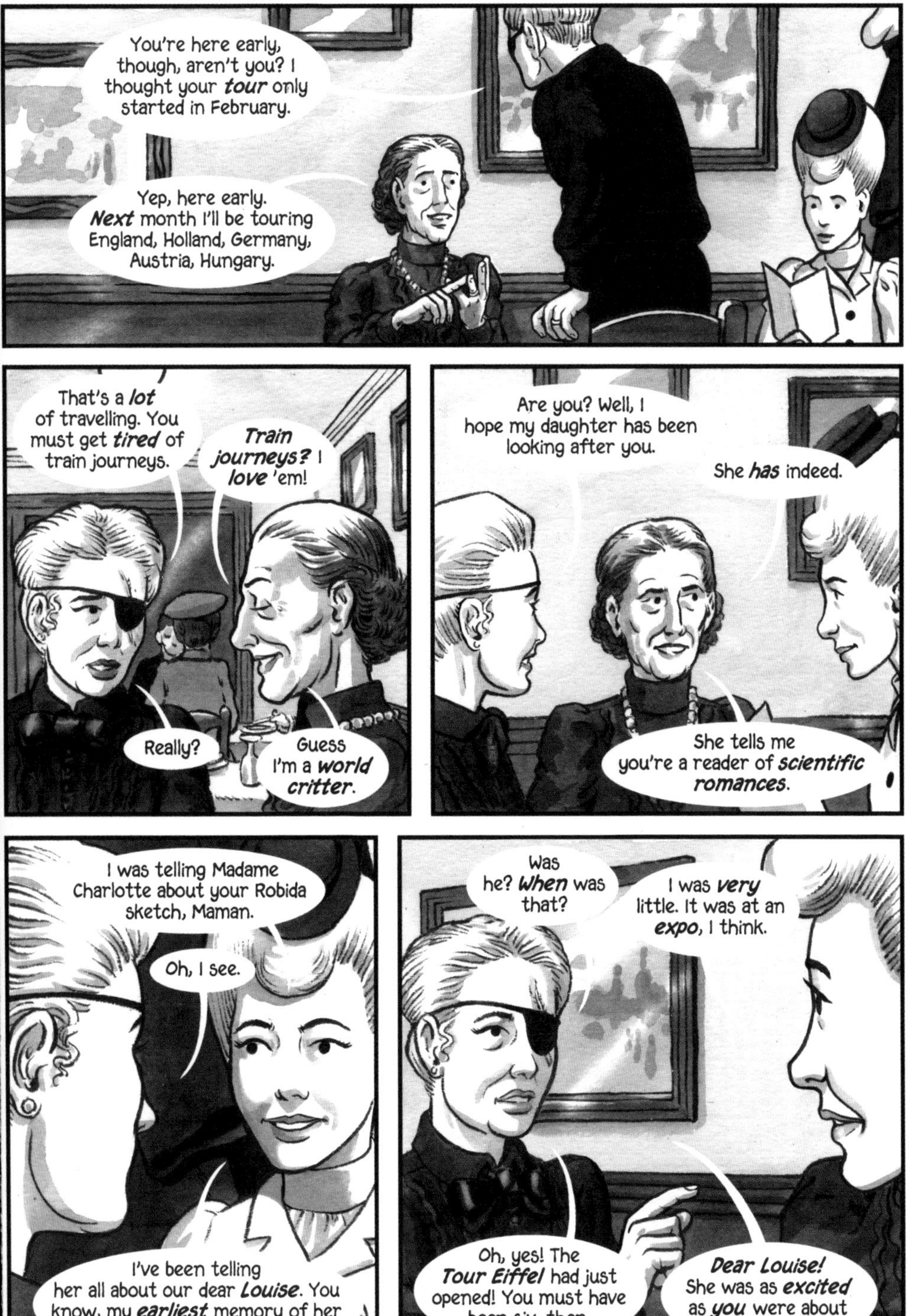
You're here early, though, aren't you? I thought your *tour* only started in February.
Yep, here early. *Next* month I'll be touring England, Holland, Germany, Austria, Hungary.
That's a *lot* of travelling. You must get *tired* of train journeys.
Train journeys? I *love* 'em!
Really?
Guess I'm a *world critter*.
Are you? Well, I hope my daughter has been looking after you.
She *has* indeed.
She tells me you're a reader of *scientific romances*.
I was telling Madame Charlotte about your Robida sketch, Maman.
Oh, I see.
I've been telling her all about our dear *Louise*. You know, my *earliest* memory of her - Albert Robida was there.
Was he? *When* was that?
I was *very* little. It was at an *expo*, I think.
Oh, yes! The *Tour Eiffel* had just opened! You must have been six, then.
Dear Louise! She was as *excited* as *you* were about it all.

Universal Exposition, Paris.
Summer 1889.

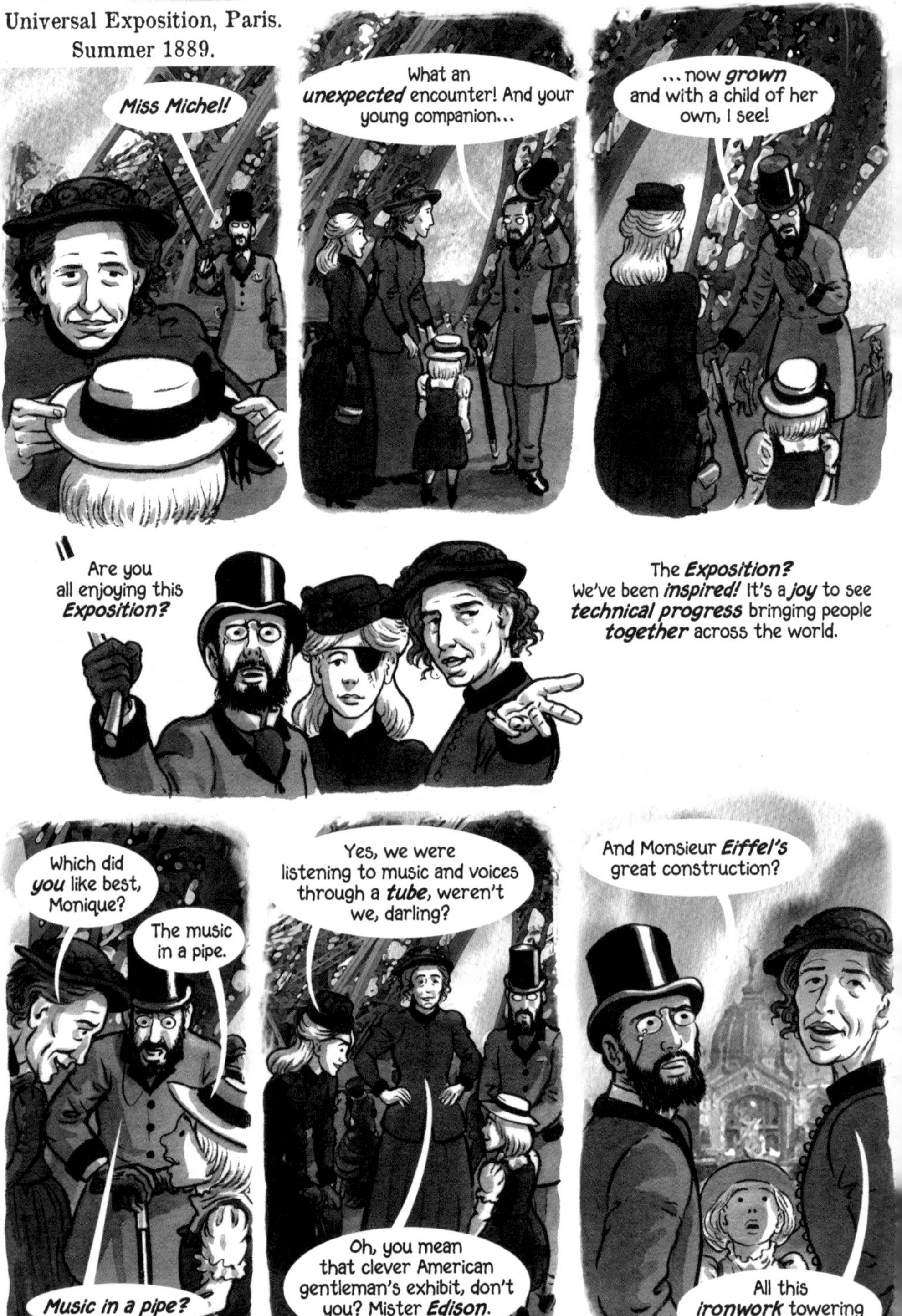
Miss Michel!
What an unexpected encounter! And your young companion...
...now grown and with a child of her own, I see!
Are you all enjoying this Exposition?
The Exposition? We've been inspired! It's a joy to see technical progress bringing people together across the world.
Which did you like best, Monique?
The music in a pipe.
Music in a pipe?
Yes, we were listening to music and voices through a tube, weren't we, darling?
Oh, you mean that clever American gentleman's exhibit, don't you? Mister Edison.
And Monsieur Eiffel's great construction?
All this ironwork towering above us?

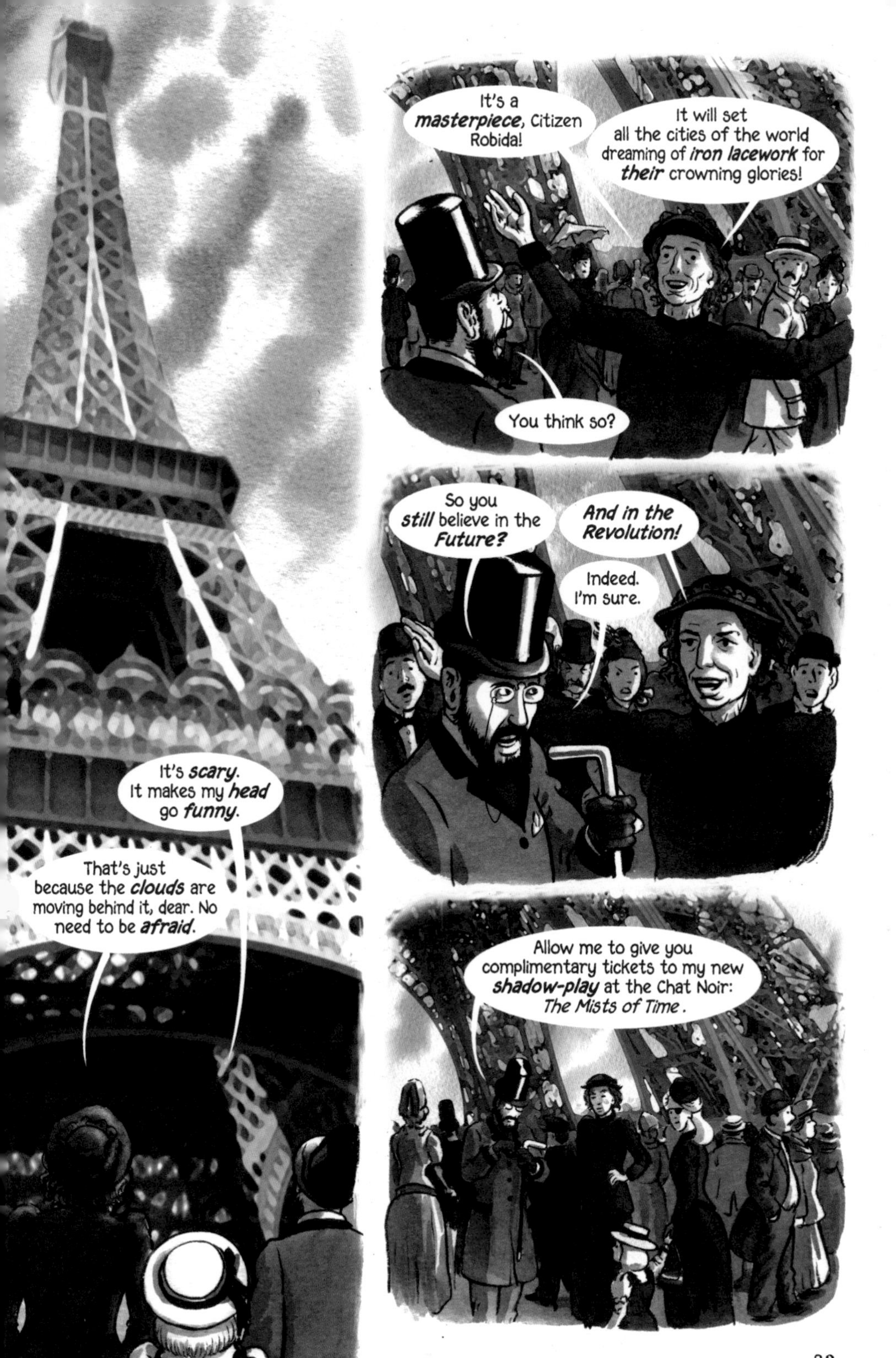
It's scary. It makes my head go funny.
That's just because the clouds are moving behind it, dear. No need to be afraid.
It's a masterpiece, Citizen Robida!
It will set all the cities of the world dreaming of iron lacework for their crowning glories!
You think so?
So you still believe in the Future?
And in the Revolution!
Indeed. I'm sure.
Allow me to give you complimentary tickets to my new shadow-play at the Chat Noir: The Mists of Time.

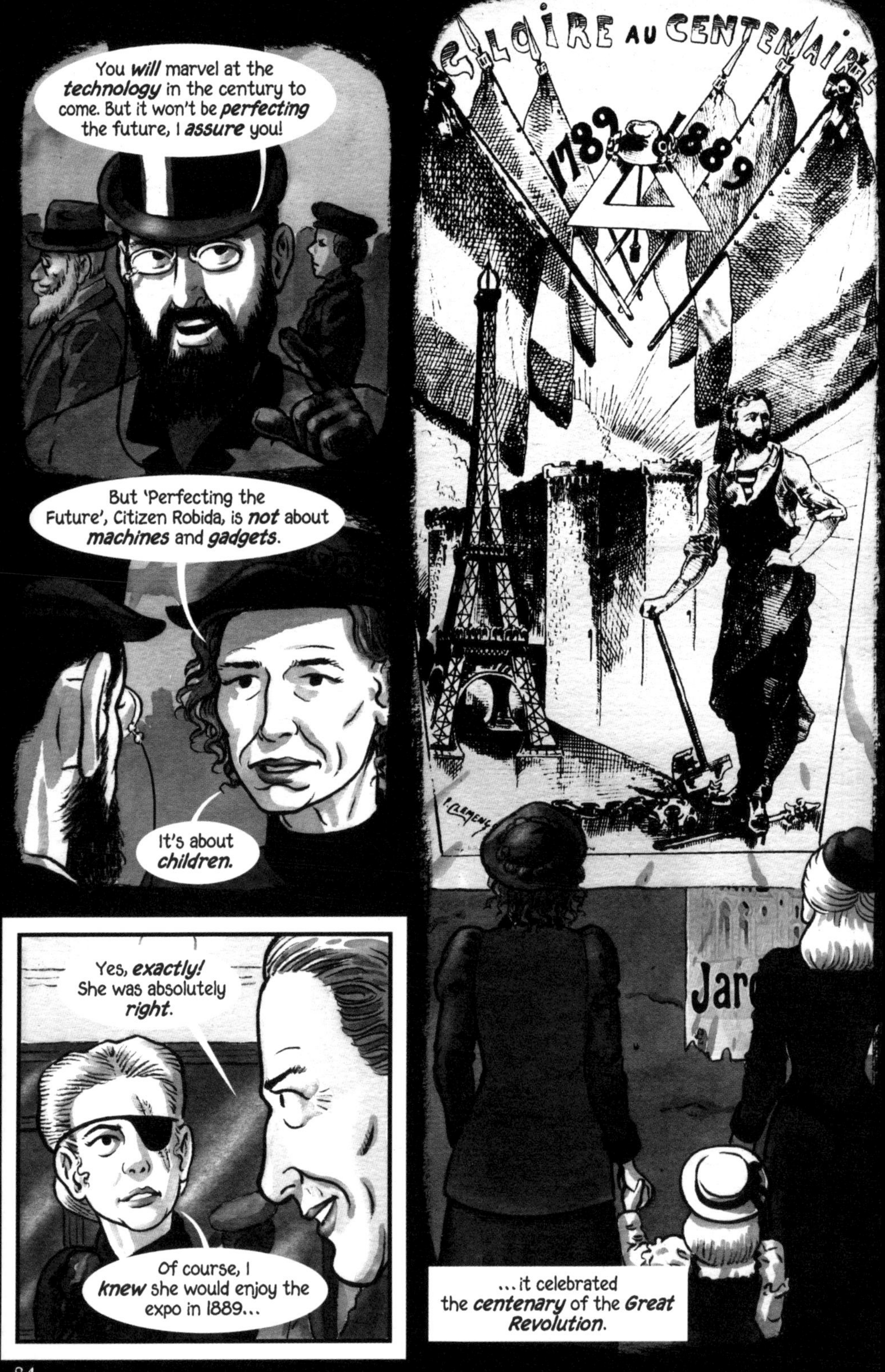
You *will* marvel at the *technology* in the century to come. But it won't be *perfecting* the future, I *assure* you!
But 'Perfecting the Future', Citizen Robida, is *not* about *machines* and *gadgets*.
It's about *children.*
Yes, *exactly!* She was absolutely *right*.
Of course, I *knew* she would enjoy the expo in 1889...
GLOIRE AU CENTENAIRE
1789 1889
...it celebrated the *centenary* of the *Great Revolution*.
Jar

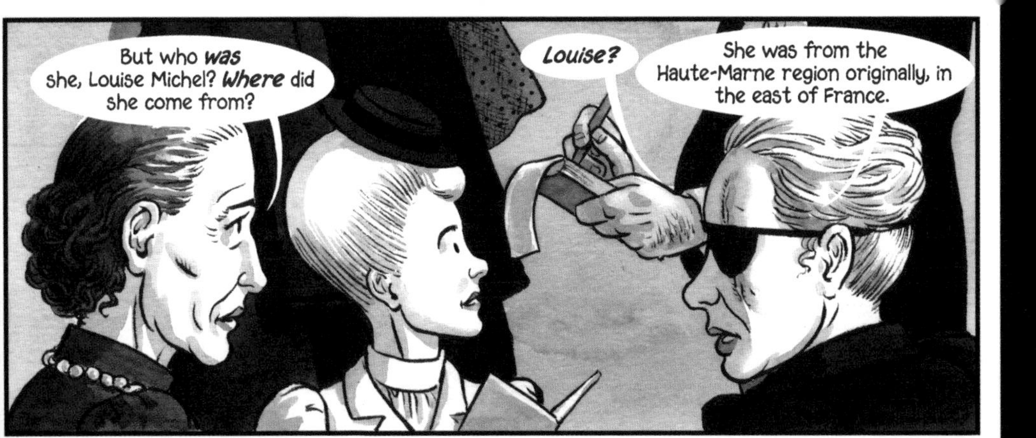

But who *was* she, Louise Michel? *Where* did she come from?
Louise?
She was from the Haute-Marne region originally, in the east of France.

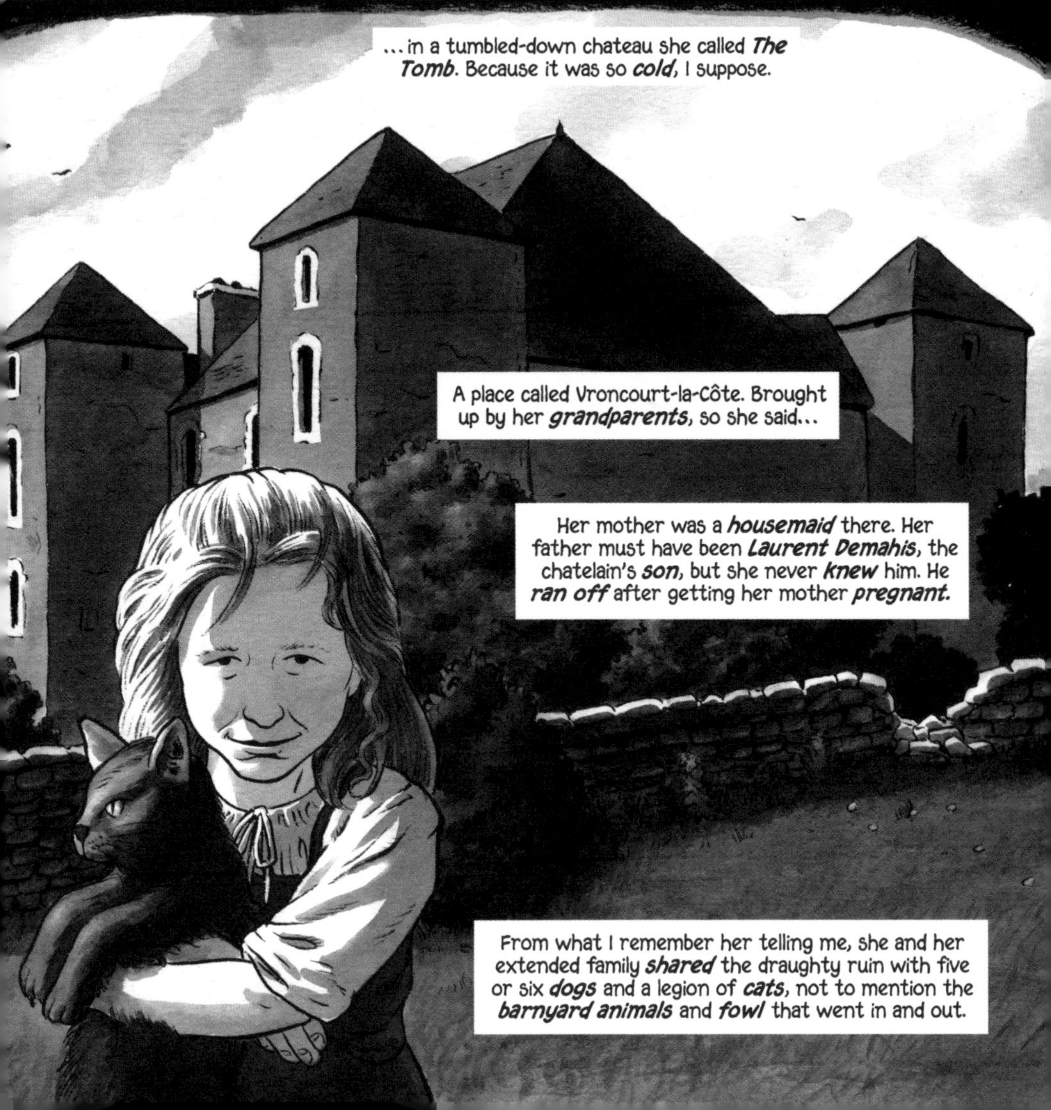

A place called Vroncourt-la-Côte. Brought up by her *grandparents*, so she said...
...in a tumbled-down chateau she called *The Tomb*. Because it was so *cold*, I suppose.
Her mother was a *housemaid* there. Her father must have been *Laurent Demahis*, the chatelain's *son*, but she never *knew* him. He *ran off* after getting her mother *pregnant*.
From what I remember her telling me, she and her extended family *shared* the draughty ruin with five or six *dogs* and a legion of *cats*, not to mention the *barnyard animals* and *fowl* that went in and out.

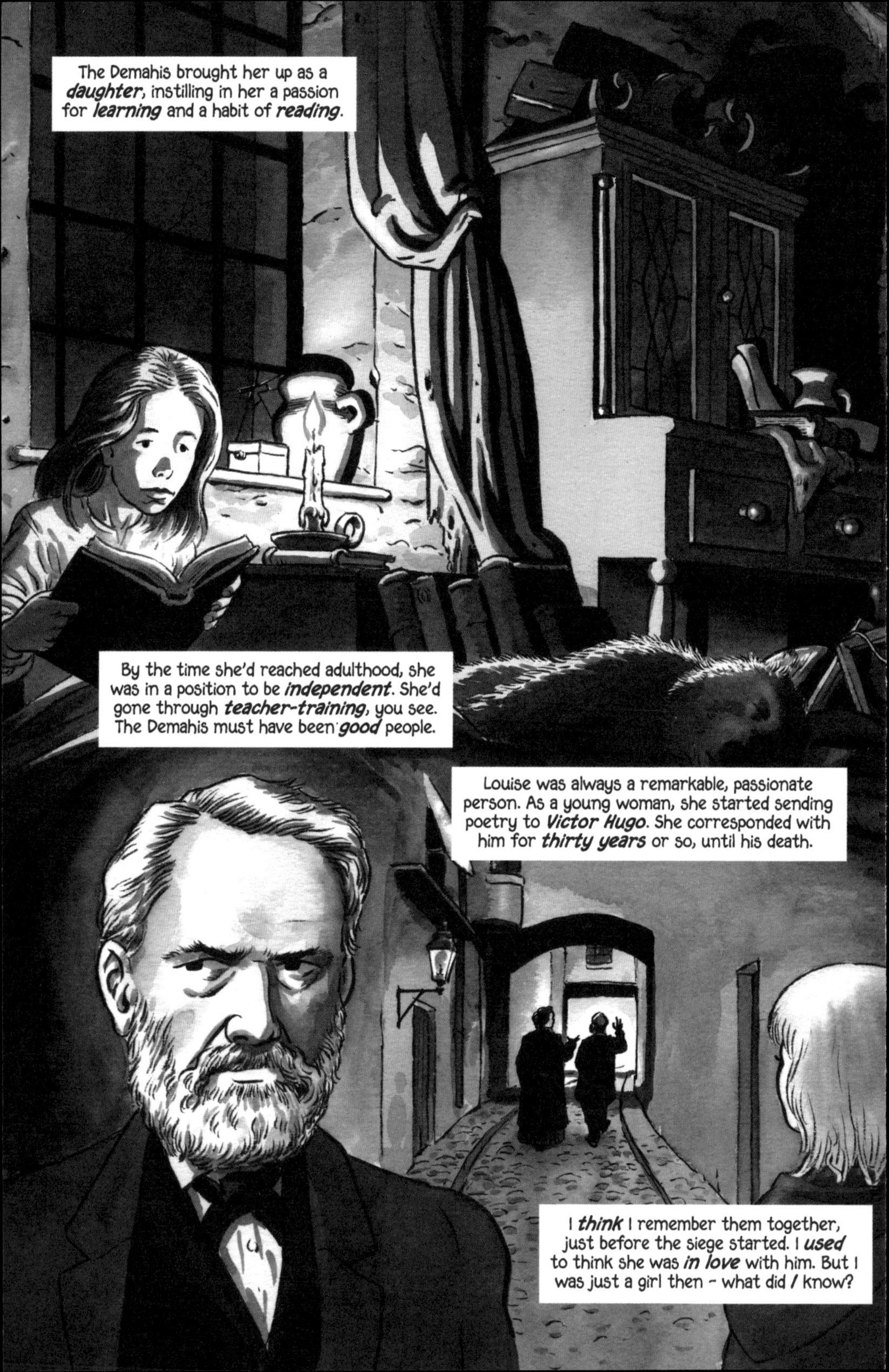
The Demahis brought her up as a *daughter*, instilling in her a passion for *learning* and a habit of *reading*.
By the time she'd reached adulthood, she was in a position to be *independent*. She'd gone through *teacher-training*, you see. The Demahis must have been *good* people.
Louise was always a remarkable, passionate person. As a young woman, she started sending poetry to *Victor Hugo*. She corresponded with him for *thirty years* or so, until his death.
I *think* I remember them together, just before the siege started. I *used* to think she was *in love* with him. But I was just a girl then - what did *I* know?

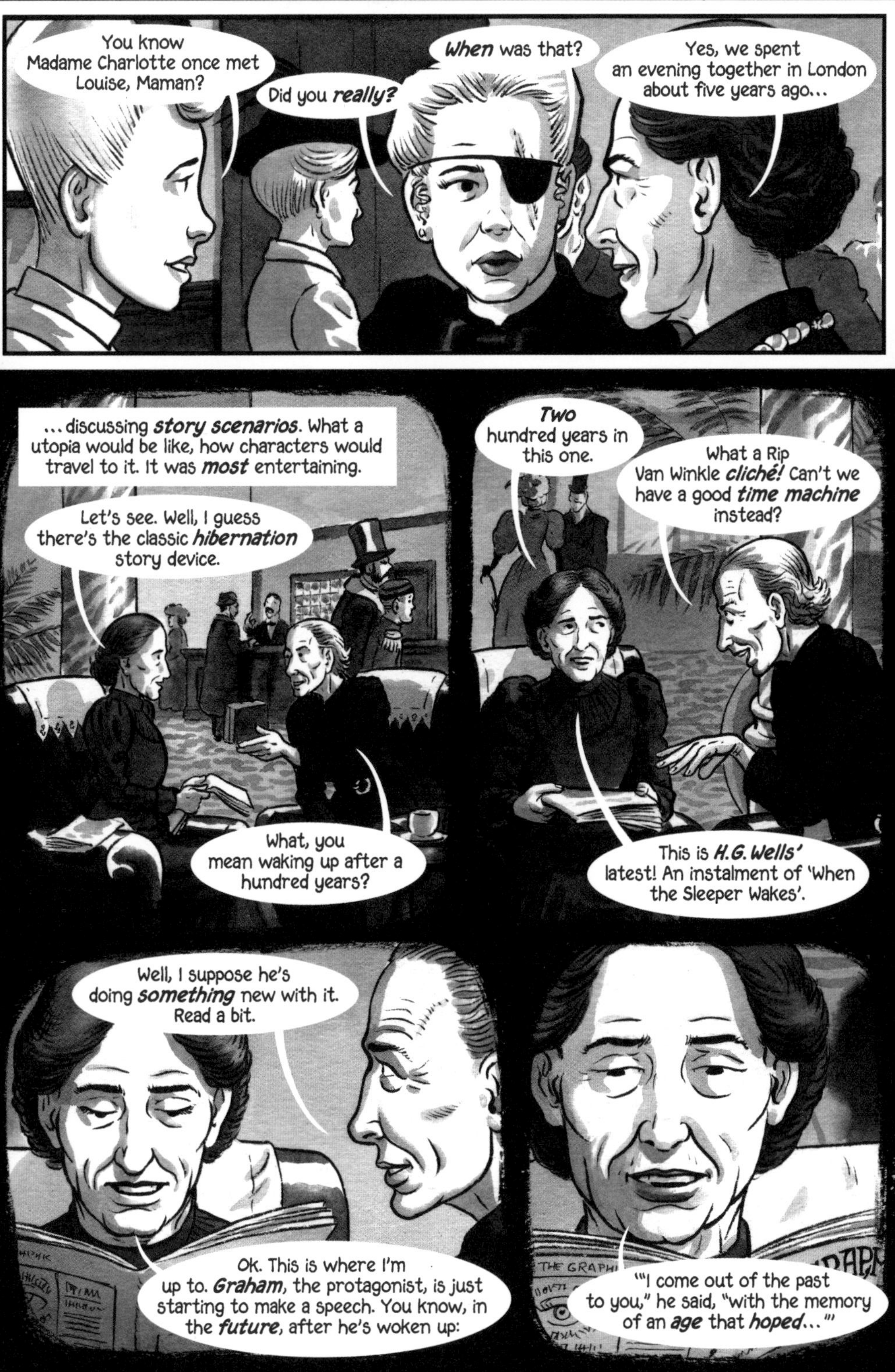
You know Madame Charlotte once met Louise, Maman?
Did you *really?*
When was that?
Yes, we spent an evening together in London about five years ago...
... discussing *story scenarios*. What a utopia would be like, how characters would travel to it. It was *most* entertaining.
Let's see. Well, I guess there's the classic *hibernation* story device.
What, you mean waking up after a hundred years?
Two hundred years in this one.
What a Rip Van Winkle *cliché!* Can't we have a good *time machine* instead?
This is *H.G. Wells'* latest! An instalment of 'When the Sleeper Wakes'.
Well, I suppose he's doing *something* new with it. Read a bit.
Ok. This is where I'm up to. *Graham*, the protagonist, is just starting to make a speech. You know, in the *future*, after he's woken up:
THE GRAPHI
"'I come out of the past to you," he said, "with the memory of an *age* that *hoped*...'"

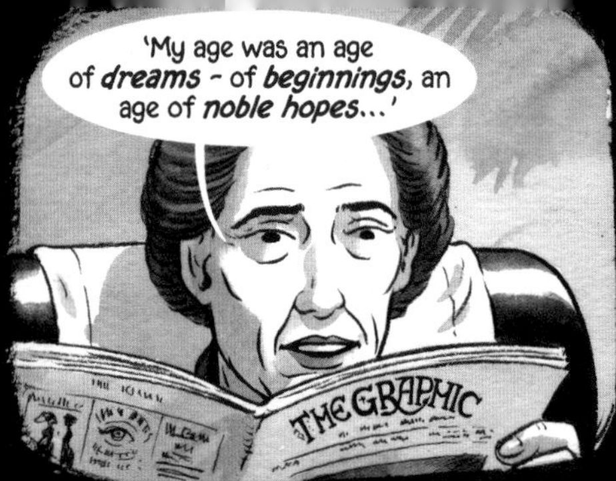
'My age was an age of *dreams* - of *beginnings*, an age of *noble hopes*...'
THE GRAPHIC

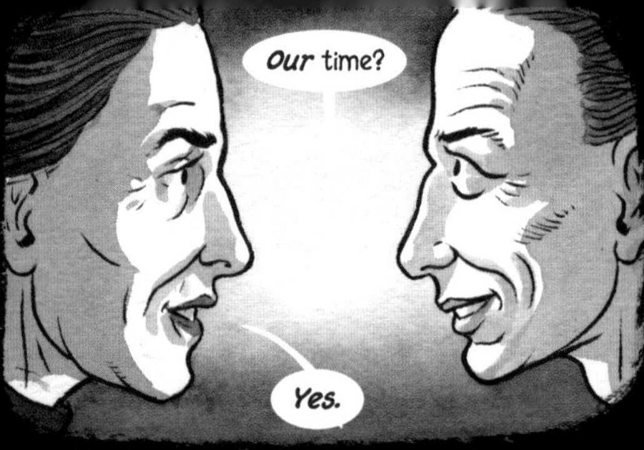
Our time?
Yes.

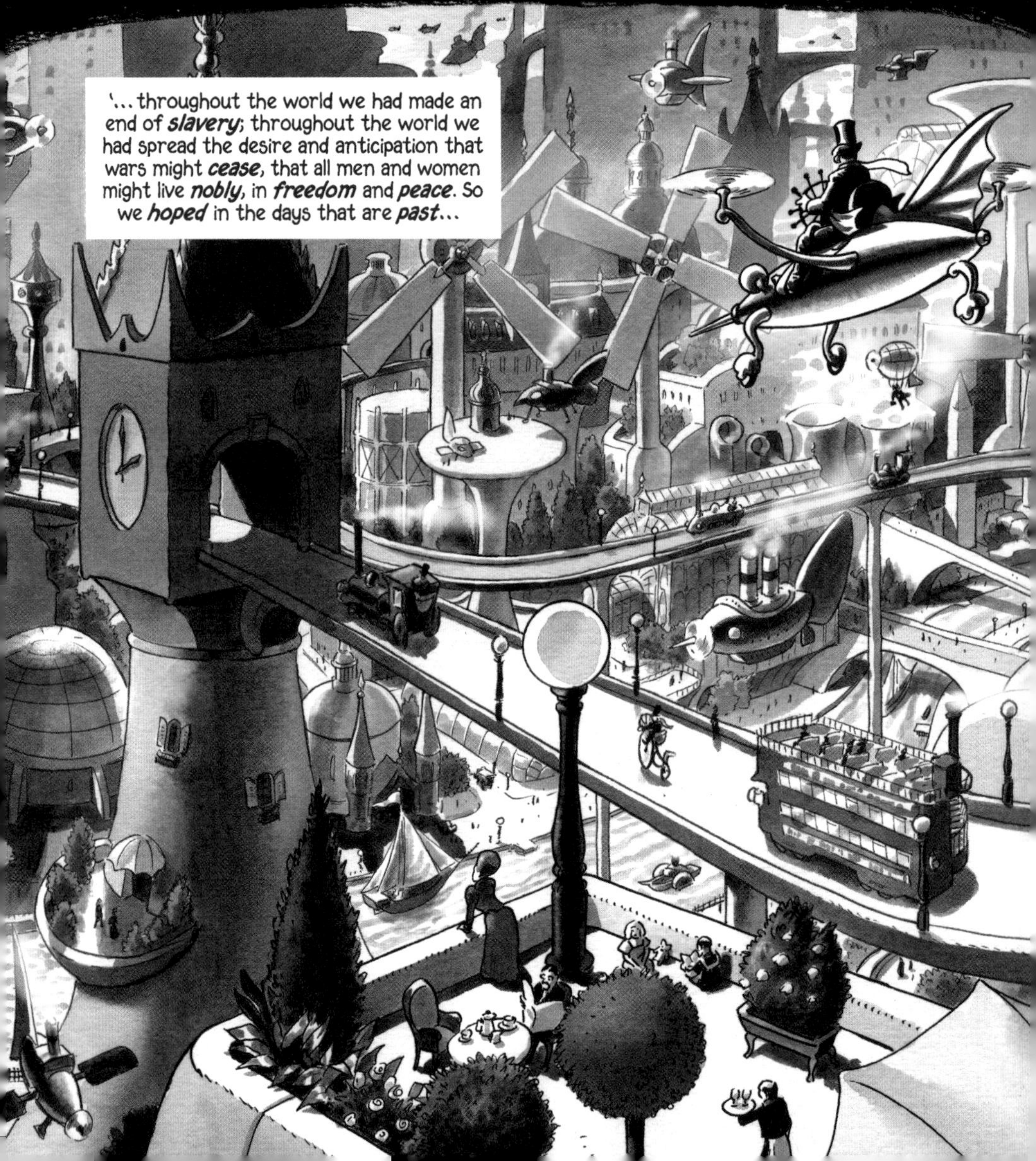
'... throughout the world we had made an end of *slavery*; throughout the world we had spread the desire and anticipation that wars might *cease*, that all men and women might live *nobly*, in *freedom* and *peace*. So we *hoped* in the days that are *past*...

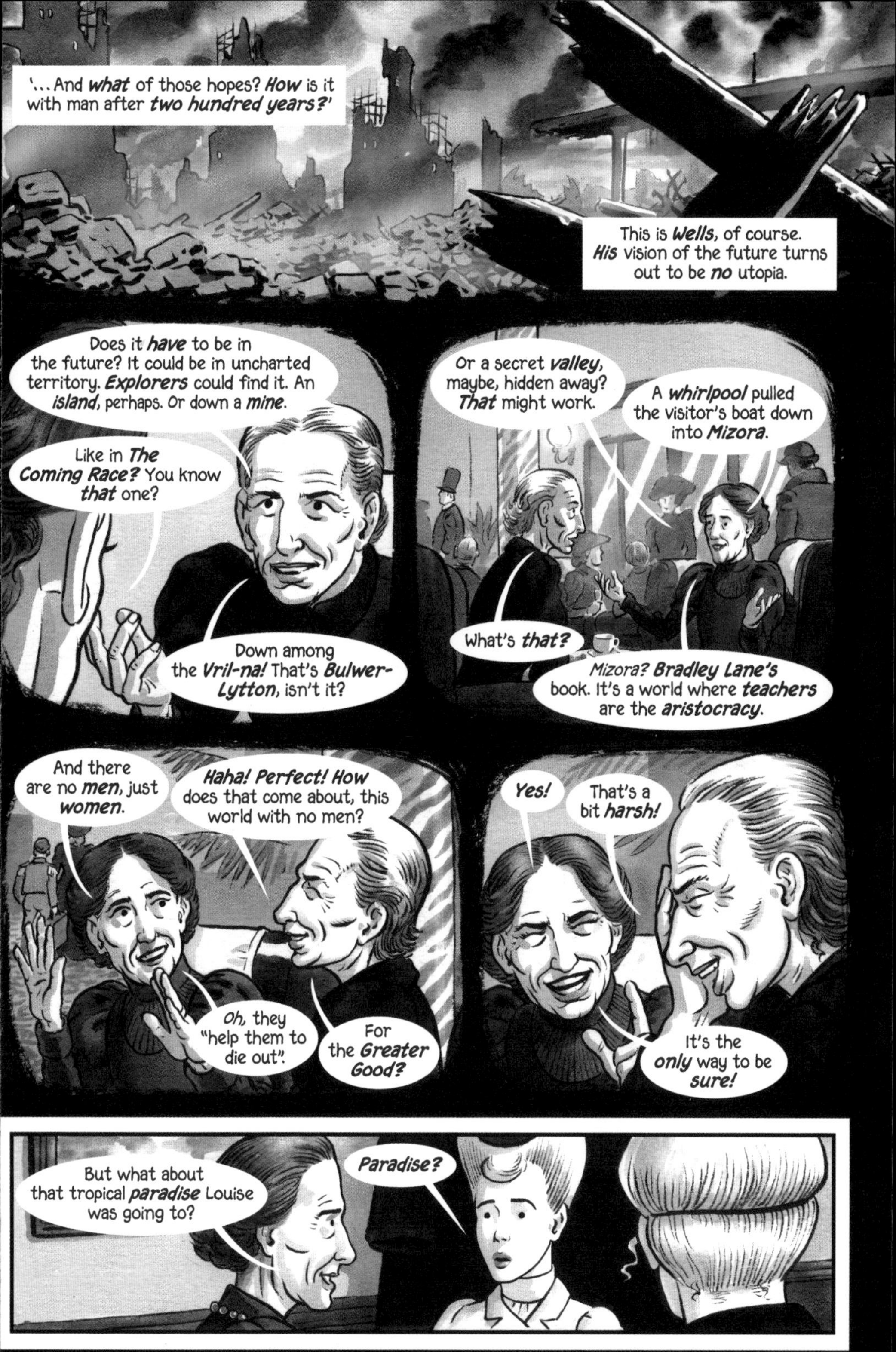
'...And what of those hopes? How is it with man after two hundred years?'
This is Wells, of course. His vision of the future turns out to be no utopia.
Does it have to be in the future? It could be in uncharted territory. Explorers could find it. An island, perhaps. Or down a mine.
Like in The Coming Race? You know that one?
Down among the Vril-na! That's Bulwer-Lytton, isn't it?
Or a secret valley, maybe, hidden away? That might work.
A whirlpool pulled the visitor's boat down into Mizora.
What's that?
Mizora? Bradley Lane's book. It's a world where teachers are the aristocracy.
And there are no men, just women.
Haha! Perfect! How does that come about, this world with no men?
Oh, they "help them to die out".
For the Greater Good?
Yes!
That's a bit harsh!
It's the only way to be sure!
But what about that tropical paradise Louise was going to?
Paradise?

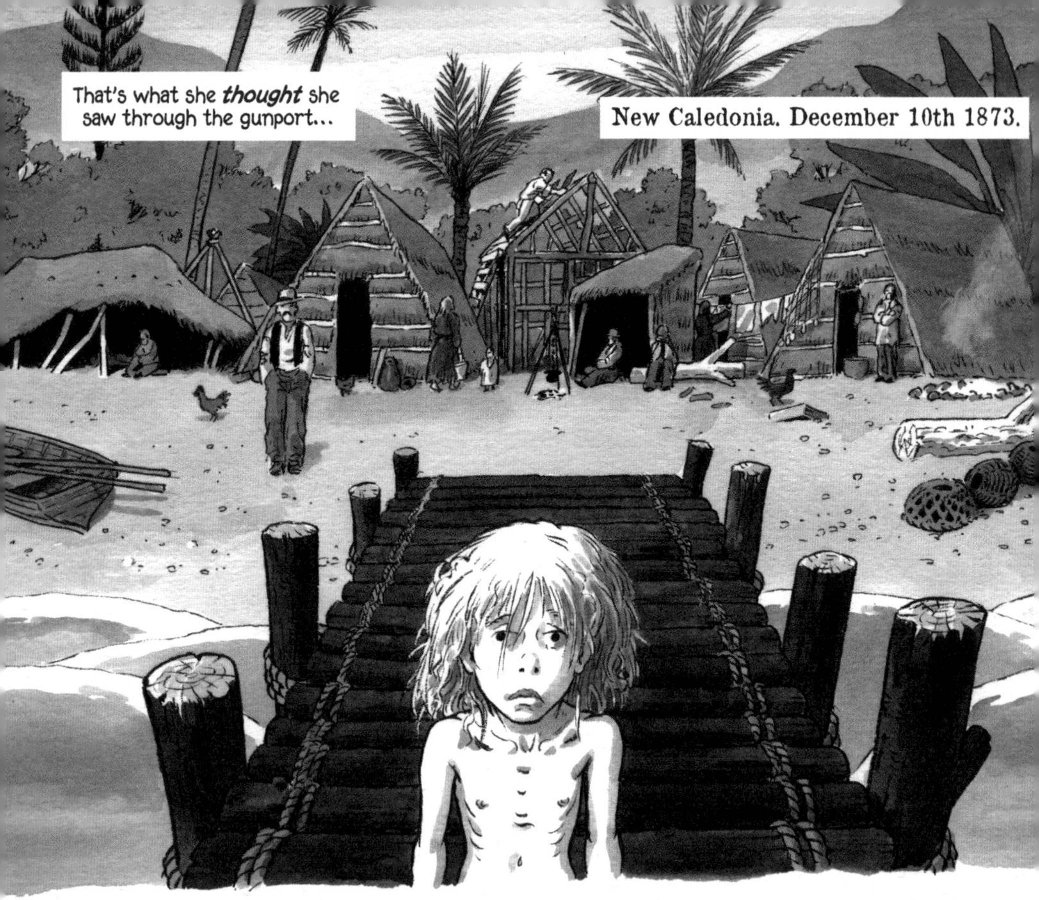
That's what she *thought* she saw through the gunport...
New Caledonia. December 10th 1873.

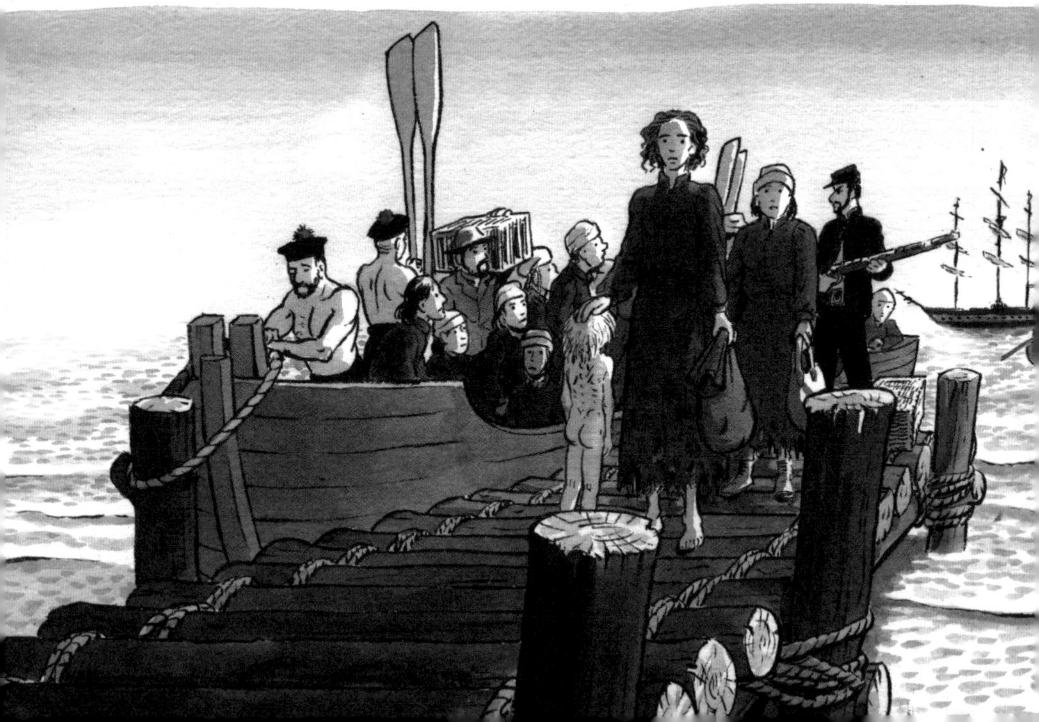

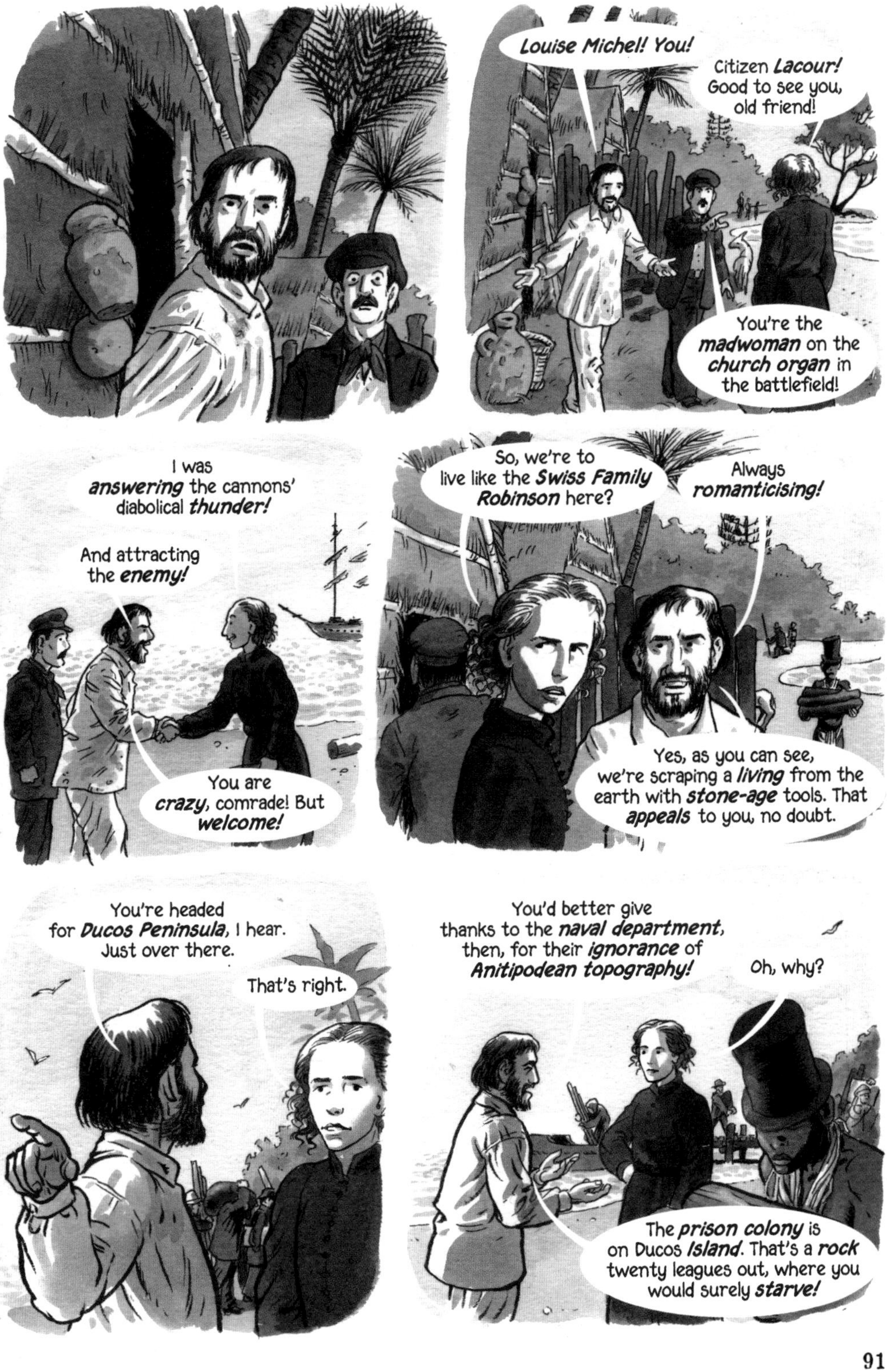
Louise Michel! You!
Citizen Lacour! Good to see you, old friend!
You're the madwoman on the church organ in the battlefield!
I was answering the cannons' diabolical thunder!
And attracting the enemy!
You are crazy, comrade! But welcome!
So, we're to live like the Swiss Family Robinson here?
Always romanticising!
Yes, as you can see, we're scraping a living from the earth with stone-age tools. That appeals to you, no doubt.
You're headed for Ducos Peninsula, I hear. Just over there.
That's right.
You'd better give thanks to the naval department, then, for their ignorance of Anitipodean topography!
Oh, why?
The prison colony is on Ducos Island. That's a rock twenty leagues out, where you would surely starve!

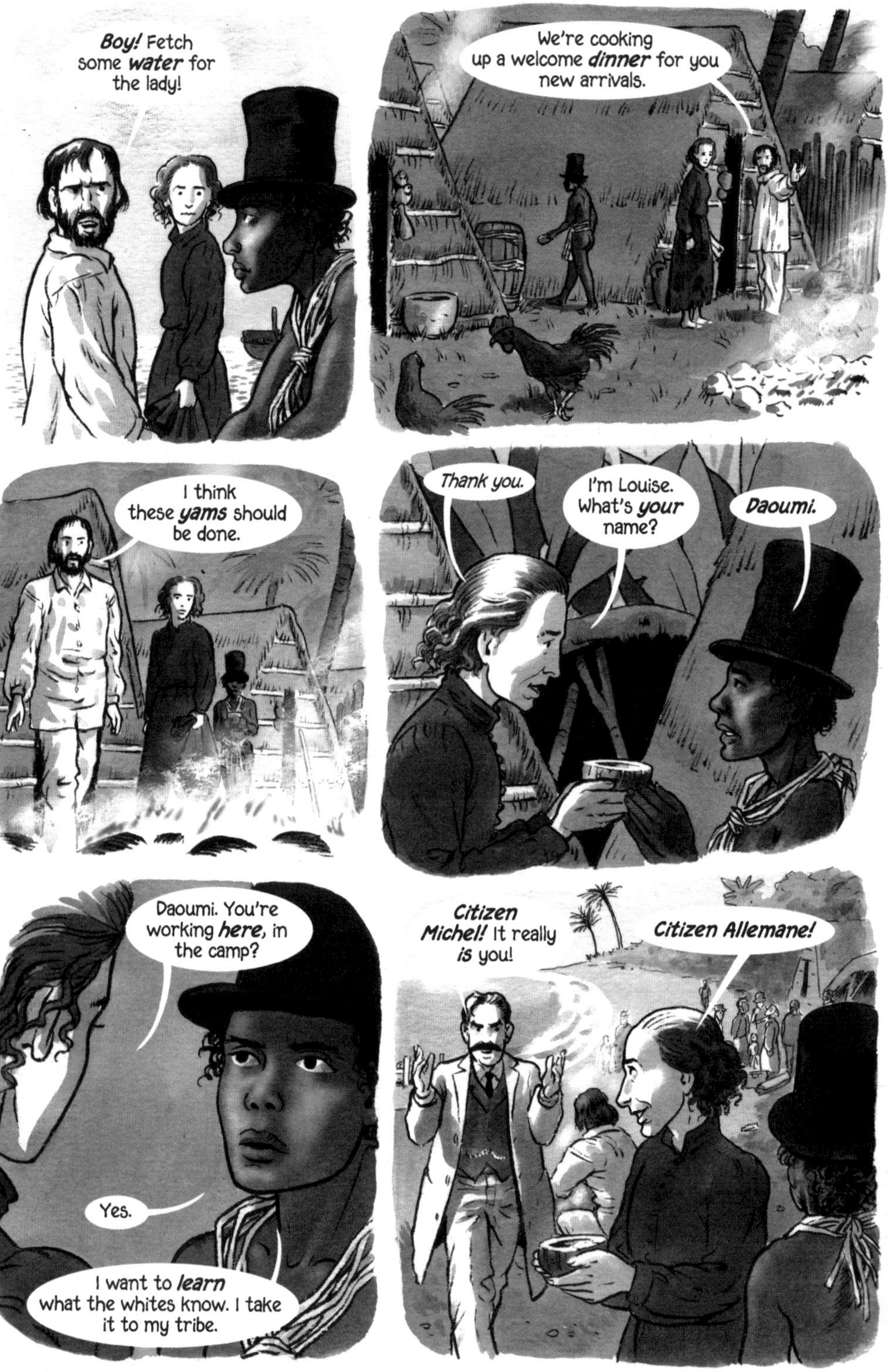
Boy! Fetch some water for the lady!
We're cooking up a welcome dinner for you new arrivals.
I think these yams should be done.
Thank you.
I'm Louise. What's your name?
Daoumi.
Daoumi. You're working here, in the camp?
Yes.
I want to learn what the whites know. I take it to my tribe.
Citizen Michel! It really is you!
Citizen Allemane!

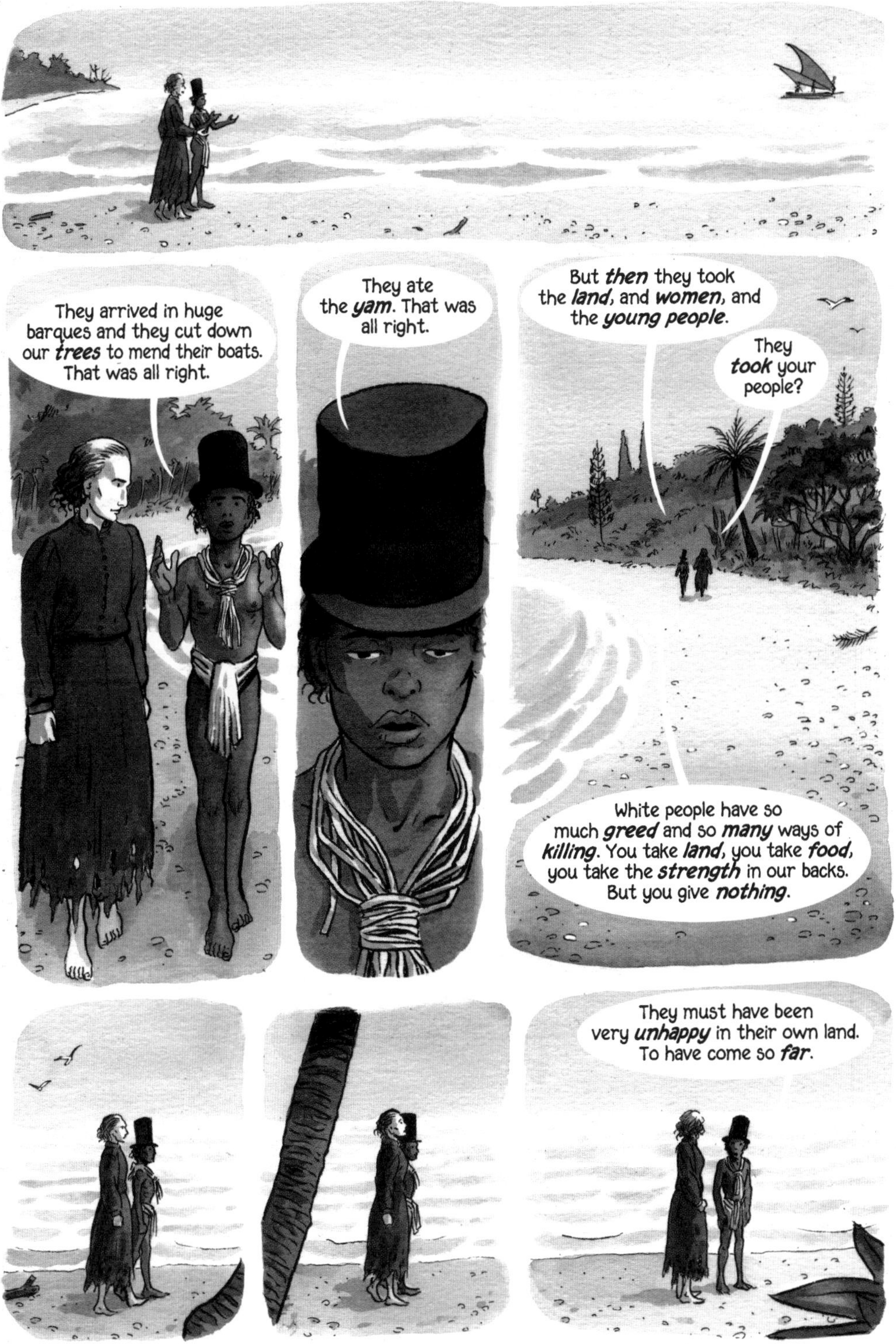
They arrived in huge barques and they cut down our *trees* to mend their boats. That was all right.
They ate the *yam*. That was all right.
But *then* they took the *land*, and *women*, and the *young people*.
They *took* your people?
White people have so much *greed* and so *many* ways of *killing*. You take *land*, you take *food*, you take the *strength* in our backs. But you give *nothing*.
They must have been very *unhappy* in their own land. To have come so *far*.

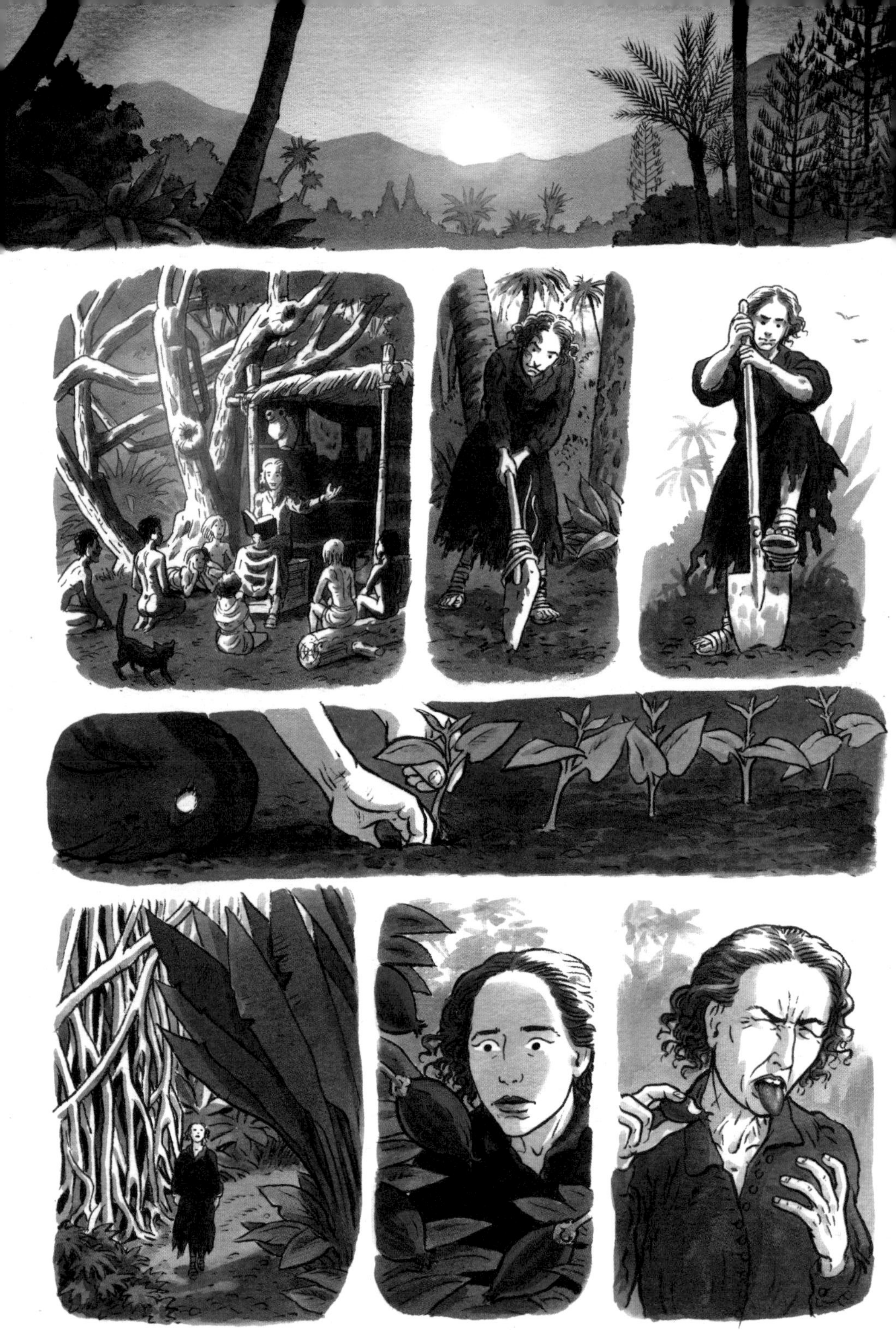

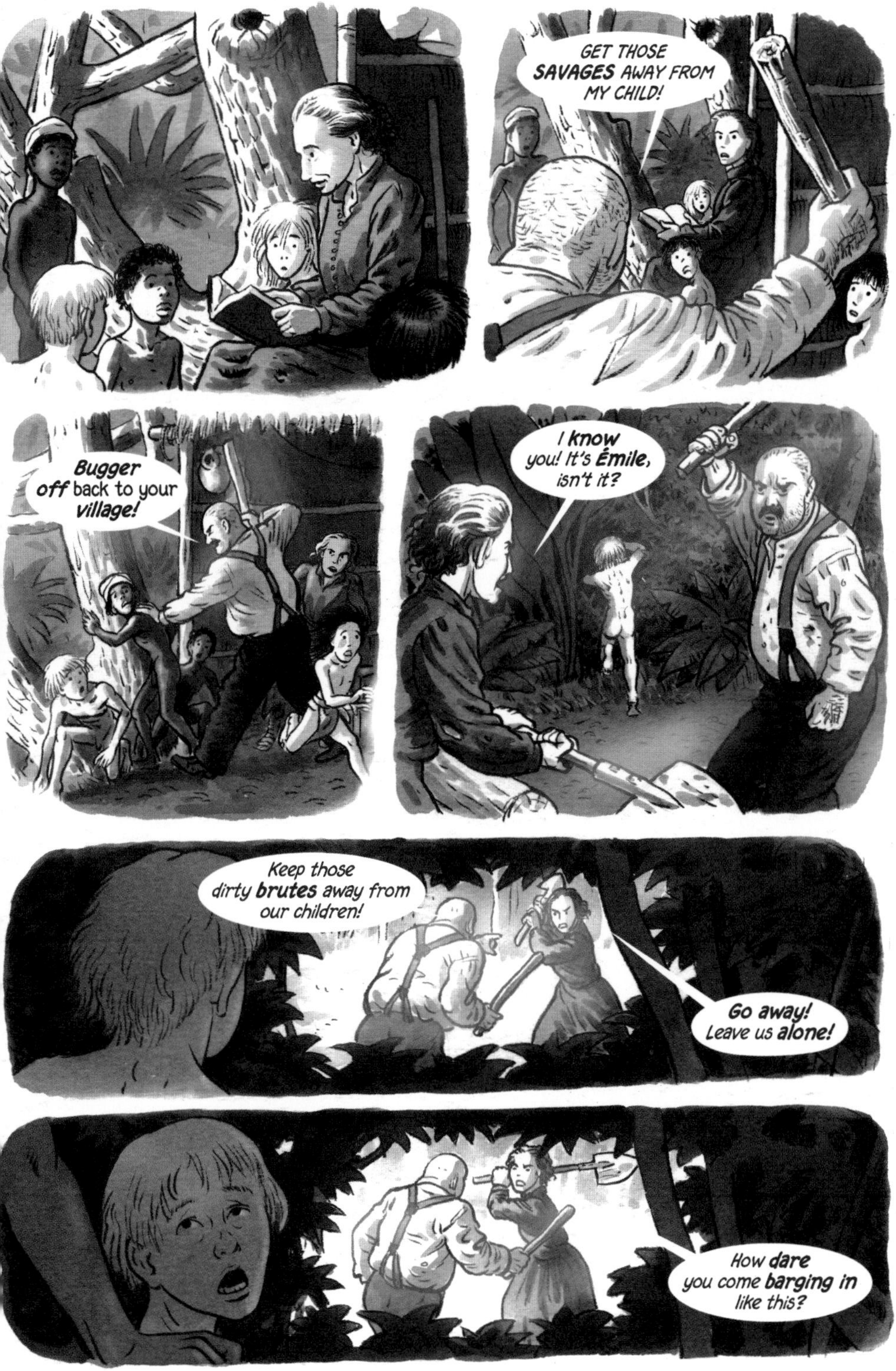
GET THOSE SAVAGES AWAY FROM MY CHILD!
Bugger off back to your village!
I know you! It's Émile, isn't it?
Keep those dirty brutes away from our children!
Go away! Leave us alone!
How dare you come barging in like this?

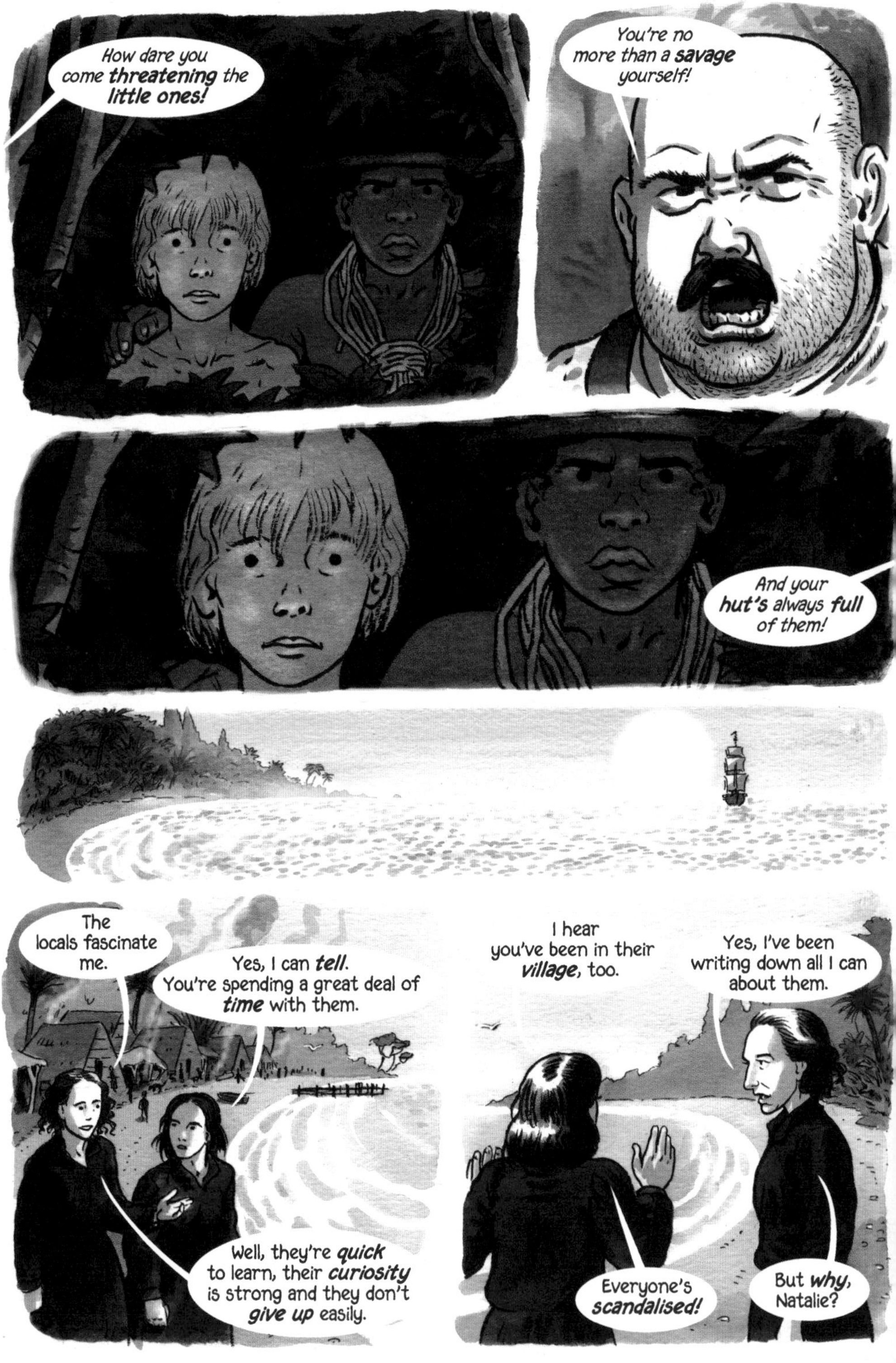
How dare you come threatening the little ones!
You're no more than a savage yourself!
And your hut's always full of them!
The locals fascinate me.
Yes, I can tell. You're spending a great deal of time with them.
Well, they're quick to learn, their curiosity is strong and they don't give up easily.
I hear you've been in their village, too.
Yes, I've been writing down all I can about them.
Everyone's scandalised!
But why, Natalie?

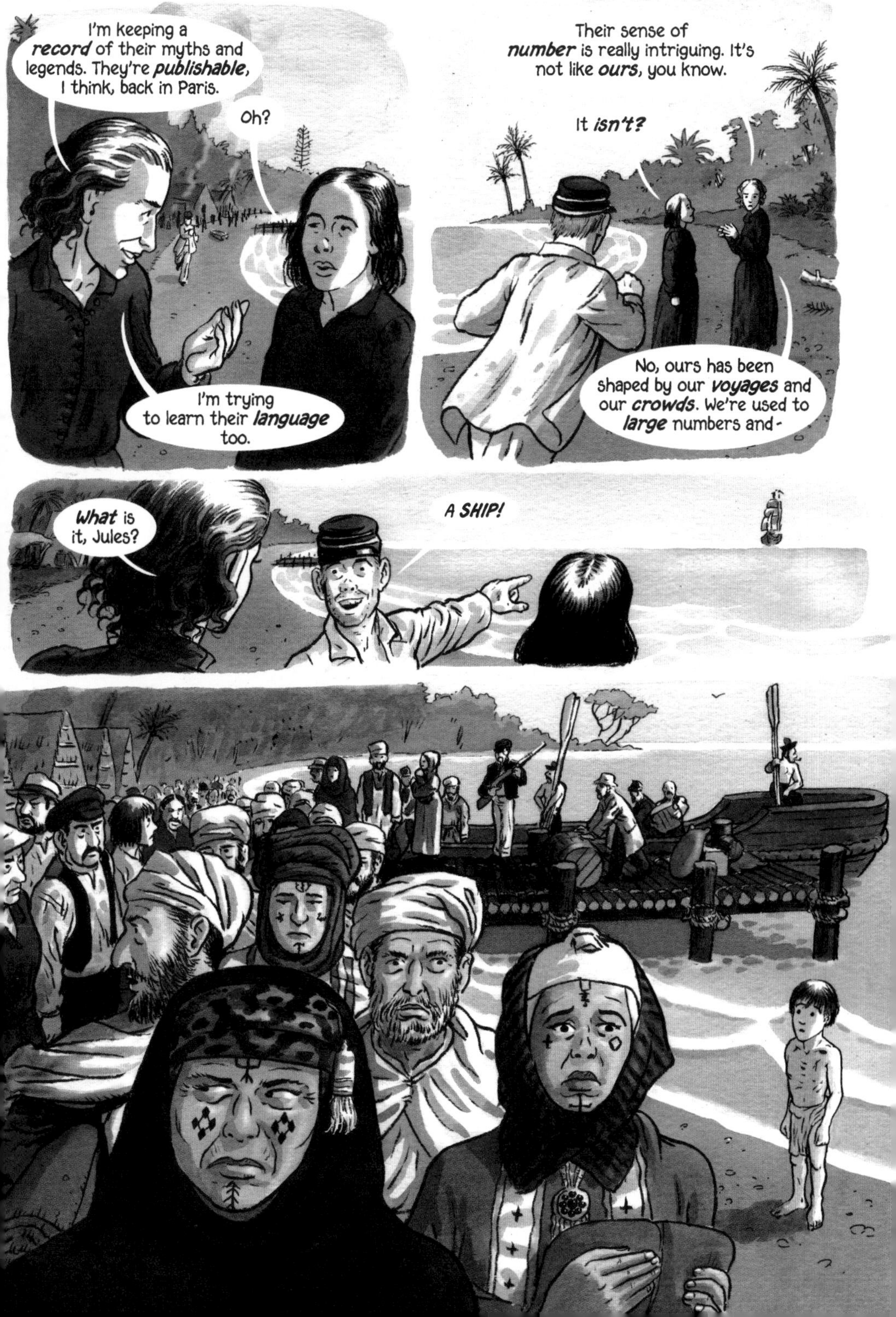
I'm keeping a record of their myths and legends. They're publishable, I think, back in Paris.
Oh?
I'm trying to learn their language too.
Their sense of number is really intriguing. It's not like ours, you know.
It isn't?
No, ours has been shaped by our voyages and our crowds. We're used to large numbers and-
What is it, Jules?
A SHIP!

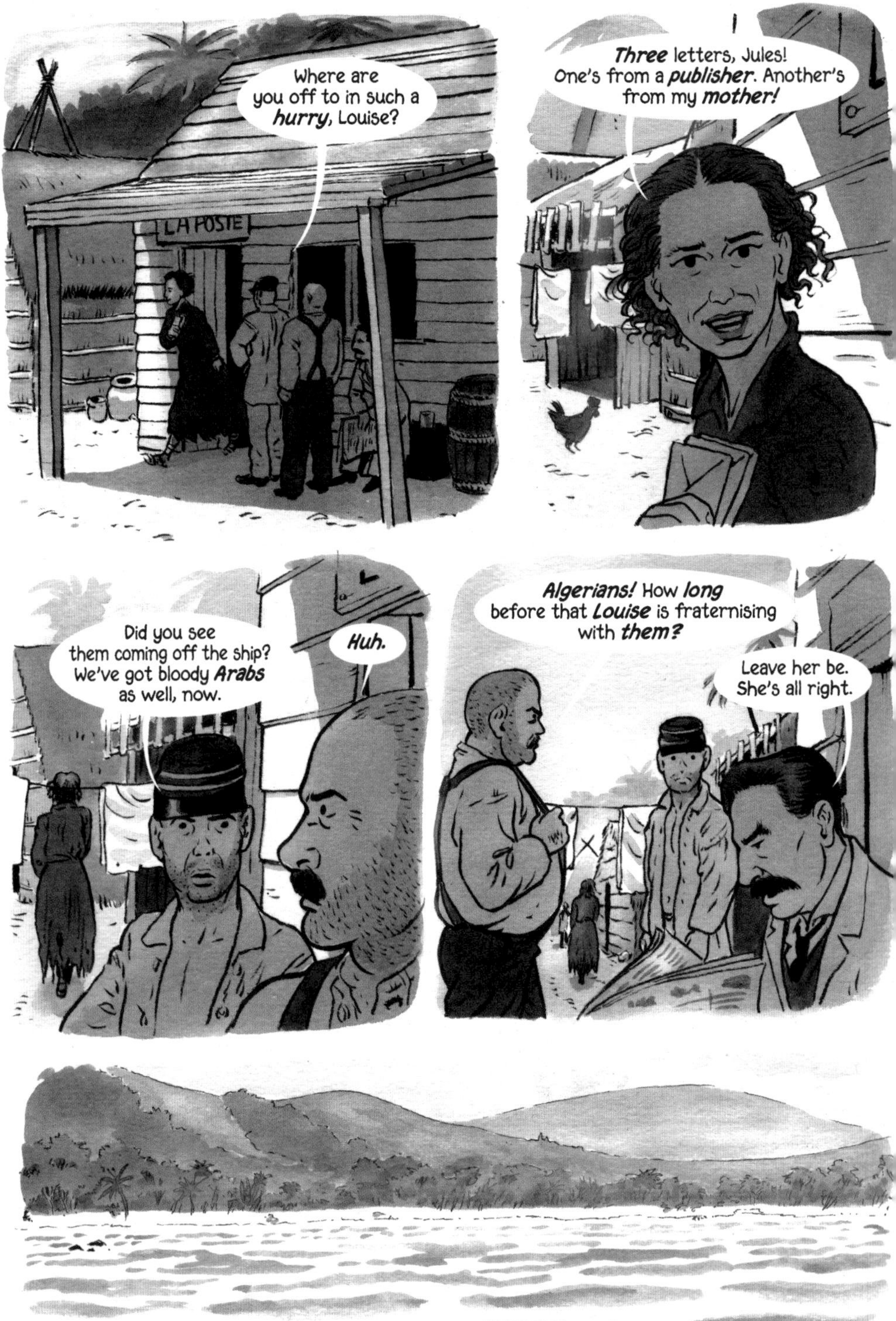
LA POSTE
Where are you off to in such a *hurry*, Louise?
Three letters, Jules! One's from a *publisher*. Another's from my *mother!*
Did you see them coming off the ship? We've got bloody *Arabs* as well, now.
Huh.
Algerians! How *long* before that *Louise* is fraternising with *them?*
Leave her be. She's all right.

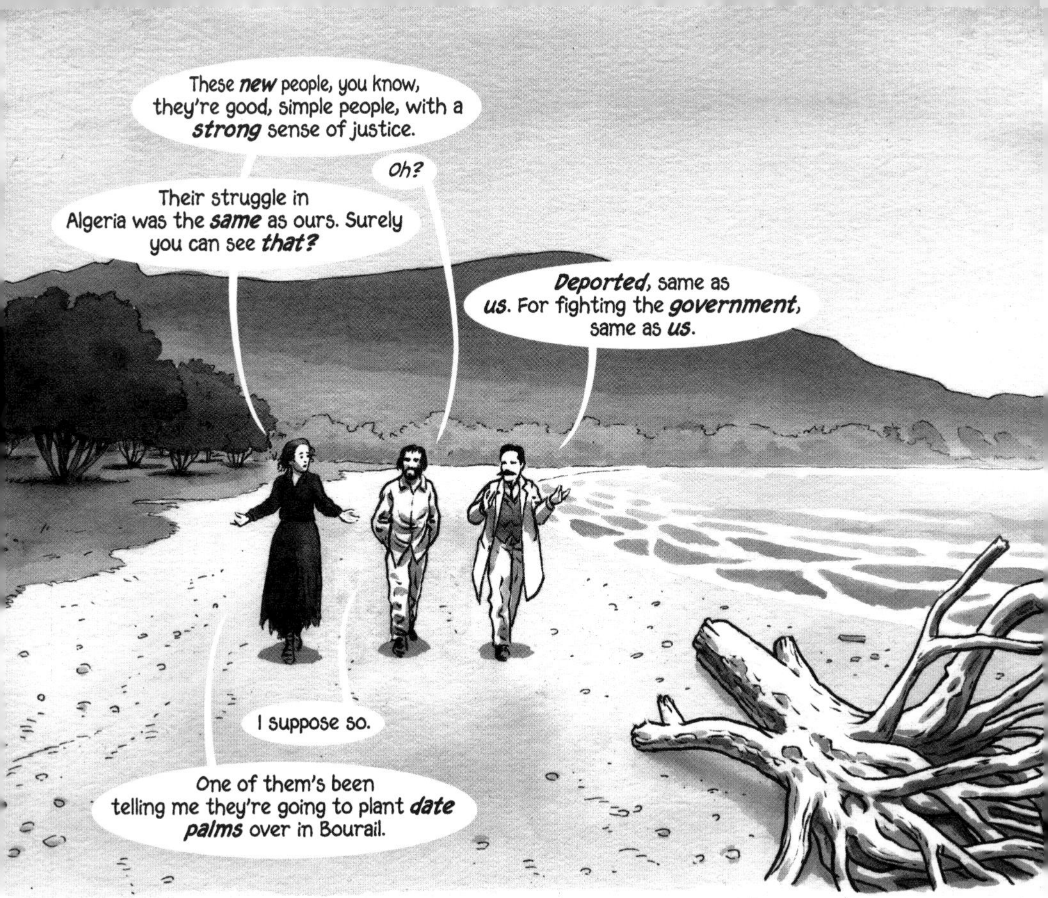
These *new* people, you know, they're good, simple people, with a *strong* sense of justice.
Oh?
Their struggle in Algeria was the *same* as ours. Surely you can see *that?*
Deported, same as *us*. For fighting the *government,* same as *us*.
I suppose so.
One of them's been telling me they're going to plant *date palms* over in Bourail.

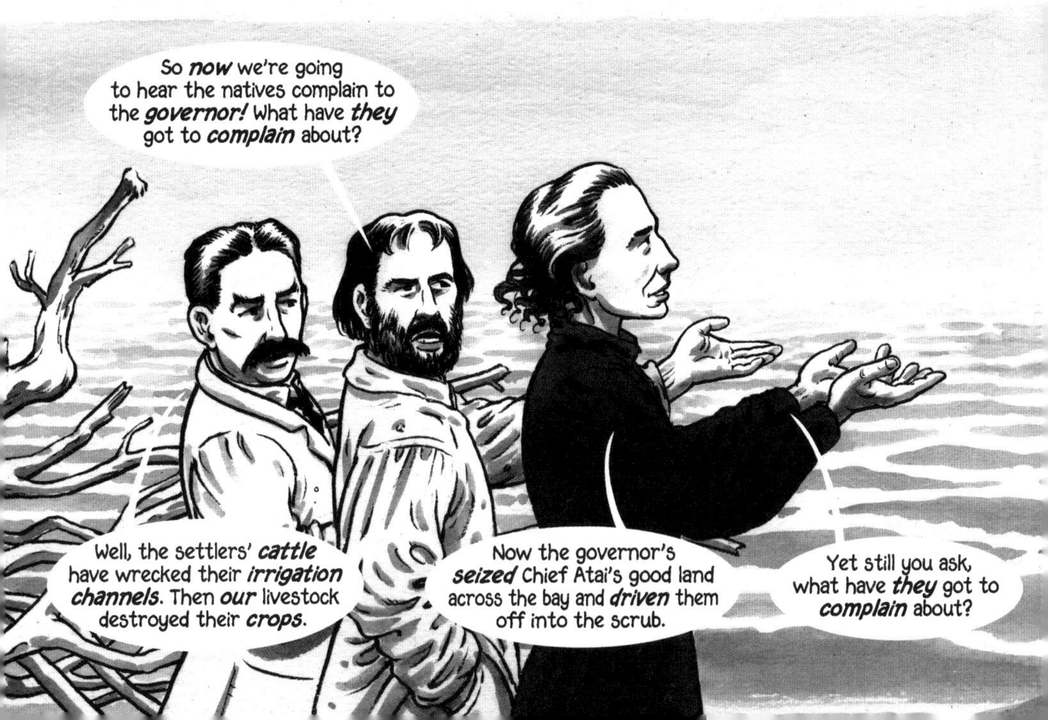
So *now* we're going to hear the natives complain to the *governor!* What have *they* got to *complain* about?
Well, the settlers' *cattle* have wrecked their *irrigation channels*. Then *our* livestock destroyed their *crops*.
Now the governor's *seized* Chief Atai's good land across the bay and *driven* them off into the scrub.
Yet still you ask, what have *they* got to *complain* about?

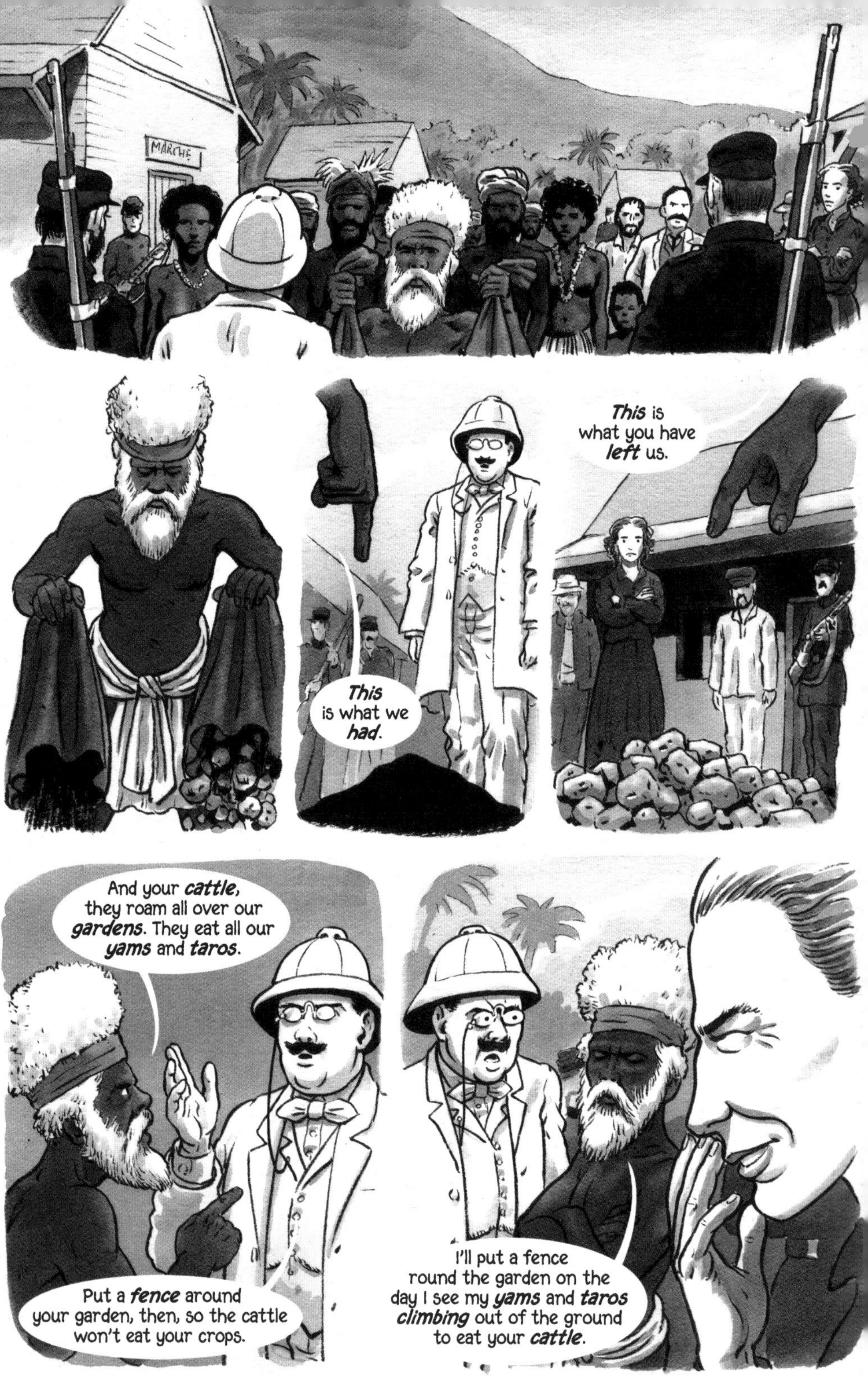
MARCHE
This is what we had.
This is what you have left us.
And your cattle, they roam all over our gardens. They eat all our yams and taros.
Put a fence around your garden, then, so the cattle won't eat your crops.
I'll put a fence round the garden on the day I see my yams and taros climbing out of the ground to eat your cattle.

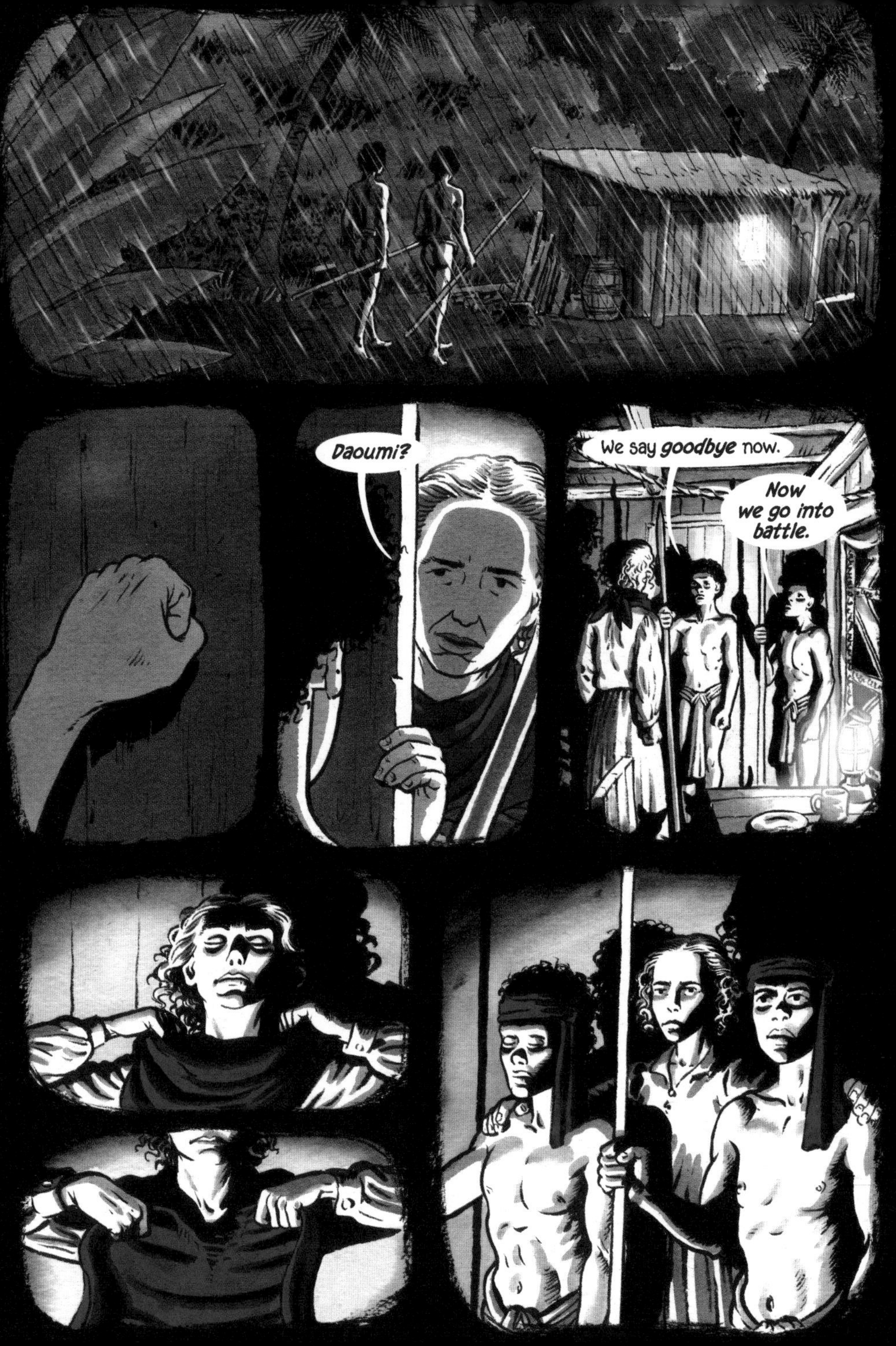
Daoumi?
We say goodbye now.
Now we go into battle.

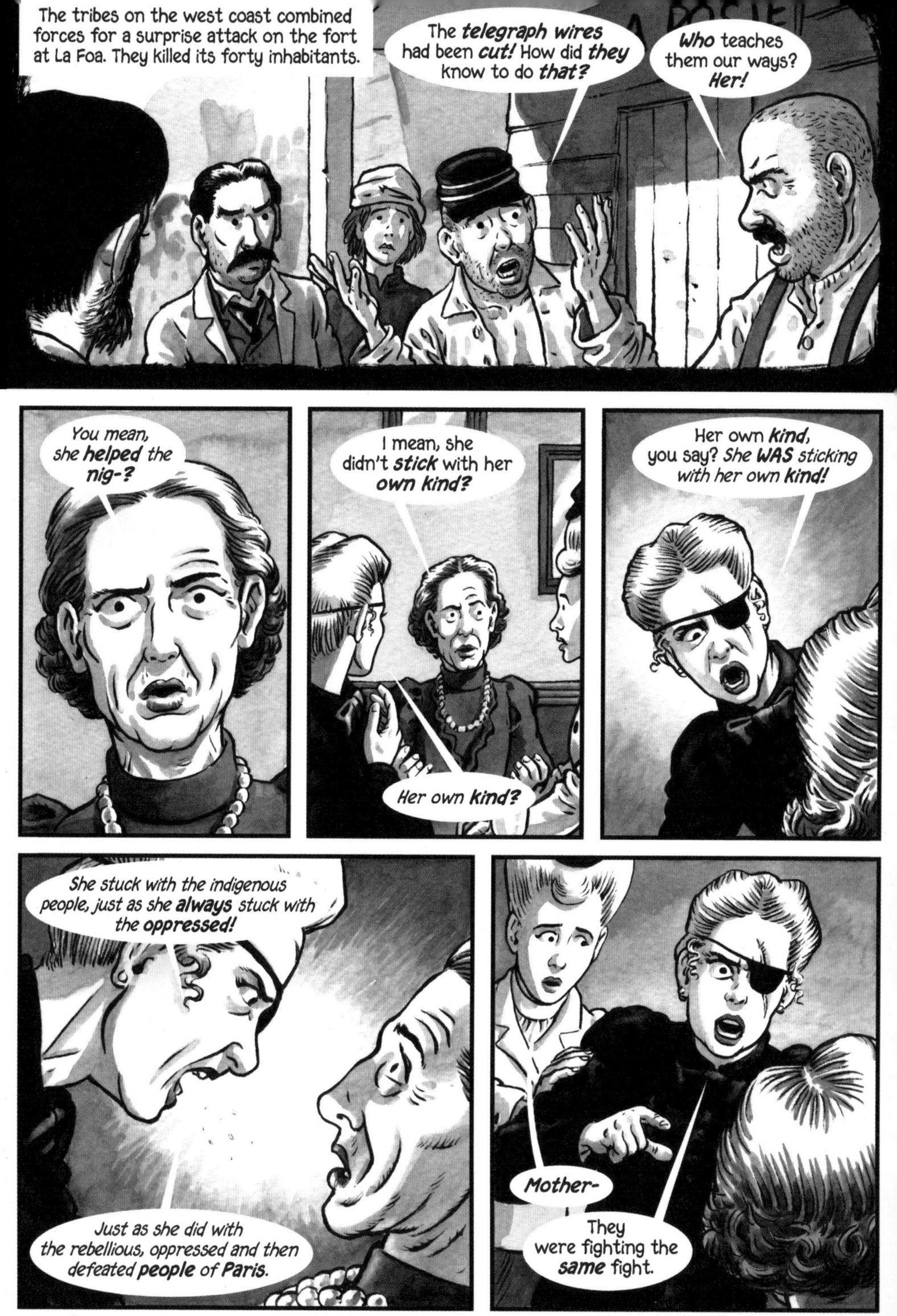

The tribes on the west coast combined forces for a surprise attack on the fort at La Foa. They killed its forty inhabitants.
The *telegraph wires* had been *cut!* How did *they* know to do *that?*
Who teaches them our ways? *Her!*
You mean, she **helped** the **nig-?**
I mean, she didn't ***stick*** with her ***own kind?***
Her own **kind?**
Her own **kind**, you say? She **WAS** sticking with her own **kind!**
She stuck with the indigenous people, just as she **always** stuck with the **oppressed!**
Just as she did with the rebellious, oppressed and then defeated **people** of **Paris.**
Mother-
They were fighting the ***same*** fight.

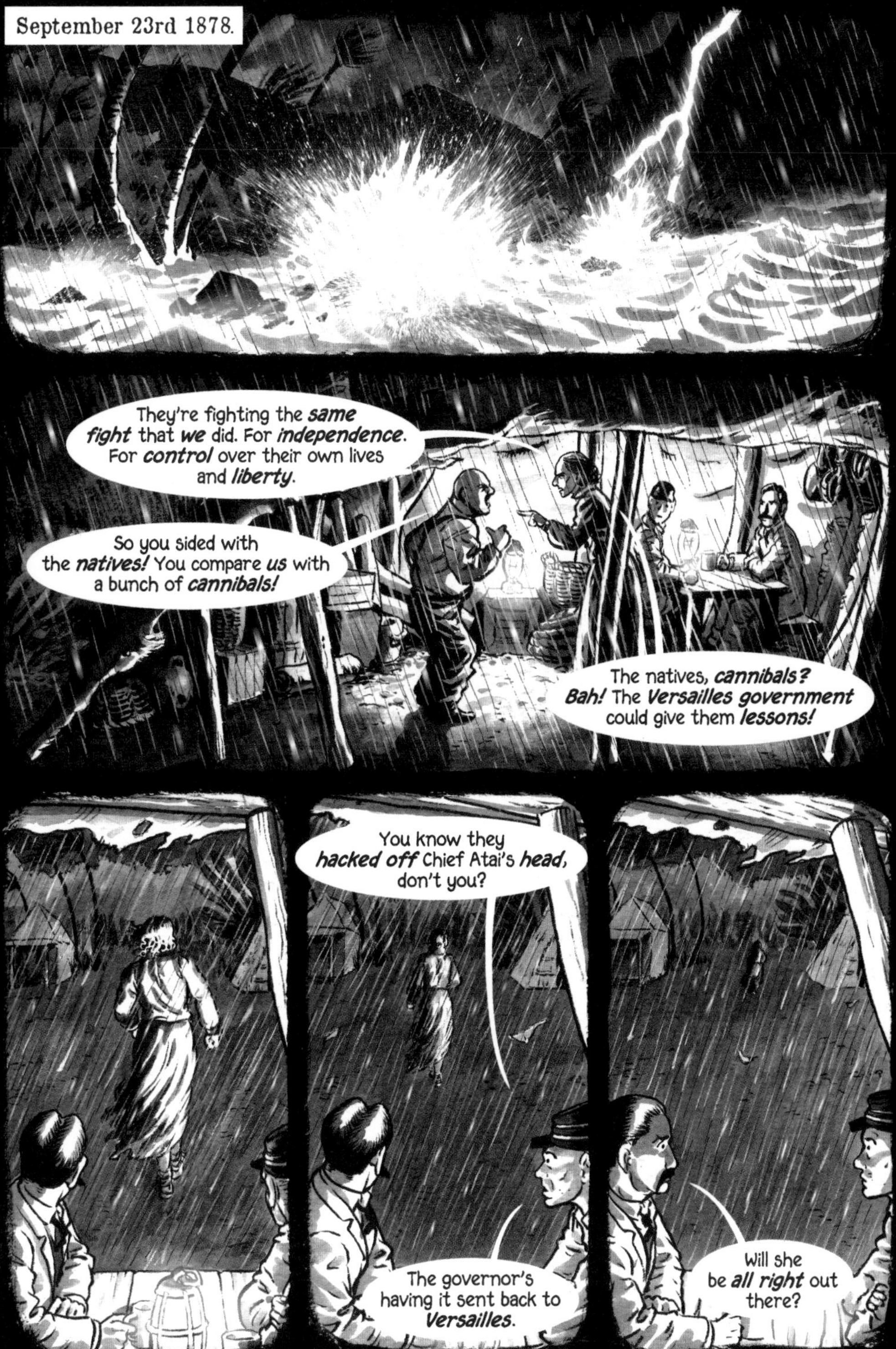
September 23rd 1878.
They're fighting the *same fight* that *we* did. For *independence*. For *control* over their own lives and *liberty*.
So you sided with the *natives!* You compare *us* with a bunch of *cannibals!*
The natives, *cannibals?* *Bah!* The *Versailles government* could give them *lessons!*
You know they *hacked off* Chief Atai's *head*, don't you?
The governor's having it sent back to *Versailles*.
Will she be *all right* out there?

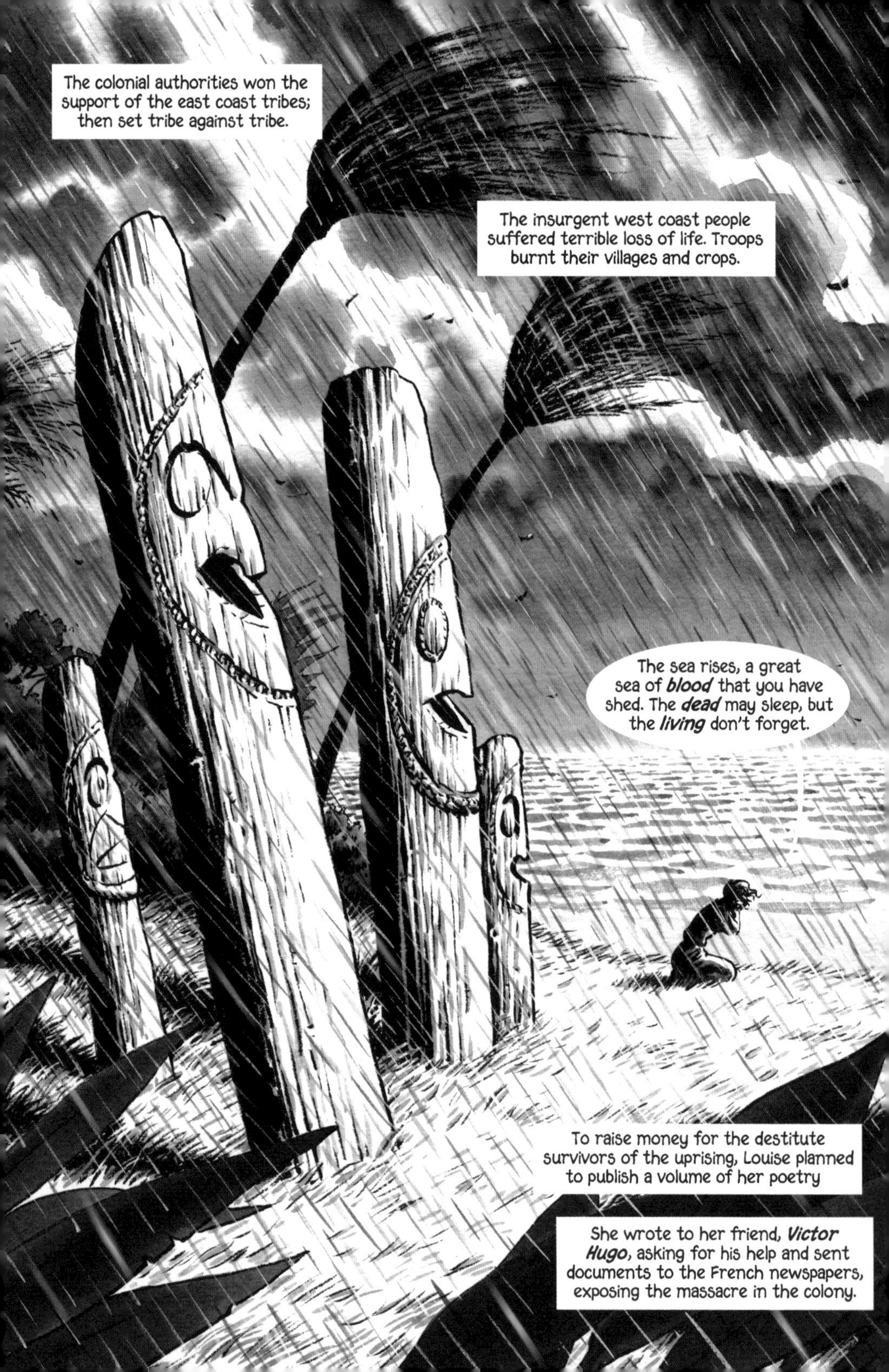
The colonial authorities won the support of the east coast tribes; then set tribe against tribe.
The insurgent west coast people suffered terrible loss of life. Troops burnt their villages and crops.
The sea rises, a great sea of *blood* that you have shed. The *dead* may sleep, but the *living* don't forget.
To raise money for the destitute survivors of the uprising, Louise planned to publish a volume of her poetry
She wrote to her friend, *Victor Hugo*, asking for his help and sent documents to the French newspapers, exposing the massacre in the colony.

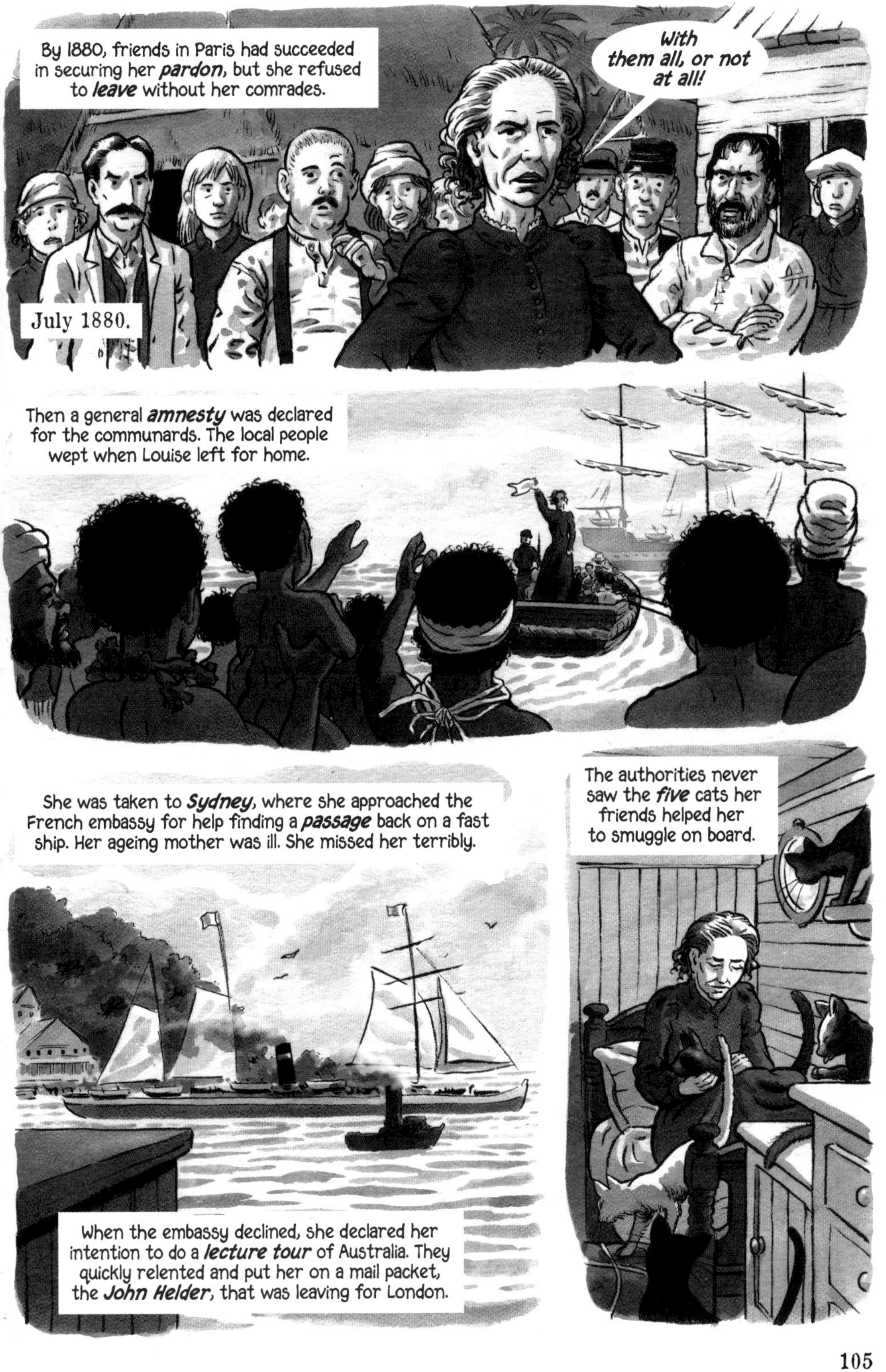
By 1880, friends in Paris had succeeded in securing her *pardon*, but she refused to *leave* without her comrades.
With them all, or not at all!
July 1880.
Then a general *amnesty* was declared for the communards. The local people wept when Louise left for home.
She was taken to *Sydney*, where she approached the French embassy for help finding a *passage* back on a fast ship. Her ageing mother was ill. She missed her terribly.
When the embassy declined, she declared her intention to do a *lecture tour* of Australia. They quickly relented and put her on a mail packet, the *John Helder*, that was leaving for London.
The authorities never saw the *five* cats her friends helped her to smuggle on board.

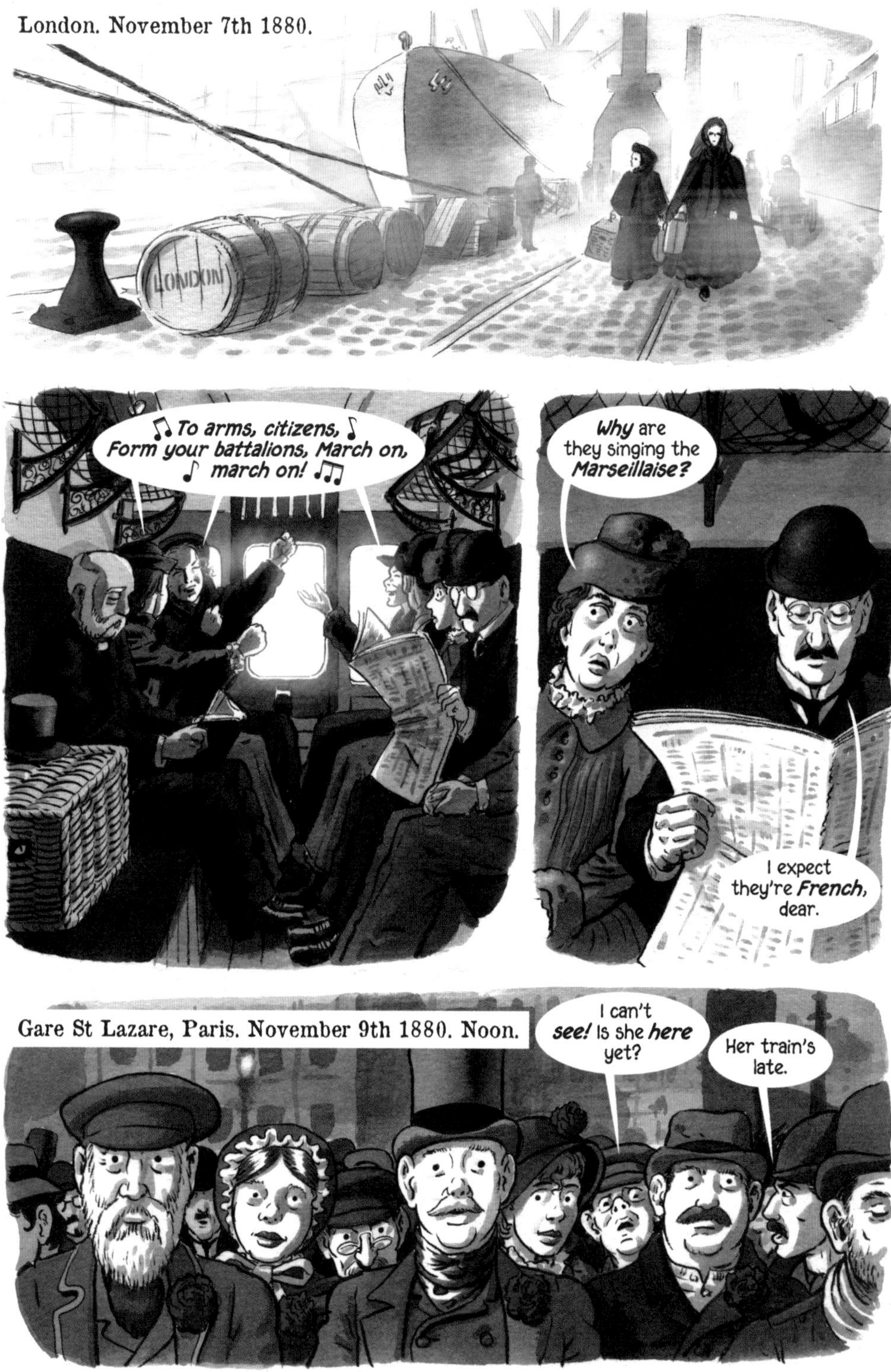
London. November 7th 1880.
LONDON
To arms, citizens, Form your battalions, March on, march on!
Why are they singing the Marseillaise?
I expect they're French, dear.
Gare St Lazare, Paris. November 9th 1880. Noon.
I can't see! Is she here yet?
Her train's late.

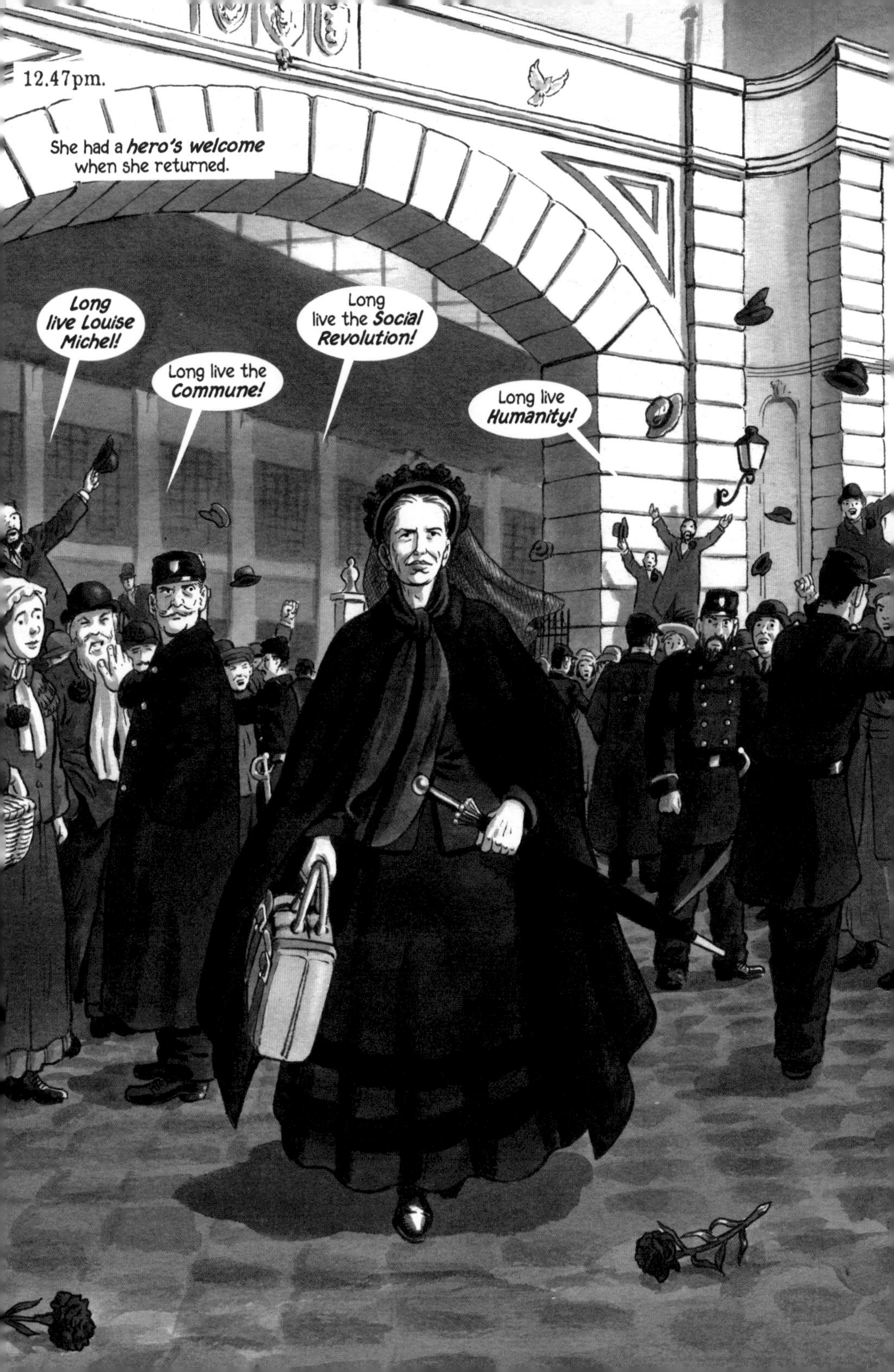
12.47pm.
She had a ***hero's welcome*** when she returned.
Long live Louise Michel!
Long live the ***Commune!***
Long live the ***Social Revolution!***
Long live ***Humanity!***

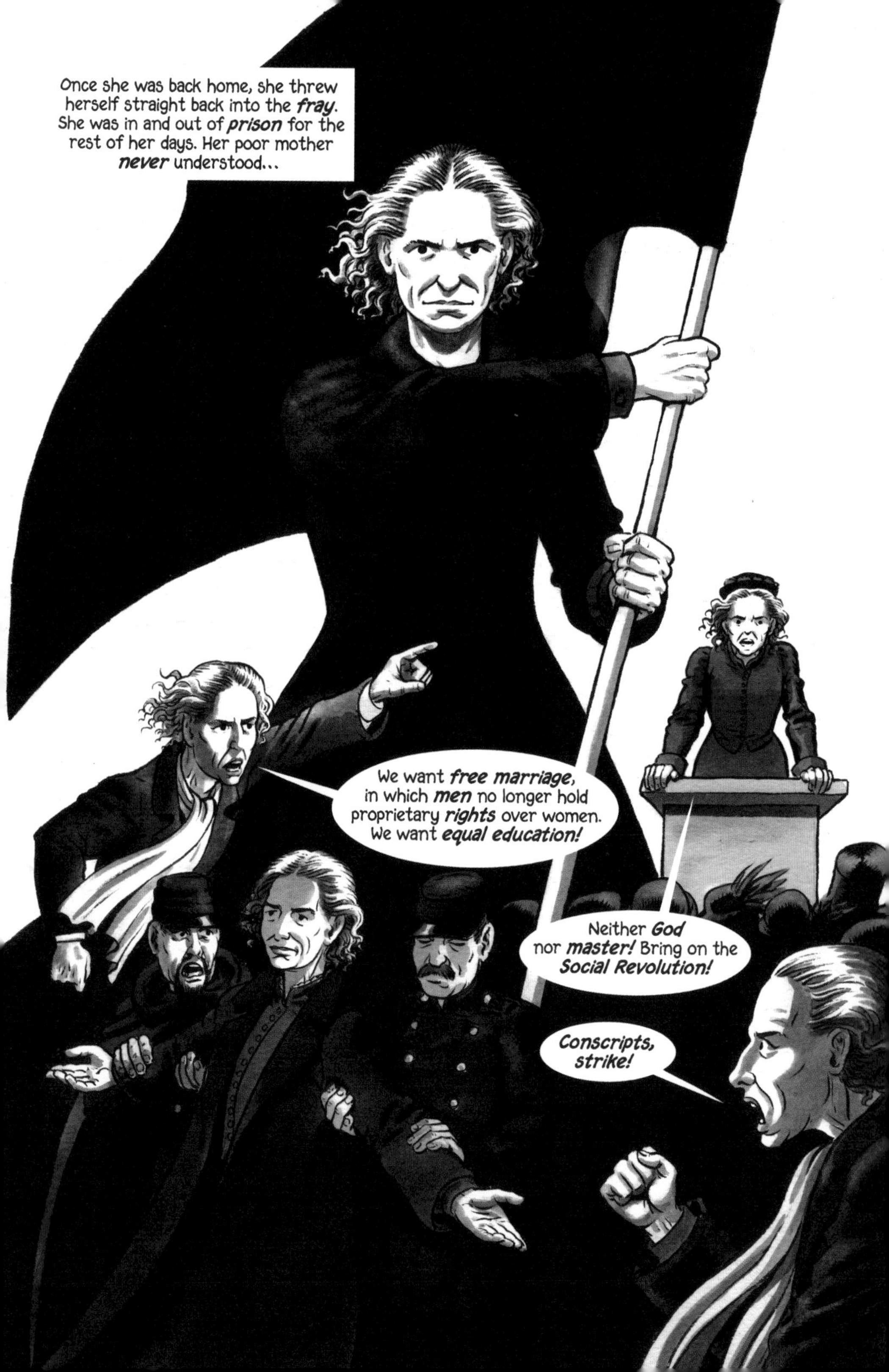
Once she was back home, she threw herself straight back into the *fray*. She was in and out of *prison* for the rest of her days. Her poor mother *never* understood...
We want *free marriage*, in which *men* no longer hold proprietary *rights* over women. We want *equal education!*
Neither *God* nor *master!* Bring on the *Social Revolution!*
Conscripts, strike!

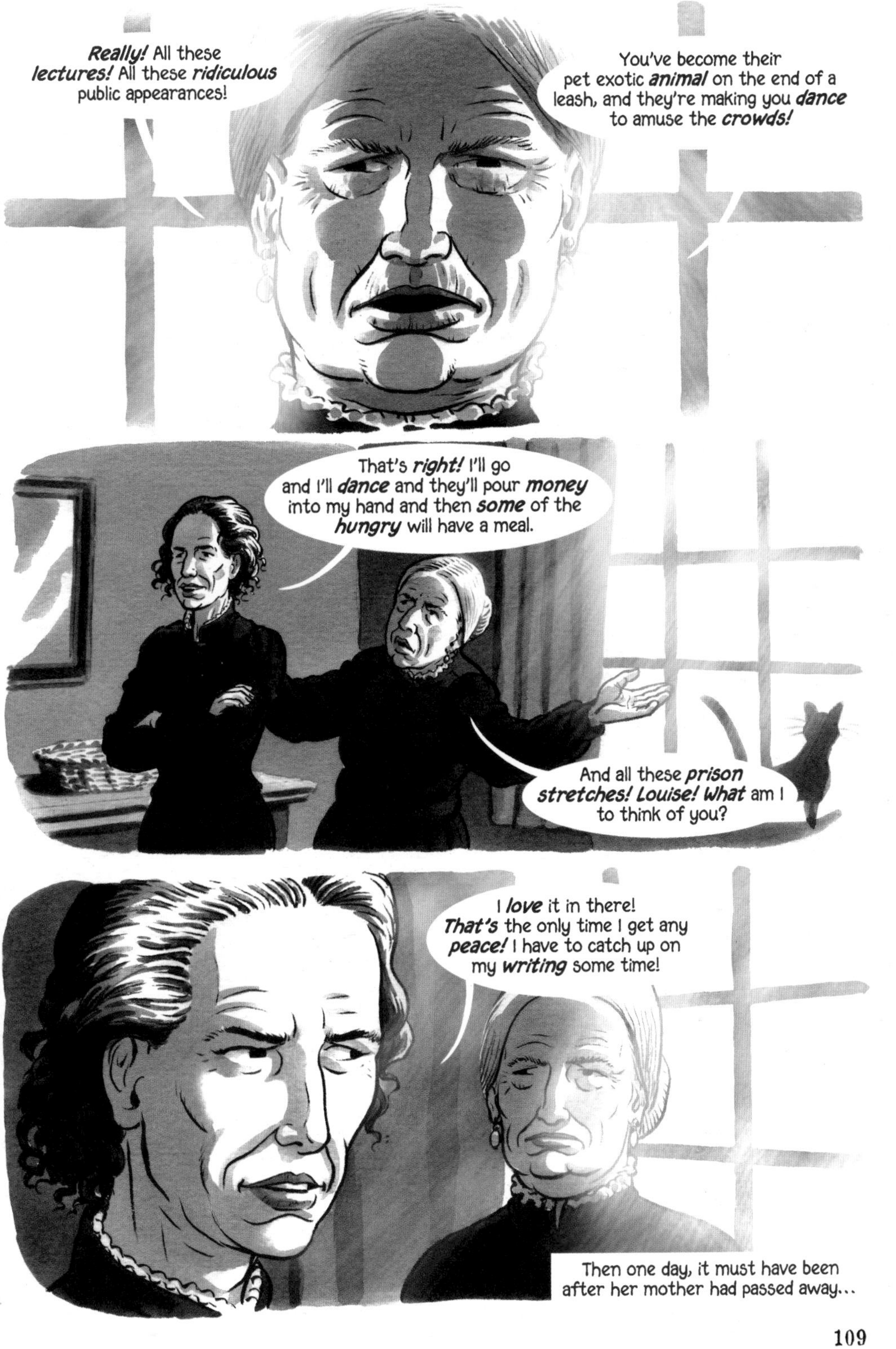
Really! All these lectures! All these ridiculous public appearances!
You've become their pet exotic animal on the end of a leash, and they're making you dance to amuse the crowds!
That's right! I'll go and I'll dance and they'll pour money into my hand and then some of the hungry will have a meal.
And all these prison stretches! Louise! What am I to think of you?
I love it in there! That's the only time I get any peace! I have to catch up on my writing some time!
Then one day, it must have been after her mother had passed away...

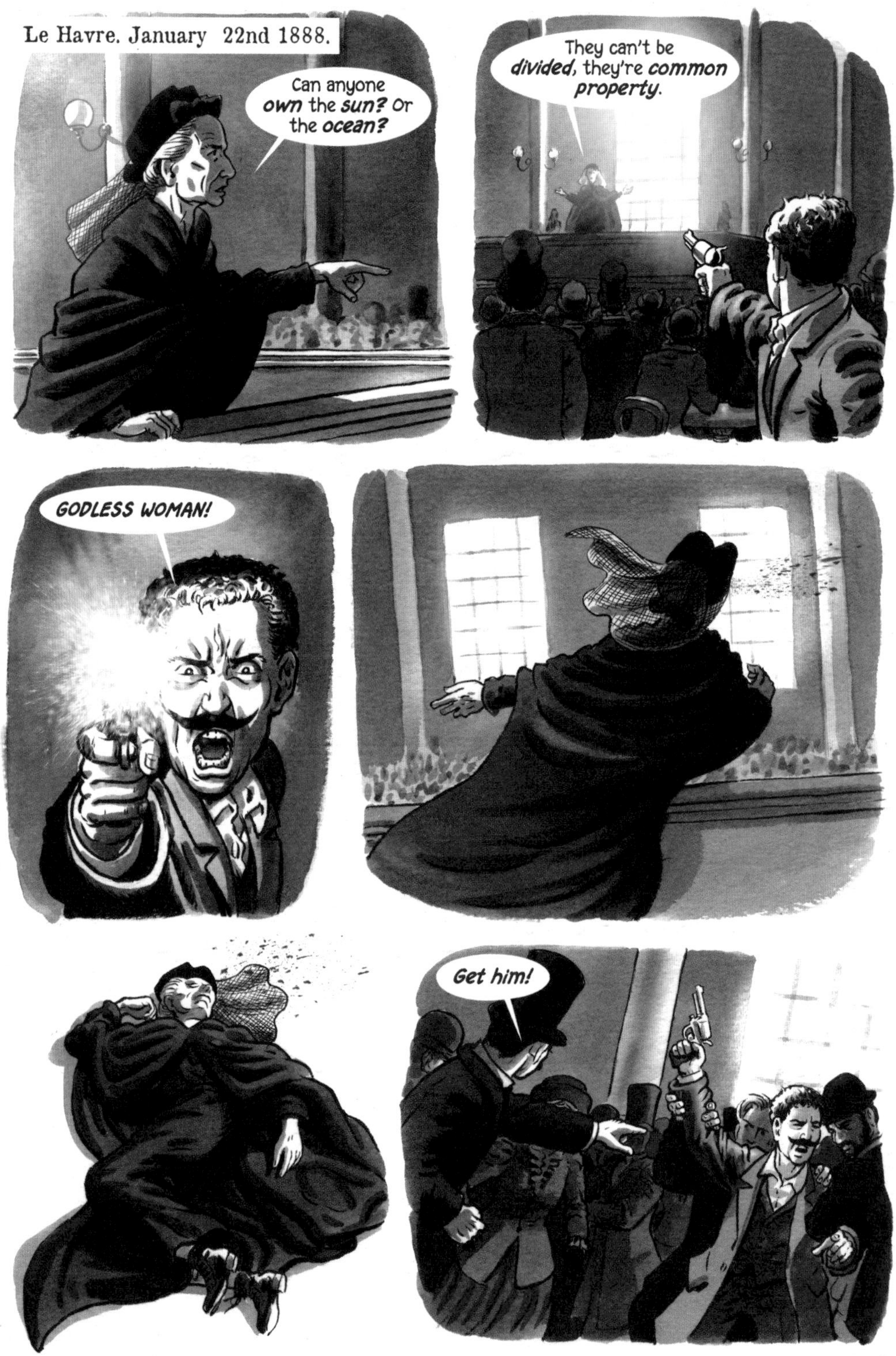
Le Havre. January 22nd 1888.
Can anyone own the sun? Or the ocean?
They can't be divided, they're common property.
GODLESS WOMAN!
Get him!

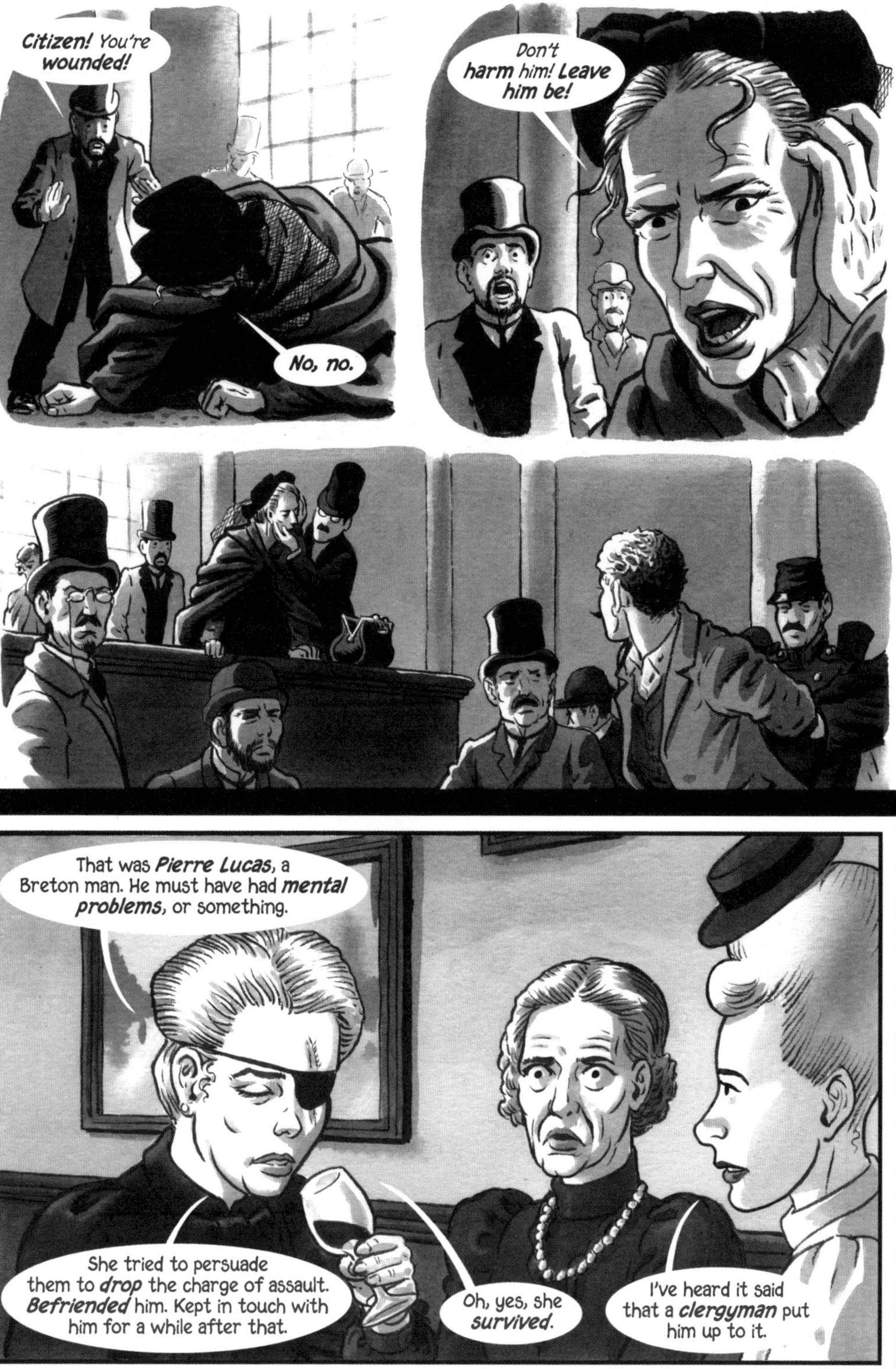
Citizen! You're wounded!
No, no.
Don't harm him! Leave him be!
That was Pierre Lucas, a Breton man. He must have had mental problems, or something.
She tried to persuade them to drop the charge of assault. Befriended him. Kept in touch with him for a while after that.
Oh, yes, she survived.
I've heard it said that a clergyman put him up to it.

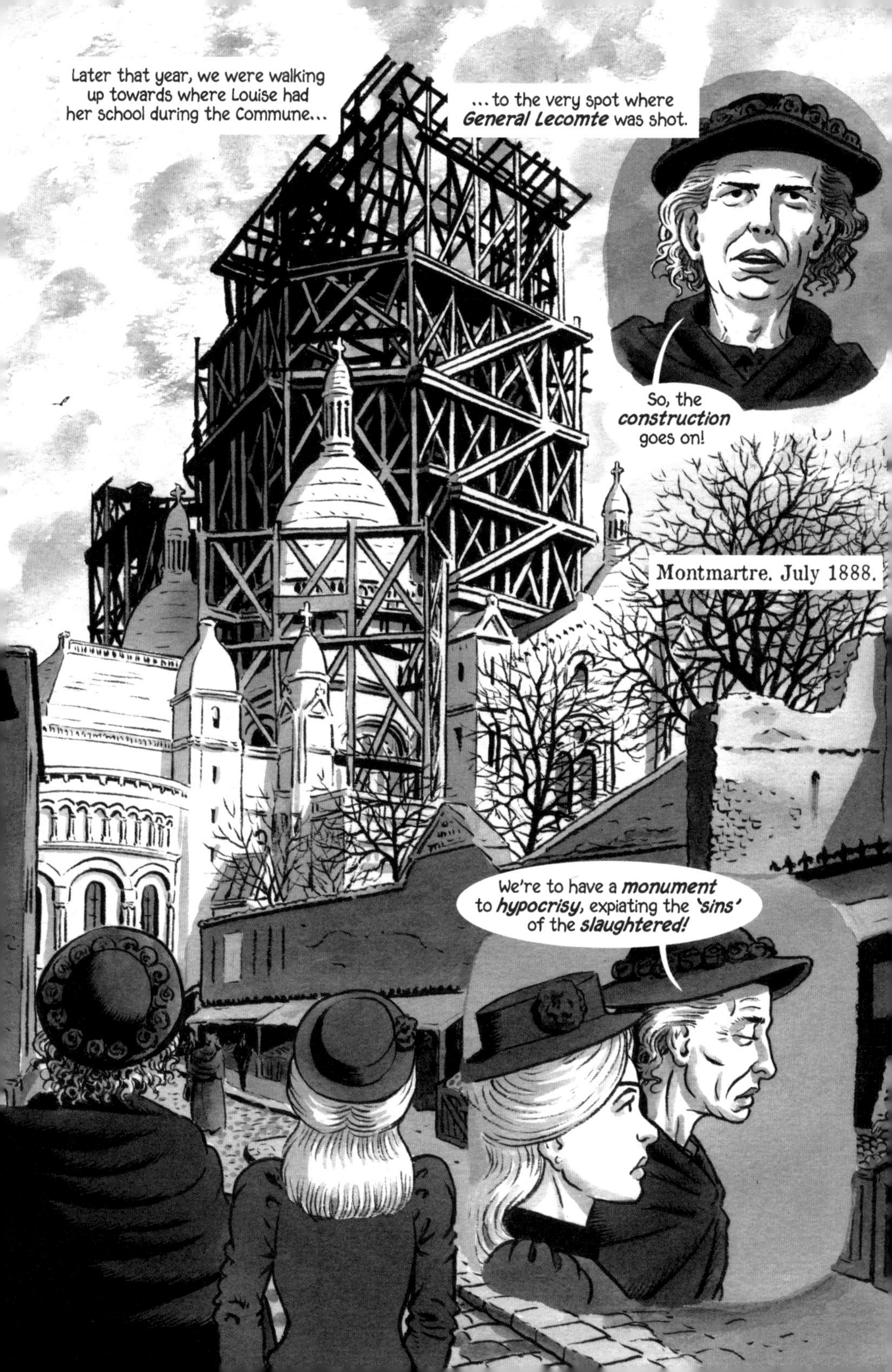
Later that year, we were walking up towards where Louise had her school during the Commune...
...to the very spot where *General Lecomte* was shot.
So, the *construction* goes on!
Montmartre. July 1888.
We're to have a *monument* to *hypocrisy*, expiating the *'sins'* of the *slaughtered!*

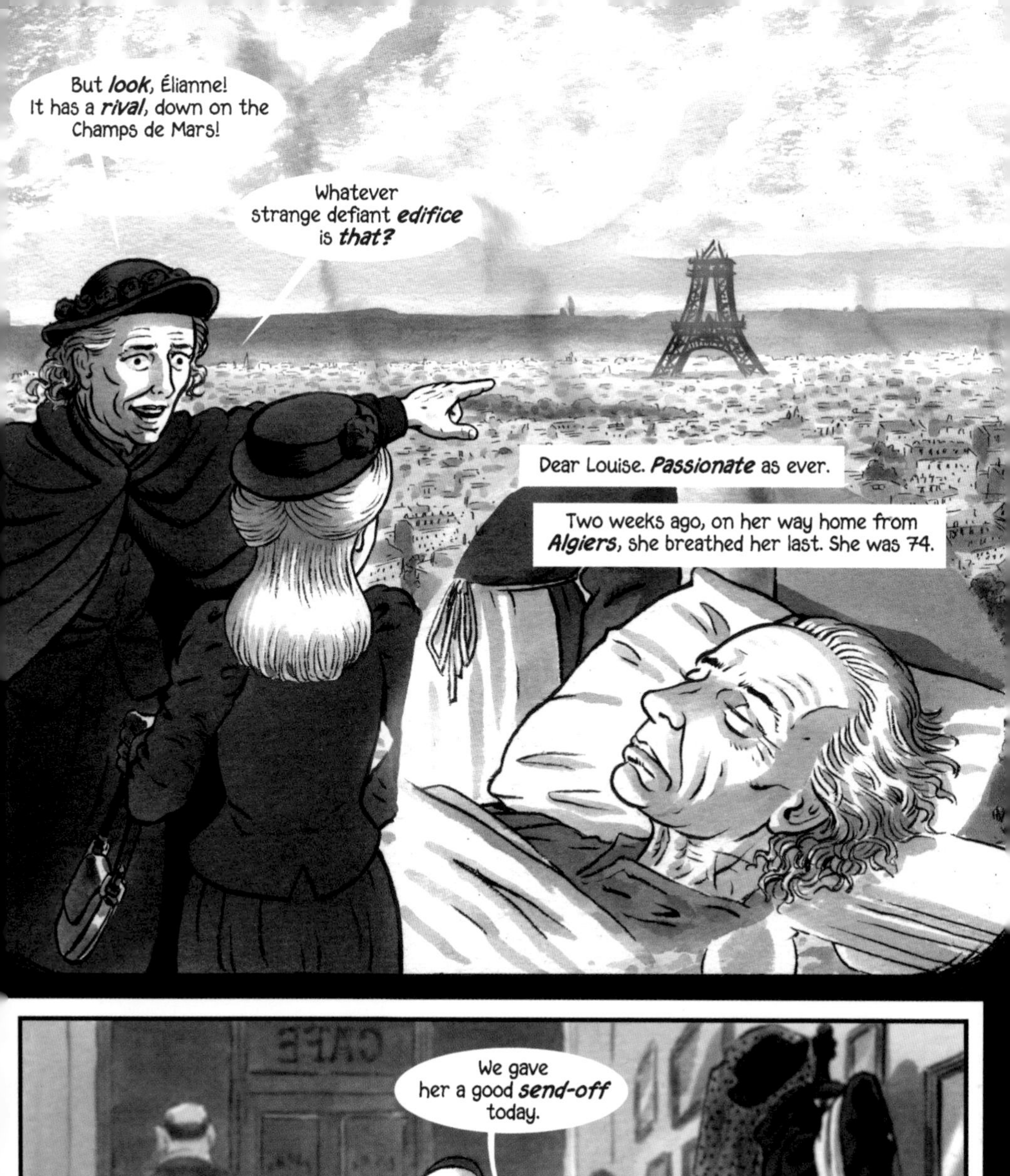
But *look*, Élianne! It has a *rival*, down on the Champs de Mars!
Whatever strange defiant *edifice* is *that?*
Dear Louise. *Passionate* as ever.
Two weeks ago, on her way home from *Algiers*, she breathed her last. She was 74.

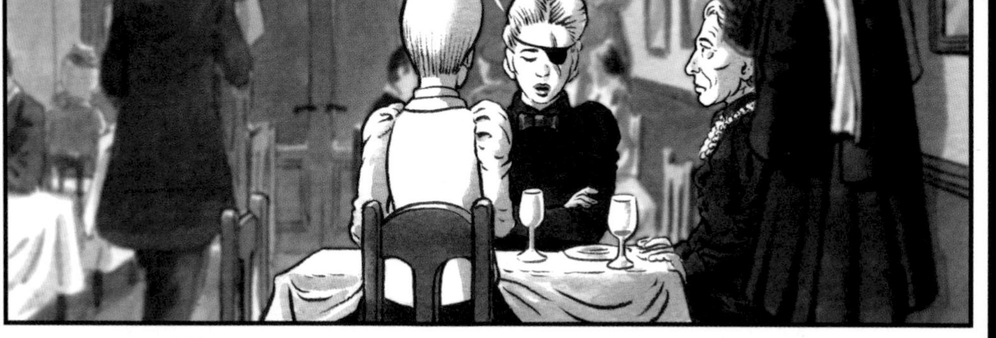
CAFE
We gave her a good *send-off* today.

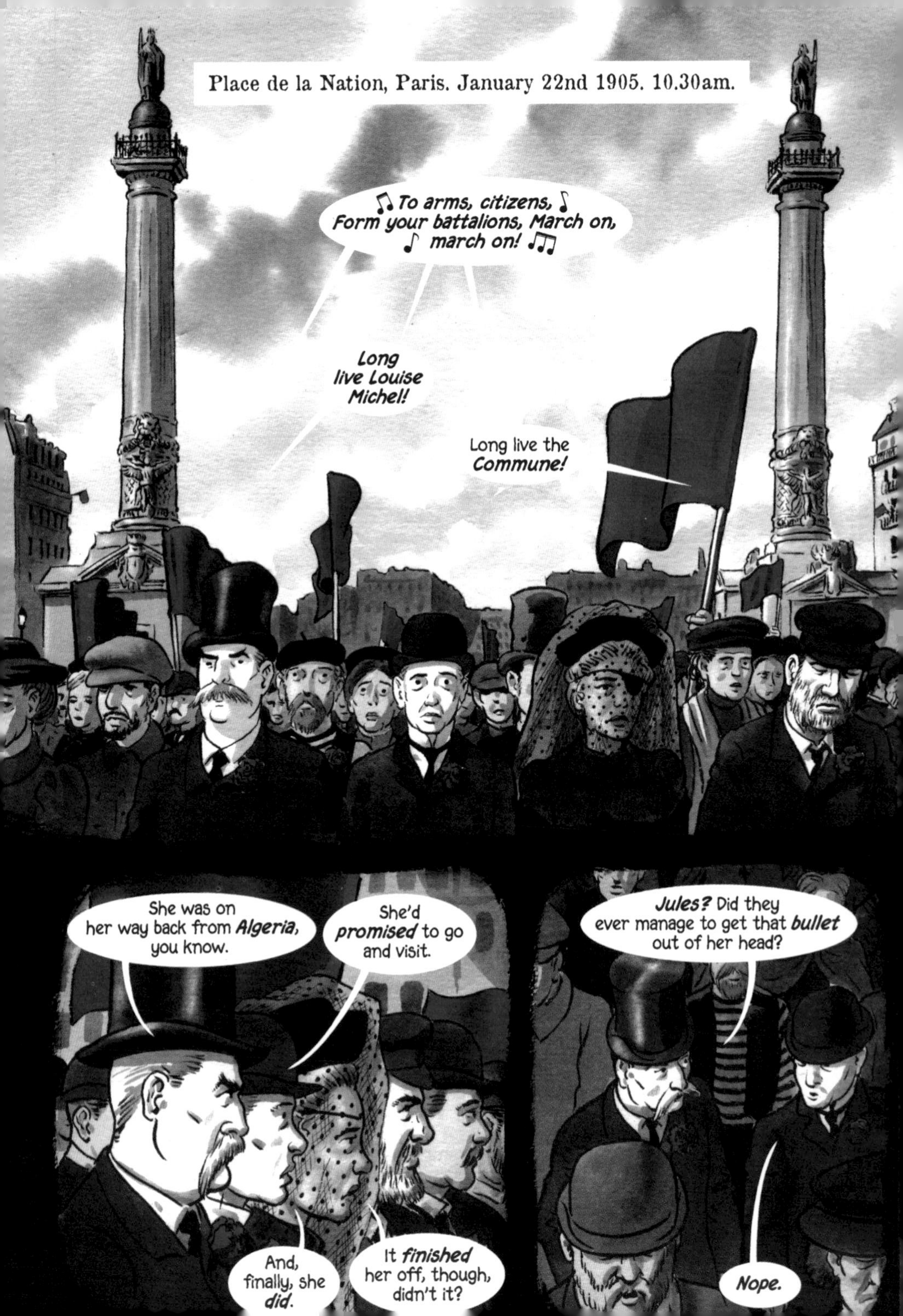
Place de la Nation, Paris. January 22nd 1905. 10.30am.
♫ To arms, citizens, ♪ Form your battalions, March on, ♪ march on! ♫
Long live Louise Michel!
Long live the Commune!
She was on her way back from Algeria, you know.
She'd promised to go and visit.
And, finally, she did.
It finished her off, though, didn't it?
Jules? Did they ever manage to get that bullet out of her head?
Nope.

Boulevard de la Villette. Noon.

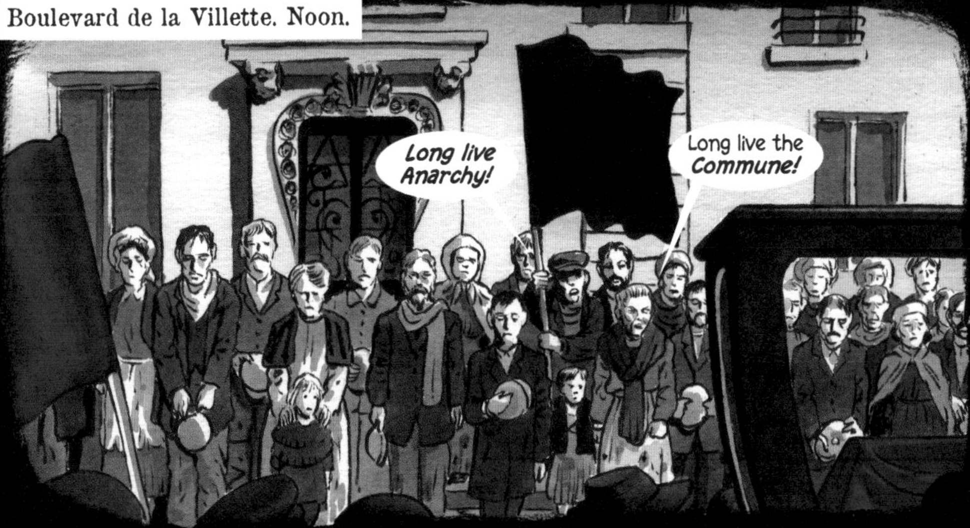

Long live Anarchy!
Long live the Commune!

Lavallois-Perret Cemetery. 2.20pm.

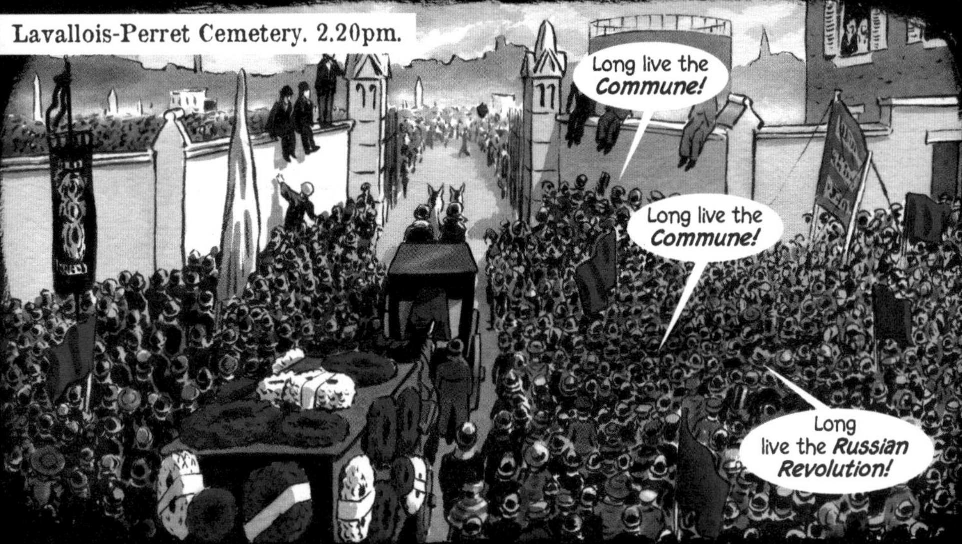

Long live the Commune!
Long live the Commune!
Long live the Russian Revolution!

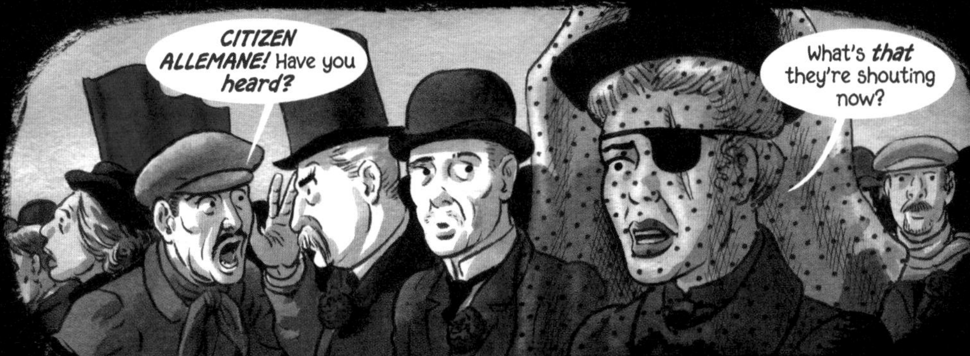

CITIZEN ALLEMANE! Have you heard?
What's that they're shouting now?

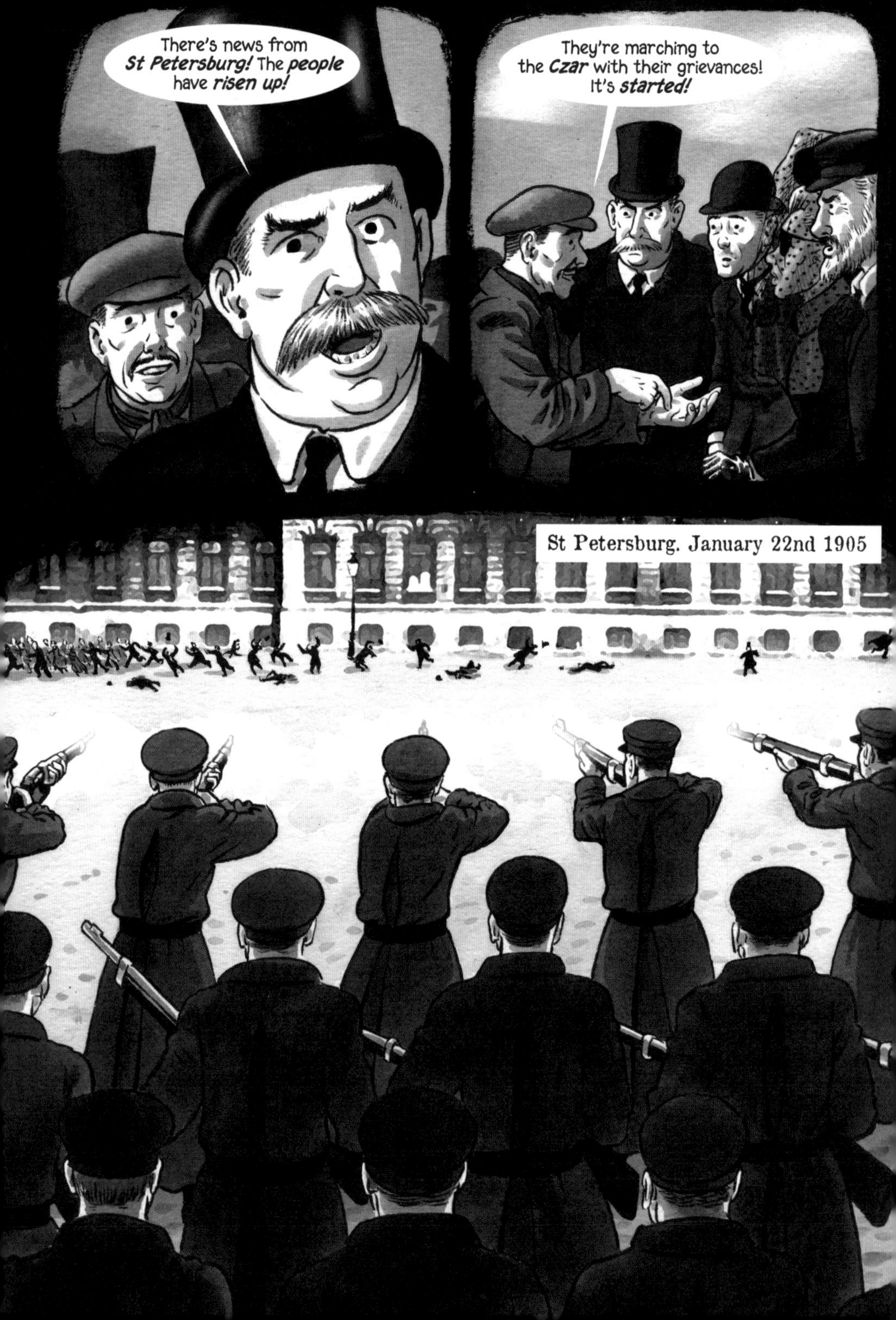
There's news from
St Petersburg! The people
have risen up!
They're marching to
the Czar with their grievances!
It's started!
St Petersburg. January 22nd 1905

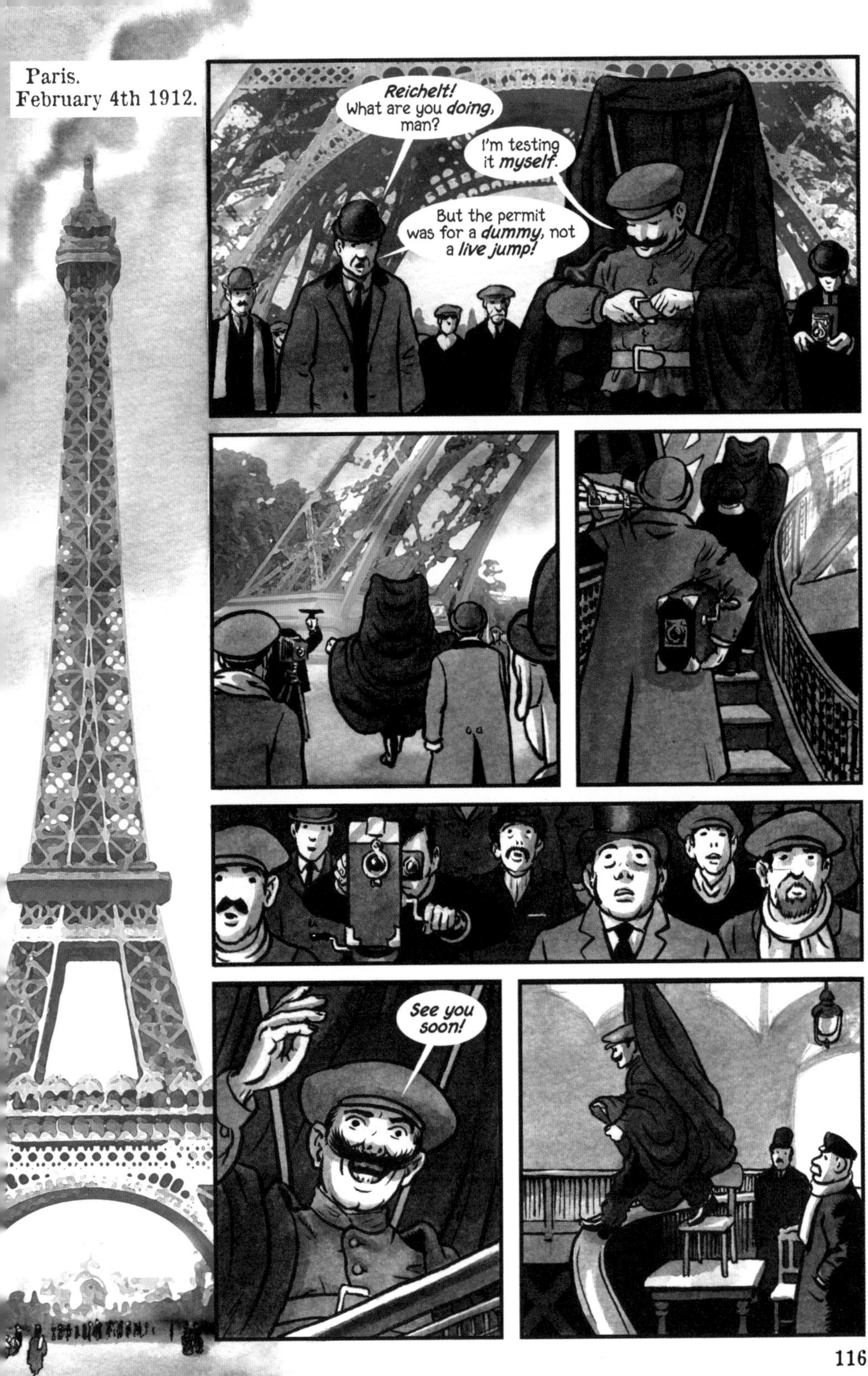

Paris.
February 4th 1912.
Reichelt! What are you doing, man?
I'm testing it myself.
But the permit was for a dummy, not a live jump!
See you soon!

SOURCES

Bullard, Alice, *Exile to Paradise: Savagery and Civilization in Paris and the South Pacific 1790-1900*, Stanford University Press, 2000

Butterworth, Alex, *The World That Never Was*, London: Bodley Head, 2010

Clayson, Hollis, *Paris in Despair: Art and Everyday Life under Siege (1870-1871)*, University of Chicago Press, 2002

Edwards, Stewart (ed.), *The Communards of Paris, 1871*, London: Thames & Hudson, 1973

Eichner, Carolyn J, *Surmounting the Barricades: Women in the Paris Commune*, Indiana University Press, 2004

Kessler, Carol Farley, *Charlotte Perkins Gilman: Her Progress toward Utopia*, Syracuse University Press, 1995

Kessler, Carol Farley, *Daring to Dream: Utopian Stories by United States Women: 1836-1919*, Pandora Press, 1984

Kumar, Krishan, *Utopia and Anti-Utopia in Modern Times*, Basil Blackwell, 1987

Leighton, John, *Paris under the Commune: or, the Seventy-Three Days of the Second Siege*, Project Gutenberg EBook, 2004 (first published in 1871)

Lemoine, Bertrand, *La Tour de Monsieur Eiffel [Mr Eiffel's Tower]*, Paris: Gallimard, Undated

Lissagaray, Prosper-Olivier, *History of the Paris Commune of 1871* (translated by Eleanor Marx) New Park Publications, 1976 (first published in 1876),

Lutsky, Vladimir Borisovich, *Modern History of the Arab Countries* (translated by Lika Nasser) (first published by Progress Publisher, Moscow, in 1969), https://www.marxists.org/subject/arab-world/lutsky/index.htm Accessed 20 June 2015

Mellor, Anne K, *Mary Shelley: Her Life, Her Fiction, Her Monsters*, New York/London: Routledge, 1988

Michel, Louise, *Je vous écris de ma nuit: correspondance générale 1850-1904* [*I'm writing to you about my night: general correspondence 1850-1904*] (edited by Xavière Gauthier), Éditions de Paris, 1999

Michel, Louise, *La Commune*, 1971 (first published in 1891 by Stock)

Michel, Louise, *The Red Virgin: Memoirs of Louise Michel* (edited and translated by Bullitt Lowry and Elizabeth Ellington Gunter), University of Alabama Press, 1981 (first published in 1886 by F Roy)

Nasseline, Nidoish, 'We Are Kanaks', *New Internationalist*, Issue 101, 1981

Oliver, Douglas, *Whisper 'Louise'* Hastings: Reality Street Editions, 2005

Planche, Fernand, *La Vie ardente et intrepide de Louise Michel* [*The ardent and intrepid life of Louise Michel*], Paris: Chez l'auteur, 1946

Robida, Albert, *The Twentieth Century* (translated by Philippe Willems; edited by Arthur B Evans), Middletown CT: Wesleyan University Press, 2004 (first published in 1882 by Decaux)

Rochefort, Henri, *The Adventures of my Life Vol.2* (arranged for English readers by the author and Ernest W Smith), London: Edward Arnold, 1896

Thomas, Edith, *Louise Michel* (translated by Penelope Williams), Montreal: Black Rose Books, 1980

Tombs, Robert, *The Paris Commune 1871*, London: Longman, 1999

http://gallica.bnf.fr   http://www.commune1871.org

http: www.parisrevolutionnaire.com

http://www.histoire-en-ligne.com

http://www.toureiffel.paris

http://www.thehistoryblog.com

The Times Digital Archive 1785-1985

http://www.en.wikipedia.org   http://www.fr.wikipedia.org

ANNOTATIONS

Page 1. 'A map of the world that does not include Utopia is not even worth glancing at, for it leaves out the one country at which Humanity is always landing. And when Humanity lands there, it looks out, and, seeing a better country, sets sail. Progress is the realisation of Utopias.' Oscar Wilde, *The Soul of Man under Socialism*, 1891.

'All of old. Nothing else ever. Ever tried. Ever failed. No matter. Try again. Fail again. Fail better.' Samuel Beckett, *Worstward Ho*, 1983.

Page 5. The details of the funeral procession are taken from a contemporary French newspaper article, 'Les obsèques de Louise Michel' (*Le Temps*, 23 January 1905).

Page 7. Charlotte Perkins Gilman was an American writer, public speaker and feminist reformer. She came from a Connecticut reformer family and inherited their missionary zeal. One of her aunts was Harriet Beecher Stowe, author of *Uncle Tom's Cabin*.

Gilman is probably best known now for a single short story, 'The Yellow Wallpaper', that was first published in January 1892 in *The New England Magazine*. Loosely based on first-hand experience, it deals critically with the repressive 'rest cure' treatment for depression to which women in the nineteenth century were often subjected. This has led to it being regarded as an important early example of feminist literature.

Her highly acclaimed *Women and Economics* critically examines women's powerlessness and financial dependence in marriage and challenges the Victorian Angel-in-the-House myth. It was first published in 1898 and immediately made her a well-known if controversial figure. When she spoke at the 1904 congress of the International Council of Women in Berlin, she received a standing ovation. Cynthia J. Davis's *Charlotte Perkins Gilman: A Biography* (Stanford University Press, 2010) is a thorough, theoretically informed account of her life and thought.

Louise Michel

My favourite work of Gilman's is the feminist utopia *Herland*, which first appeared in serial form in her own publication (*The Forerunner*, 1915). It is a story of three men who travel to a hidden valley that is inhabited by a society consisting entirely of women. The book is a critical, and sometimes highly amusing, exploration of gender identities, roles and relationships. It does not advocate separatism; rather, Gilman uses the device of an all-female society to show women functioning effectively and independently as full citizens. It's unfortunate that she didn't extend her optimism about the capacities of white women to African Americans, however. In 1908 her 'Suggestion on the Negro Problem' appeared in the *American Journal of Sociology* (volume 14, pp.78-85). As her biographer remarks, 'Whereas to improve (white) women she advocated their immediate and full integration into society, to improve "Negroes" she argued for their temporary segregation. Charlotte prided herself on her logical mind, but in this instance prejudice blinded her to her own illogic' (Davis, 2010, p.276).

Page 9. In 1890 Louise Michel put together a booklet on the topics of her public lectures for a Saint-Denis anarchist group publication. *Prise de possession* included science-fiction speculations about the glittering future for humanity once emancipated. Various sources have written about her science-fiction writer's percipience regarding scientific advances (Oliver, 2005; Thomas, 1980). Fernand Planche even claims that she began writing *Twenty Thousand Leagues Under the Sea* and, being unable to complete it, sold the draft to Jules Verne for 100 francs (Planche, 1946). I haven't read the source for this claim directly and rely on Douglas Oliver, who goes on to add that it 'seems an extreme version of the legend, probably of some foundation, that she sold Jules Verne the idea for his "Nautilus"' (Oliver, 2005, p. 313). She was definitely *au courant.*

Page 12. As much as possible, I've turned to Louise Michel herself as my primary source, both directly and through her biographer (Michel, 1971, 1981, 1999; Thomas, 1980). Other sources for the Siege of Paris and the Paris Commune included Butterworth (2010), Clayson (2002), Edwards (1973), Eichner (2004), Leyton (2004), Lissagaray (1976), Oliver (2005) and Tombs (1999) and the various websites noted under Sources.

Paris's gas supply was restricted during the Siege, plunging the City of Light into darkness. Much of the supply was redirected for use in hot air balloons, which were the city's principal means of communication with the outside world for the duration of the Siege.

Page 15. Napoleon III was captured by the Prussians after the fall of Sedan on 4 September 1870. A group of elected deputies, led by Léon Gambetta, immediately seized power, declaring the Republic and installing themselves at the Hôtel de Ville as the Government of National Defence. At the same time the Prussian Siege of Paris began.

Page 17. At the beginning of the Siege in September, the newly formed government resolved to increase the Paris National Guard by 90,000, roughly doubling it. By October there were 194 new battalions, making the National Guard the main employer in Paris. These battalions were in place in all *arrondissements* as local, democratic organisations and they were armed. As they were federally linked, National Guardsmen were often known as 'Federals', though regular soldiers disparagingly called them the 'thirty sous', in reference to their daily wage (Tombs, 1999).

Page 22. Albert Robida was a French writer and illustrator, best known for his humorous science-fiction work *Le vingtième siècle* (*The Twentieth Century*), first published in 1882, and *La vie électrique* (*The Electric Life*), among others. His comic SF stories are distinctive in the way he imagined the impact of technological innovations on everyday life. *The Twentieth Century* features telecommunications and rapid global transport, as well as the gastronomic engineering of the illustration.

As a Paris resident during the Siege, Robida was recruited into the National Guard, along with many other artists, with whom he probably rubbed shoulders, including Gustave Courbet, Edgar Degas, Gustav Doré, Edouard Manet and Henri Regnault.

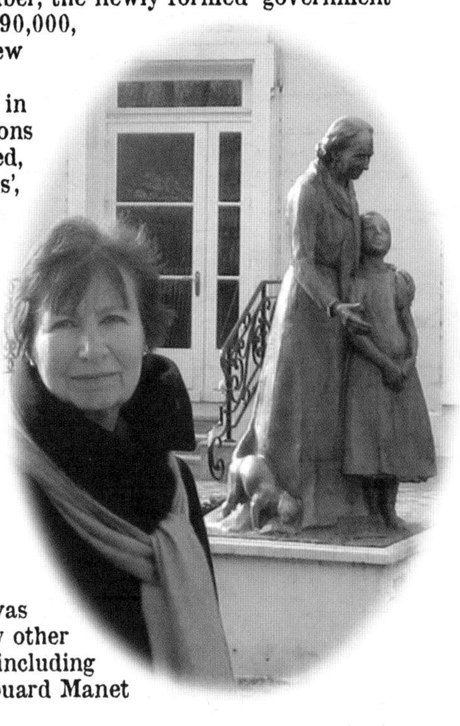

At the statue of Louise in Parc de la Planchette, Levallois

Page 23. Mary Shelley's "poor abused monster" was of course Victor Frankenstein's creature. The French Revolution would have been recent history for Shelley and she would have learned about it from her father, William Godwin. Her mother, Mary Wollstonecraft, died of puerperal fever ten days after her birth (Mellor, 1988).

Page 24. The image of a club-wielding Herculean giant is loosely based on an engraving entitled *Le Peuple Mangeur de Rois* (The People, Eater of Kings) done in 1793, as a design for a proposed colossus statue to commemorate the Revolution (Mellor, 1988).

Page 27. The bourgeois governments that had taken over after the collapse of Empire had two enemies: the Prussians and Paris workers. There was gross disparity between rich and poor's experience of the Siege. It was a grim ordeal for the poor, especially for women, and had the effect of politicising them. This announcement by the National Guard's Central Committee was a direct challenge on the behalf of the Parisian poor. The full text appears in translation in Edwards (1973), pp.48-9.

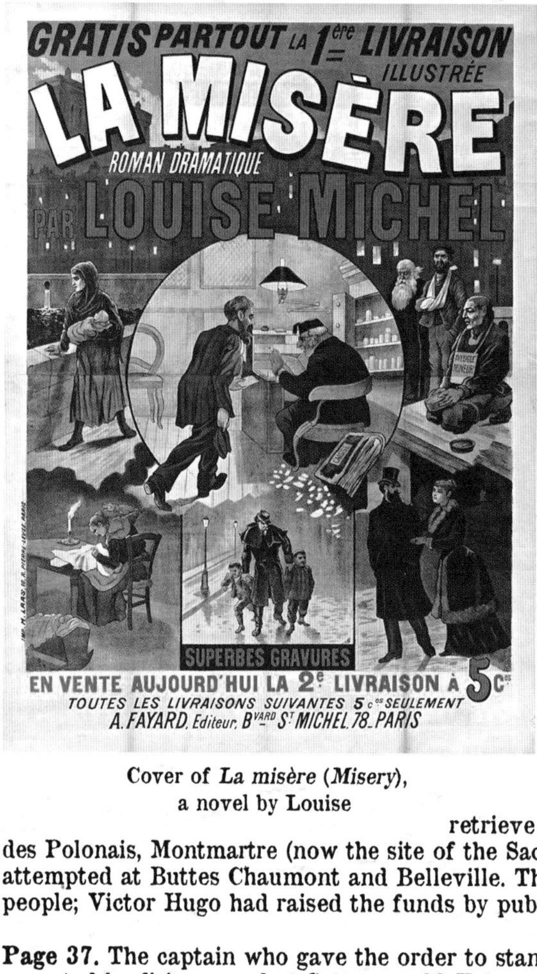
GRATIS PARTOUT LA 1ère LIVRAISON
ILLUSTRÉE
LA MISÈRE
ROMAN DRAMATIQUE
PAR LOUISE MICHEL
SUPERBES GRAVURES
EN VENTE AUJOURD'HUI LA 2e LIVRAISON À 5c
TOUTES LES LIVRAISONS SUIVANTES 5 c SEULEMENT
A. FAYARD, Éditeur, Bvard St MICHEL 78_PARIS

Cover of *La misère* (*Misery*), a novel by Louise

Page 30. The first Prussian troops had arrived in Versailles on 19 September 1870. Wilhelm I and Chancellor Bismarck went there on 5 October, in preparation for the proclamation of the German Empire. This proclamation of German unity as a state took place in the Hall of Mirrors in the Château on 18 January 1871.

The Prussians did not invade the city of Paris. The victory march down the Champs-Élysées on 1 March was one of the conditions of the armistice. As a symbolic crushing of the French, it was an insult, presumably performed for the benefit of the triumphant Prussian army. It was after the announcement of this intended march through the capital that the National Guard indignantly hauled their cannons up to Montmartre.

Page 34. General Claude Lecomte led 250 soldiers of the 88th regiment to retrieve 171 pieces of artillery from the Champ des Polonais, Montmartre (now the site of the Sacré-Coeur). Similar operations were being attempted at Buttes Chaumont and Belleville. These cannons had been paid for by the people; Victor Hugo had raised the funds by public subscription.

Page 37. The captain who gave the order to stand down was Galdric Verdaguer. He was executed by firing squad at Satory on 22 February 1872.

Page 39. The sequence of events here is condensed. Lecomte was arrested and taken to the National Guard's local headquarters at 6 rue des Rosiers for court-martial, along with Jacques Clément-Thomas, another hated general recognised by the crowd (Clément-Thomas had ordered a massacre in the uprising of June 1848). Lecomte was commanded to sign an order to evacuate the Buttes of Montmartre, which he readily did. However, by the afternoon an angry crowd had surrounded the building and was demanding the death of the prisoners. In the crowd were enraged soldiers who'd been disciplined by imprisonment in Solferino Tower by their commanding officer, Lecomte. The officers of the National Guard posted sentinels and tried to appease the crowd, urging them to 'Wait for the Committee', as Louise did. However, the crowd eventually seized both generals and executed them.

There is an old photograph supposedly depicting the assassination by firing squad of General Lecomte. It seems to be an inaccurate reconstruction. None of the accounts by onlookers report any such orderly execution. According to Louise, 'Tempers flared, there was a scuffle, guns went off'. Prosper-Olivier Lissagaray's account of the whole episode is a good deal more detailed:

> No member of the Committee had arrived when, at half-past four, formidable cries filled the street, and hunted by a fierce multitude, a man with a white beard was thrust against the wall of the house. It was Clément-Thomas, the man of June, 1848, the insulter of the revolutionary battalions. He had been recognized and arrested at the Chaussée des Martyrs, where he was examining the barricades.
>
> Some officers of the National Guard, a Garibaldian captain, Herpin-Lacroix, and some franc-tireurs had tried to stop the deadly mass, repeating a thousand times, 'Wait for the Committee! Constitute a court-martial!' They were jostled, and Clément-Thomas was again seized and hurled into the little garden of the house. Twenty muskets levelled at him battered him down. During this execution the soldiers broke the windows of the room where General Lecomte was confined, threw themselves upon him, dragging him towards the garden. This man, who in the morning had three times given the order to fire upon the people, wept, begged for pity, and spoke of his family. He was forced against the wall and fell under the bullets.

(Lissagaray 1976)

The dialogue on this page ('Would I fire on a Frenchman?' etc) is derived from an account in *The Times* (20 March 1871).

Page 40. With Louise Michel and Paule Minck in this crowd are men who went on to form the Commune Council: Théophile Ferré, Gustav Tridon, Jules Vallès, Léo Fränkel and Élisée Reclus. Jean Allemane (who reappears later in the New Caledonia section) is also present.

Louise is calling for the assassination of Adolphe Thiers, who was the new Head of State following national elections in February 1871. There was no love lost between him and the common people or 'vile multitude', as he liked to call them (Edwards, 1973, p.24). The order to retrieve the cannon on 18 March came directly from him, as did the command to retreat to Versailles.

Page 44. H.G. Wells' *A Modern Utopia* came out in 1905. Charlotte did review several of his books – she disliked his *Ann Veronica* intensely but praised *The History of Mr. Polly*. I haven't been able to find a review of his *Modern Utopia*, however. Perhaps she was too busy touring that year. Wells, for his part, seems to have been something of a fan – on visiting the United States, his first request was to meet her (Eichner, 2004, p.xii).

Page 45. Louise was a prodigious letter writer. There's only a handful from during the Commune to be found in her collected correspondence, however. Given the events that followed, it's rather surprising any survived at all. In her letter to Citizen Mayor (the young Dr. Georges Clemenceau, Mayor of Montmartre) she is making six numbered requests, writing in her capacity as provisional president of the Montmartre Women's Vigilance Committee (Michel, 1999).

Pages 48-49. Political clubs flourished, using the emptied churches for meetings. Extracts from the women's speeches, including Paule Minck's here and Louise's on page 52, came from Carolyn Eichner's study of the position and roles of women during the Commune (Eichner, 2004).

Page 50. Edward Bellamy's utopian novel *Looking Backward: 2000-1887* was published in 1888. Its protagonist, Julian West, wakes from drug-induced slumber to find himself in a utopian society that has abandoned capitalism and embraced principles of cooperativeness and public ownership. It triggered a Bellamy craze, with hundreds of nationalist clubs starting up across the United States. Charlotte became an ardent supporter, lecturing and writing on nationalism until the movement and its magazine folded in 1894.

Paule Minck

While Bellamy's book was an international bestseller, it wasn't without its critics. Prominent among them was William Morris, whose utopian *News from Nowhere* (1890) was an anti-Bellamy rebuttal.

Page 54. John Leighton gives an eye-witness account of heavy shelling of the Champs-Élysées, troops sheltering under the Arc de Triomphe and a battalion on the move, 'fully equipped, with blankets and saucepans strapped to their knapsacks, and loaves of bread stuck aloft on their bayonets' (ch.38).

Page 57. This scene depicts one of Louise's anecdotes. Her biographer explains:

> Her contempt for danger, her disregard for even the most elementary precautions, sometimes annoyed her comrades. Called to the barricade of Rue Peironnet in Neuilly, she went off to play the organ in the deserted Protestant church. 'I was having a wonderful time, when a captain and three or four furious Federals suddenly burst in the door. "So you're the one drawing enemy fire on this barricade. I came to find whoever was responsible, and shoot him." Thus ended my attempts to compose a few harmonies in imitation of the dancing bombs.'
>
> (Thomas, 1980, pp.86-7)

Page 58. During the hostilities, Louise was fortunate enough to sustain nothing worse than a wrist graze from a bullet and a sprained ankle, despite putting herself in harm's way on a more or less daily basis. She does seem to have been remarkably fearless under fire, but she rejected any praise for bravery:

> Some people say I'm brave. Not really. There is no heroism; people are simply entranced by events. What happens is that in the face of danger my perceptions are submerged in my artistic sense, which is seized and charmed. Tableaux of the dangers overwhelm my thoughts, and the horrors of the struggle become poetry.
>
> It wasn't bravery when charmed by the sight, I looked at the

dismantled fort of Issy, all white against the shadows, and watched
my comrades filing out in night sallies, moving away over the little
slopes of Clamart or towards the Hautes Bruyères, with the red teeth
of chattering machine guns showing on the horizon against the night
sky. It was beautiful, that's all. Barbarian that I am, I love cannon, the
smell of powder, machine-gun bullets in the air.

(Michel, 1981, pp.65-6)

Hers was a very singular aesthetic. I drew on her commentary on the fighting for some
of her lines.

Page 60. The army entered the city before dawn on 21 May and began sweeping through
it. By the afternoon of the 28th the Communard barricades had been overthrown and all
resistance ceased. It became known as la Semaine Sanglante (Bloody Week). John
Leighton, a *Times* journalist living in Paris throughout the Commune, gives an eye-witness
account:

The hours and the days pass and resemble each other horribly. To
write the history of the calamities is not yet possible. Each one sees
but a corner of the picture, and the narratives that are collected are
vague and contradictory; it appears certain now that the insurrection
is approaching the end. It is said that the fort of Montrouge is taken;
but it still hurls its shells upon Paris. Several have just fallen in the
quarter of the Banque. There is fighting still at the Halles, at the
Luxembourg, and at the Porte Saint-Martin. Neither the cannonading
nor the fusillade has ceased, and our ears have become accustomed to
the continued roar. But, in spite of the barbarous heroism of the
Federals, the force of their resistance is being exhausted. What has
become of the chiefs?

...I am told that at the Théâtre du Châtelet a court-martial has been
established on the stage. The Federals are brought up twenty at a time,
judged, and condemned, they are then marched out on to the Place,
with their hands tied behind their backs. A mitrailleuse, standing a
hundred yards off, mows them down like grass. It is an expeditious
contrivance. In a yard, in the Rue Saint-Denis, is a stable filled with
corpses; I have myself seen them there.

(Leighton, 2004)

Page 66. According to a biographical supplement in Albert Robida's *The Twentieth Century*,
his 'unassuming demeanour miraculously allowed him to avoid the death that was meted
out to his fellow prisoners: taking advantage of his guards' momentary inattention, he is
said to have simply walked away from the group being led to the firing squad, pretending
to be a simple passerby' (Robida, 2004, p.392).

As for Louise:

> Somehow I managed to escape from the soldiers trying to arrest me.
> Finally the victorious reactionaries took my mother and threatened to
> shoot her if I wasn't found. To set her free I went to take her place,
> although she didn't want me to do it, the poor, dear woman.
>
> (Michel, 1981, p.69)

Louise spent several weeks in the notorious Satory prison in Versailles, where the cells were overcrowded and heaving with lice. Prisoners' rations there consisted of 'siege bread'; that is, bread cut with straw and wood slivers. She was transferred to Arras until the trial in December. The move was seemingly to put an end to her constant fraternisation with fellow communards in Satory, in particular the condemned Théophile Ferré, with whom she kept up continuous correspondence (Thomas, 1980, p.97).

Page 67. The full trial dialogue was recorded in the *Gazette des Tribunaux* and Louise attached it to her memoirs as an appendix (Michel, 1980). Victor Hugo wrote the poem 'Viro Major' in admiration after her bravery on trial. Here's the opening verse:

> Ayant vu le massacre immense, le combat,
> Le peuple sur sa croix, Paris sur son grabat,
> La pitié formidable était dans tes paroles ;
> Tu faisais ce que font les grandes âmes folles,
> Et lasse de lutter, de rêver, de souffrir,
> Tu disais : J'ai tué ! car tu voulais mourir.

> Having seen the huge massacre, the combat,
> The people on their cross, Paris on its pallet,
> Tremendous pity was in your words;
> You did what the great crazy souls do
> And weary of fighting, dreaming, suffering,
> You said: 'I have killed! for you wanted to die.

Page 68. The *Virginie* was a French naval frigate built in Rochefort in 1829 and originally called the *Niobé*. As I've only managed to find one picture of it, another frigate has had to serve as a model for the scenes on board. HMS *Trincomalee* is a British naval frigate with very similar specifications. It was built in 1817 in Sri Lanka. It is now berthed in Hartlepool, beautifully restored and open to the public.

Page 69. Prior to deportation Louise made extensive preparations. Her biographer observes that she was 'determined to transform punishment into a scientific expedition' (Thomas, 1980, p.137). Indeed, she seems to have been looking forward to it very much. She had corresponded about her forthcoming trip to New Caledonia with the president of the Geographical Society, offering her services. He was very pleased to accept: 'I will perhaps be the only one – but I will congratulate you on your departure, because you have desired it so much and for so long, convinced of being useful in this new land' (Michel, 1999, p.202). Arrangements were made for her to send back observations about climate, flora and fauna. She was furnished with seed to trial and technical books to assist her. She also received, on her request, books on other subjects for study purposes, including Breton, Russian and Polish grammars. She clearly had no intention of pining away in exile!

It was on this four-month sea voyage to New Caledonia, in long conversation with her companion, Natalie Lemel, that Louise became committed to anarchism. All her life she remained committed to the belief that power is inherently evil. On trial for inciting a bread riot in 1883, she stated: 'When one person alone no longer has authority, there will be light, truth and justice. Authority vested in one person is a crime. What we want is authority vested in everyone' (Michel, 1981, p.169).

Page 70. I heard this poem in English, read out in *Great Lives: Paul Mason on Louise Michel*, which was broadcast on BBC Radio 4 on 3 September 2013.

Pages 71-72. The poem on these pages is 'L'oeillet rouge' ('The red carnation'). Louise wrote it to Théophile Ferré, a Communard leader who was tried and executed while Louise was still imprisoned in the infamous Satory prison awaiting trial in 1871. Here it is in the original French:

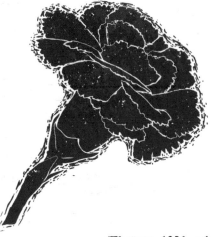

Si j'allais au noir cimetière,
Frères, jetez sur votre soeur
Comme une espérance dernière
De rouges oeillets tout en fleur.

Aujourd'hui, va fleurir dans l'ombre
Des noires et tristes prisons.
Va fleurir près du captif sombre
Et dis-lui bien que nous l'aimons.

Dis-lui que par le temps rapide
Tout appartient à l'avenir;
Que le vainqueur au front livide
Plus que le vaincu peut mourir.

(Thomas, 1980, p.104)

Page 73. Jules Verne's *Vingt milles lieues sous les mers* (*Twenty Thousand Leagues Under the Sea*) was first published in book form in 1870.

Louise's generous 'Neighbour Starboard Aft' was actually the aristocratic radical journalist and politician Henri Rochefort, who had also been sentenced to deportation. I decided not to include him in Louise's story because I felt that if I gave him a voice it would start to dominate. He's the kind of character who takes over any story he's involved in.

During the Second Empire, Rochefort's radical pro-republican journalism frequently landed him in jail but also made him popular with the people. When the Empire fell in September 1870, he was serving a prison sentence. On the day the Republic was proclaimed, he was liberated and borne in triumph to the provisional government at the Hôtel de Ville.

Though he was elected as a member of the Government of National Defence, his position became untenable after an attempted coup on 31 October and he resigned. As Louise observed, 'There was only one red sash of the Revolution being worn at the Hôtel de Ville, and that was worn by Henri Rochefort' (Michel, 1981, p.57). Sympathetic with the insurgents, he set up another radical newspaper. Criticising government from the margins seemed to suit him better than serving in it. When the national elections took place in February 1871, he was voted back in, along with Victor Hugo. Both of them resigned in protest at the conditions of the armistice.

Page 76. Louise is composing the first verse of 'Dans les mers polaires' ('In Polar Seas'). Here it is in the original French:

> La neige tombe, le flot roule,
> L'air est glacé, le ciel est noir,
> Le vaisseau craque sous la houle
> Et le matin se mêle au soir.

(Thomas, 1980, p.140)

The Captain's consideration for Louise and her exasperating generosity are subjects of an anecdote in Henri Rochefort's autobiography:

> Captain Launay did not know how to get her to accept a pair of warm felt boots, to prevent her from catching her death of cold, and came to beg me to help him to overcome her scruples.
> 'If I offer them to her', he said, 'she will refuse them point-blank. You must send them to her as coming from yourself.'
>
> I entered into the spirit of the thing, and had the boots handed to her with a little note, in which I explained that my daughter had given them to me before we left, but that they were too small, and I hoped she would accept them and wear them for the sake of the giver. For two days I had the satisfaction of seeing them on her feet. The third day somebody else was wearing them. The lack of this world's goods is not always a preventive against having one's kindness exploited.

(Rochefort, 1896, pp.74-5)

Page 83. The French title of Robida's play was *La Nuit des temps ou l'Elixir de rejeunissement* (*The Mists of Time or The Elixir of Youth*).

Page 84. *La Dame du Fer* (the original Iron Lady) was originally erected as a temporary construction for the Universal Exposition of 1889. Construction of the Eiffel Tower began in August 1887 and the structural work was completed by March 1889. It opened to the public on 15 May, a week after the opening of the Exposition, though the lifts weren't operational until 26 May, so the first visitors must have had plenty of exercise. During the Expo it had two million visitors.

130

Its proposed construction was not without criticism, however, including a formal written protest signed by prominent artists and writers of the period:

> **We come, we writers, painters, sculptors, architects, lovers of the beauty of Paris** which was until now intact, to protest with all our strength and all our indignation, in the name of the underestimated taste of the French, in the name of French art and history under threat, **against the erection in the very heart of our capital, of the useless and monstrous Eiffel Tower** which popular ill-feeling, so often an arbiter of good sense and justice, has already christened the Tower of Babel.
>
> (Eiffel Tower website)

Louise loved it. She praised the technical progress it stood for in a lecture she gave in the Salle des Capucines the month before: 'The Eiffel Tower has set cities dreaming of iron lacework, not stone, for their crowning glories. The twentieth century will see humanity's genius spectacularly transformed, and great strides in daring and invention' (Thomas, 1980, p.297).

Page 86. In her correspondence with Victor Hugo, Louise signed herself 'Enjolras', after the revolutionary leader of his epic *Les Misérables*. She seemed to identify with his well-known fictitious activist. Her own fame as a heroic revolutionary figure only really developed while she was in exile in New Caledonia. It was probably triggered by Hugo's poem 'Viro Major', which he wrote in admiration after her bravery on trial in December 1871.

Page 88. H.G. Wells' *When the Sleeper Wakes* was serialised in *The Graphic* from 1898 to 1903. He has its protagonist reflecting directly on the earlier sleeper-awakes story, Bellamy's *Looking Backward*: 'He thought of Bellamy, the hero of whose Socialistic Utopia had so oddly anticipated this actual experience. But here was no Utopia, no Socialistic state. He had already seen enough to realise that the ancient antithesis of luxury, waste and sensuality on the one hand and abject poverty on the other still prevailed.'

Wells reworked the story as *The Sleeper Awakes* in 1910.

Page 89. Edward Bulwer-Lytton wrote prolifically, but *The Coming Race* was his only work of science fiction. First published in 1871, it appeared in the United States as *Vril: The Power of the Coming Race* in 1872. The Vril-na are a strain of humanity living beneath the surface of Earth. They are superior to surface dwellers physically, morally and intellectually and have discovered a life force and limitless source of energy known as Vril (which, incidentally, is where the brand name of a well-known beef tea comes from: an abbreviation of 'Bovine Vril').

Bradley Lane's *Mizora: A Prophecy* was serialised in *The Cincinnati Commercial* in 1880-81. There are excerpts in an edited collection of utopian stories by United States women of 1836-1919 (Kessler, 1984).

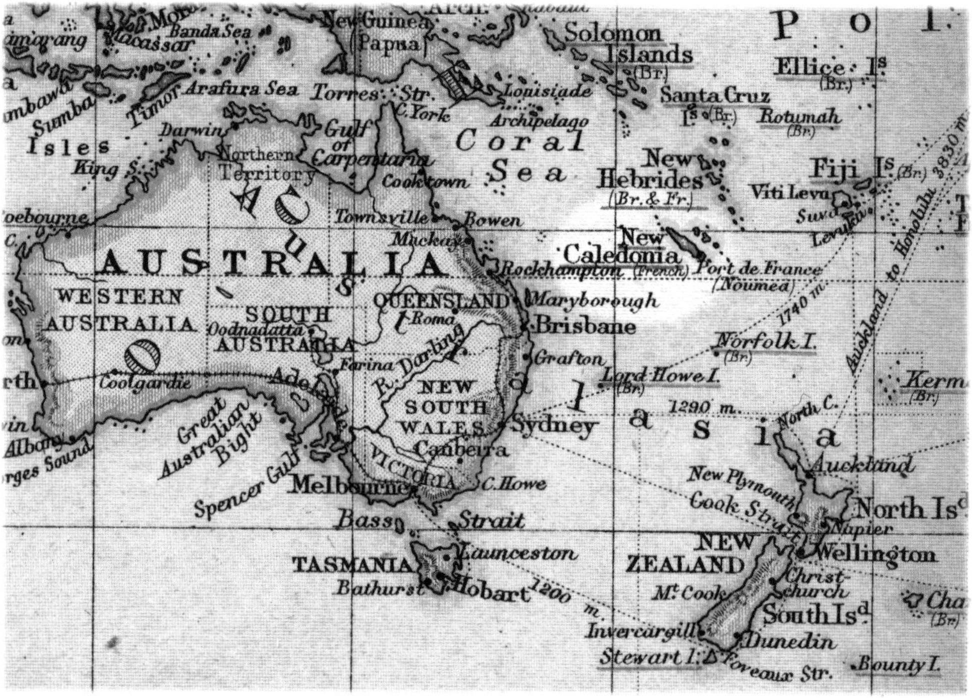
Banda Sea
New Guinea
Papua
Solomon Islands
(Br.)
Ellice Is
(Br.)
Timor
Arafura Sea
Torres Str.
Louisiade Archipelago
Santa Cruz Is (Br.)
Rotumah (Br.)
C. York
Sumba
Darwin
Gulf of Carpentaria
Coral Sea
New Hebrides
(Br. & Fr.)
Fiji Is (Br.)
Viti Levu
Northern Territory
Cooktown
Townsville
Bowen
Mackay
New Caledonia (French)
Rockhampton
Port de France
(Noumea)
AUSTRALIA
WESTERN AUSTRALIA
SOUTH AUSTRALIA
Oodnadatta
QUEENSLAND
Roma
Maryborough
Brisbane
1740 m.
Norfolk I.
(Br.)
Auckland to Honolulu
Farina
R. Darling
Grafton
Coolgardie
Lord Howe I.
(Br)
NEW SOUTH WALES
Sydney
1290 m.
North C.
Great Australian Bight
Canberra
Victoria
Melbourne
C. Howe
Auckland
New Plymouth
Cook Strait
North Isd
Spencer Gulf
Bass Strait
Napier
Wellington
NEW ZEALAND
TASMANIA
Launceston
Christchurch
Bathurst
Hobart
1200 m.
Mt Cook
South Isd
Invercargill
Dunedin
Stewart I.
Foveaux Str.
Bounty I.

Location of New Caledonia

Page 91. My source for the naval department's clerical error about the deportees' final destination was volume II of Henri Rochefort's autobiography. He opens with this gleeful observation:

> When things have looked most desperately gloomy, I have invariably been aided by luck or by the stupidity and ignorance of my adversaries. The governor of New Caledonia advised the home government to set apart the Ile des Pins, situated about ten leagues from Noumea, for the accommodation of prisoners sentenced to simple transportation, and the Ile Ducos, a desert spot at least twenty leagues distant from New Caledonia, as a place of banishment for those who had been sentenced to confinement in a fortified place. [...] But when the governmental geographers consulted their atlases they could find no mention of the island, and confounded it with a peninsula of the same name.
>
> (Rochefort, 1896, p.1)

Given that the French word for 'peninsula' is *presqu'île* (literally, 'almost-island') his adversaries were perhaps not quite as dim as he makes out. But in a sense he and Louise were more fortunate still, in that they were not sentenced to hard labour. If they had been, they would have ended up in 'le Bagne' on Dou Island, a penitentiary established in 1854, where they would probably not have survived the notoriously harsh conditions.

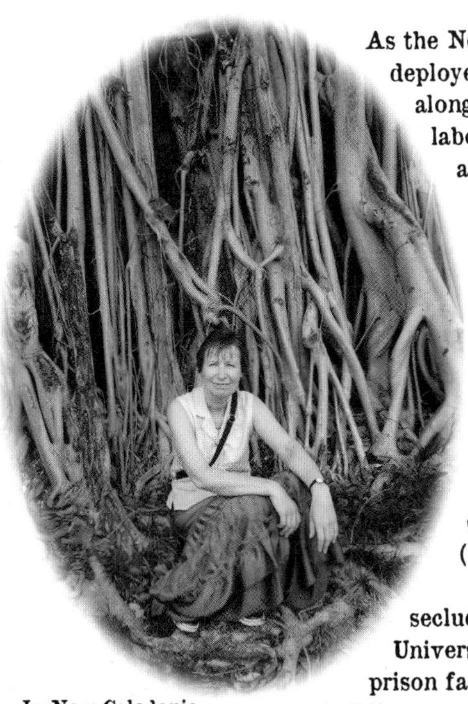

In New Caledonia

As the Noumea colony developed, deportees' labour was deployed in road building and other civic works, alongside enormous numbers brought in as cheap labour from China, Vietnam and the surrounding area. Nevertheless, when Governor Feillet was installed in 1894, he was instructed to turn off 'the tap of dirty water' to the growing colony; in other words, to put an end to deportation. The penal colonies were considered to be 'veritable founts of moral infection' and not beneficial in the establishment of a new colony. Besides, given the New Caledonian climate, the punishment wasn't deemed severe enough (which makes me think of that *Life of Brian* line: 'Crucifixion's too good for them!'). The last convoy of transportees arrived on 25 February 1897 (source: City Museum of Noumea).

These days the location of 'le Bagne' is a secluded spot popular with tourists, close by the University of New Caledonia. All that remains of the prison facility, fortunately, are some old penitentiary buildings, one of which now houses a restaurant called Le 1881. It specialises in gourmet French cuisine and cabaret.

Page 93. Daoumi taught Louise his tribal language and songs and also told her his people's legends. She wrote them down and eventually published them as *Légendes et chants de gestes canaques* (*Legends and songs of the Kanaks*) in 1885. In it she recorded Daoumi's account of the Europeans' arrival in New Caledonia, reproduced on this page (cited in Thomas, 1980, p.149).

Louise was greatly impressed by the wisdom and capacity to learn that Daoumi and his people displayed: 'I wondered which of us was the superior being: the one who assimilates foreign knowledge through a thousand difficulties for the sake of their race, or the well-armed white who annihilates those who are less well armed?' (Michel, 1981, p.117).

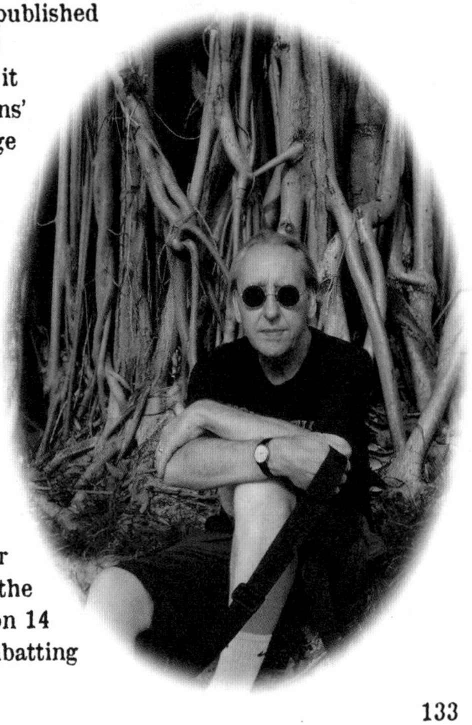

Page 99. An Algerian revolt against French colonial occupation coincided almost exactly with the Paris Commune. The Arab and Berber tribal uprising, led by Mohammed el-Mokrani, the ruler of the Kabyle region of Medjana, began on 14 March 1871. With French troops occupied combatting

the Communards in Paris, the insurgent Algerian peasants won one victory after another, but their eventual suppression was every bit as brutal. According to Vladimir Lutsky (1969):

> The Versaillists cynically admitted that they had dealt with the Algerian insurgents in the 'Parisian manner'. Thousands were executed, thrown into prison or exiled to New Caledonia to do penal servitude. The rebellious tribes paid 36,000,000 francs indemnities and 500,000 hectares of their best land were confiscated. To save the rest they had to pay the conquerors another 27,000,000 francs.

Page 101. Louise was oddly reticent about commenting on the revolt in New Caledonia, but she does mention the symbolic passing-on of her red scarf:

> The revolt of the tribes was deadly serious, but it is better if I say little about it. The Kanaks were seeking the same liberty we had sought in the Commune. Let me say only that my red scarf, the red scarf of the Commune that I had hidden from every search, was divided in two pieces one night. Two Kanaks, before going to join the insurgents against the whites, had come to say goodbye to me.
>
> (Michel, p.112)

In 1969 a political movement of Kanak youth formed, calling themselves les Foulards Rouges (the Red Scarves). Another in 1974 was known as the 1878 Group. From these beginnings, as well as related groups for Kanak workers' rights, an independent political party was eventually established: Kanak Socialist Liberation. While Louise was an anarchist rather than a socialist, she would surely have approved.

Page 103. In 2011, Chief Atai's head was found in an anthropological museum in Paris and finally returned to New Caledonia in 2014. In a solemn ceremony on August 28, France's Overseas Territories Minister George Pauangevin presented the skull to Bergé Kawa, a direct descendant of Atai.

Page 110. Originally from Finistère in Brittany, Pierre Lucas worked in Le Havre as a warehouseman. According to police reports, he had listened to Louise speaking earlier in the day and, offended by her blasphemy, returned with a revolver to 'assassinate that devil in female skin' (Thomas, 1980, p.281). 'It was being said', Thomas continues, 'that Lucas belonged to the Union of the Sacred Heart (presided over by the Count and Countess of Paris) and had been provoked to his deed by a rural clergyman' (p.283).

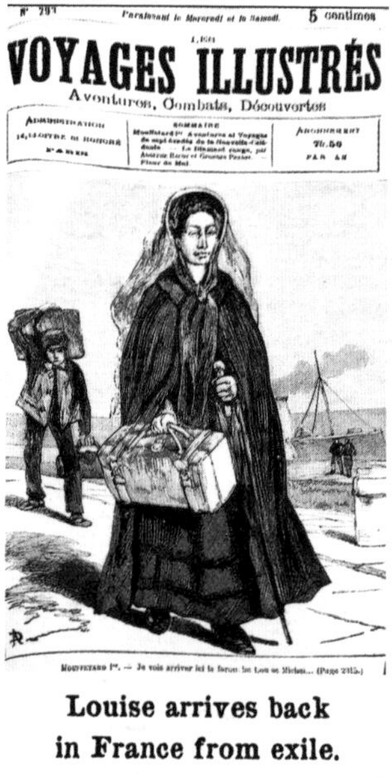
5 centimes
VOYAGES ILLUSTRÉS
Aventures, Combats, Découvertes

Louise arrives back in France from exile.

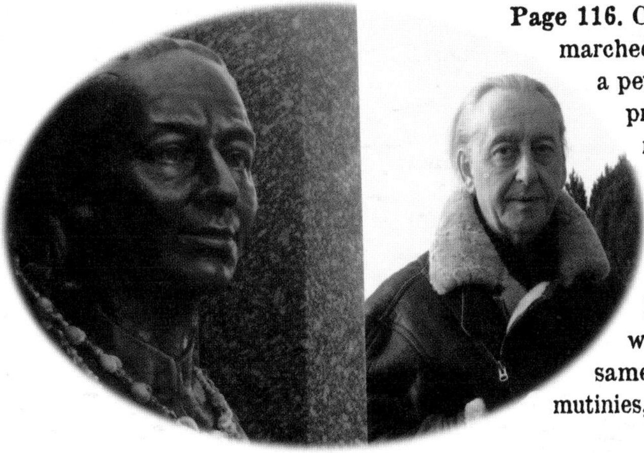

Page 116. On 22 January 1905 a huge crowd marched to the Winter Palace to deliver a petition to the Czar. With orders to prevent the demonstrators from reaching the Palace, troops opened fire, killing up to a thousand unarmed people. The massacre came to be known as Bloody Sunday. It triggered mass strikes, involving factory and railway workers but also teachers. In the same year there were also naval mutinies, including on battleship *Potemkin.*

At Louise's grave, Levallois-Perret Cemetary

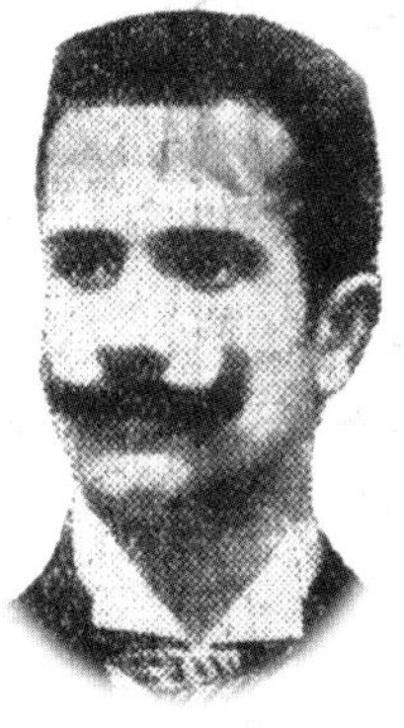

Franz Reichelt

Page 118. Franz Reichelt, an Austrian-born tailor living in France, had been given permission to test a prototype parachute-suit from the first stage of the Eiffel Tower, using a dummy. He fell to his death while trying out the invention himself. The preparation and fatal jump were captured on film and can be seen on YouTube. He seems to have been undeterred by previous failures and injuries from much smaller jumps, which I reckon makes him a worthy candidate for a Darwin Award.

In 1946, Louise's remains were exhumed and reburied in a more central spot in Levallois-Perret Cemetery. In the same year, a metro station in Levallois-Perret was renamed Louise Michel. Over 160 schools and colleges now bear her name, including Louise Michel College in Païta, New Caledonia. Innumerable streets and squares are named after her, including Square Louise Michel in Montmartre, which was renamed on 8 March 2004 in an International Women's Day commemorative event.

Mary Talbot, 2015

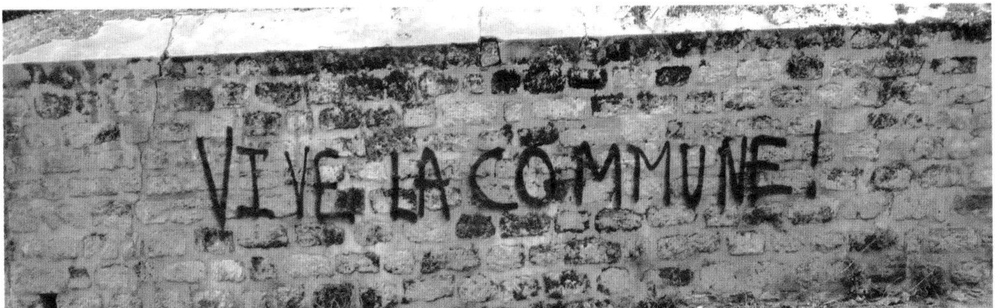
VIVE LA COMMUNE!

Graffiti in Montmartre, January 2015

Dotter of her Father's Eyes

Mary M Talbot
Bryan Talbot

SALLY HEATHCOTE SUFFRAGETTE

MARY M TALBOT
KATE CHARLESWORTH
BRYAN TALBOT

MARY M TALBOT

Now a freelance writer, Mary Talbot is an internationally acclaimed scholar of gender and language who previously held academic posts for over twenty-five years. She gained her PhD at Lancaster University in 1990, with a thesis entitled *Language, Intertextuality and Subjectivity: Voices in the Construction of Consumer Femininity*. Since then she has published extensively in her field. Her first graphic novel, *Dotter of Her Father's Eyes* (with Bryan Talbot), won the 2012 Costa Biography Award. Her second, *Sally Heathcote, Suffragette* (with Kate Charlesworth and Bryan Talbot), brings a strong narrative approach to complex historical material. She has also collaborated with Kate Charlesworth on a chapter for the dystopian SF graphic novel *IDP: 2043*, with Alwyn Talbot on a short strip for *Cross: A Political Satire Anthology* and with Kate and Bryan again for an upcoming Amnesty International anthology.

Mary and Bryan Talbot are founder patrons of the Lakes International Comics Arts Festival.

www.mary-talbot.co.uk

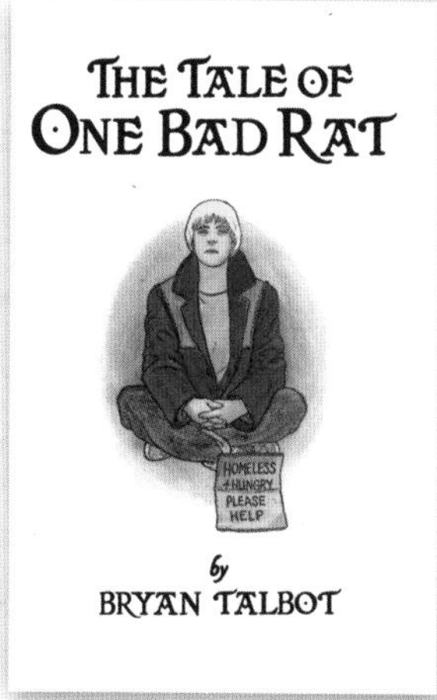
THE TALE OF
ONE BAD RAT
HOMELESS
+ HUNGRY
PLEASE
HELP
by
BRYAN TALBOT

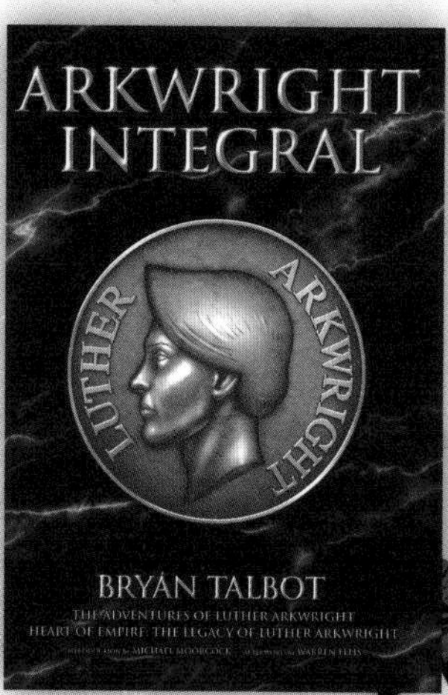
ARKWRIGHT
INTEGRAL
LUTHER ARKWRIGHT
BRYAN TALBOT
THE ADVENTURES OF LUTHER ARKWRIGHT
HEART OF EMPIRE: THE LEGACY OF LUTHER ARKWRIGHT

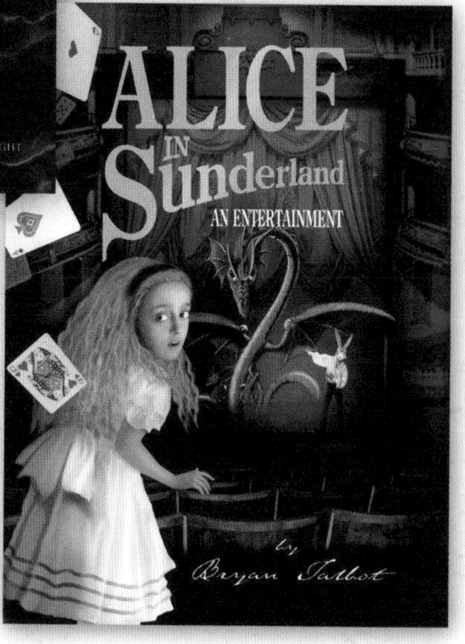
ALICE
IN
Sunderland
AN ENTERTAINMENT
by
Bryan Talbot

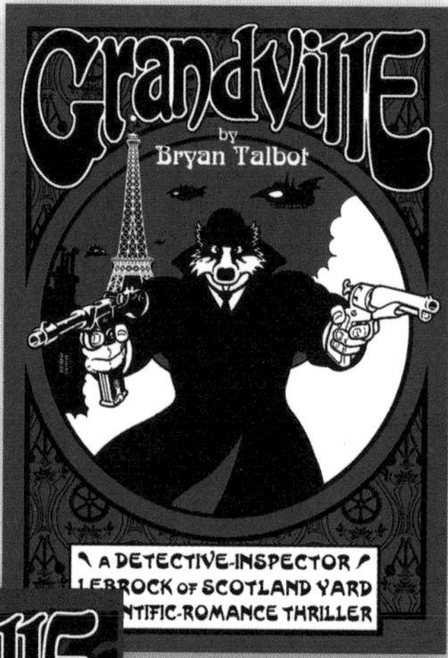
Grandville
by
Bryan Talbot
A DETECTIVE-INSPECTOR
LEBROCK OF SCOTLAND YARD

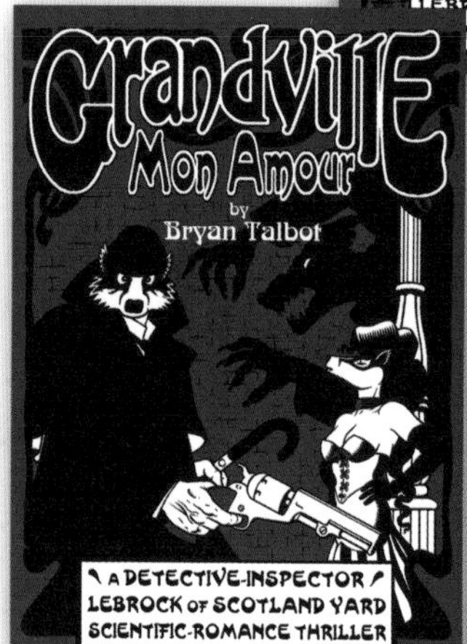
Grandville
Mon Amour
by
Bryan Talbot
A DETECTIVE-INSPECTOR
LEBROCK OF SCOTLAND YARD
SCIENTIFIC-ROMANCE THRILLER

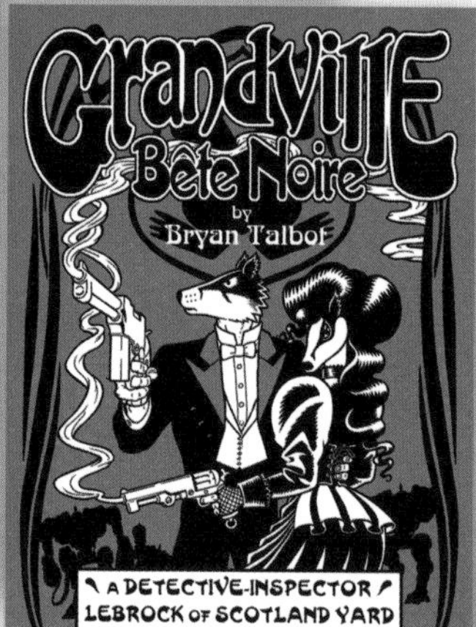
Grandville
Bête Noire
by
Bryan Talbot
A DETECTIVE-INSPECTOR
LEBROCK OF SCOTLAND YARD
SCIENTIFIC-ROMANCE THRILLER

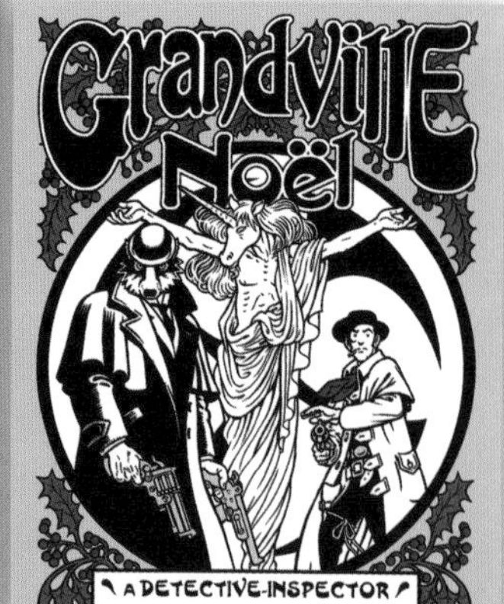
Grandville
Noël
A DETECTIVE-INSPECTOR
LEBROCK OF SCOTLAND YARD
SCIENTIFIC-ROMANCE THRILLER
Bryan Talbot

BRYAN TALBOT

Eisner and Eagle Award winner Bryan Talbot has produced underground and alternative comics, notably *Brainstorm!*, science-fiction and superhero stories such as *Judge Dredd*, *Nemesis the Warlock*, *Teknophage*, *The Nazz* and *Batman: Legends of the Dark Knight*. He's worked on DC/Vertigo titles including *Hellblazer*, *Sandman*, *The Dreaming* and *Fables* and has written and drawn the graphic novels for which he is best known, including *The Adventures of Luther Arkwright*, *Heart of Empire*, *The Tale of One Bad Rat* and *Alice in Sunderland*. He is published in over eighteen countries and is a frequent guest at international comic festivals. He was awarded an honorary Doctorate in Arts by Sunderland University in 2009 and a Doctorate in Letters by Northumbria University in 2012. The *Grandville* series has been twice nominated for a Hugo Award and the French edition of *Grandville Mon Amour* won the Prix SNCF for best graphic novel in 2012. *Dotter of Her Father's Eyes*, a collaboration with Mary Talbot, was the first British graphic novel to win a major literary prize, the Costa Biography Award for 2012.

http://www.bryan-talbot.com

OTHER BOOKS BY MARY M TALBOT

Academic Books

Fictions at Work

Language and Gender

Media Discourse: Representation and Interaction

Language, Intertextuality and Subjectivity:
Voices in the Construction of Consumer Femininity

All the World and Her Husband:
Women in Twentieth-Century Consumer Culture
(with Maggie Andrews)

Language and Power in the Modern World
(with David Atkinson and Karen Atkinson)

Graphic Novels

Dotter of Her Father's Eyes
(with Bryan Talbot)

Sally Heathcote, Suffragette
(With Kate Charlesworth and Bryan Talbot)